About the Author

Throughout her teaching career Pat Andrews has specialized in American history and government. Currently an American government instructor at West Valley College in Saratoga, California, she has also been a faculty member at Cabrillo College and Presentation High School, both in California, and a guest lecturer at Repton and Greylands Colleges in England. Following completion of her B.A. at San Jose State University and attaining lifetime teaching credentials in history and government from California Community College, Pat Andrews earned M.A. degrees in social science and political science at California State University, San Jose. An active member of the teachers' unions at West Valley and Cabrillo Colleges, she also served as coordinator of West Valley's Cultural Diversity Task Force and has been honored with several outstanding teacher awards. In addition to this book, she has written a number of freelance articles on politics and current issues.

Pat Andrews and her family make their home in San Jose.

Voices of Diversity

Perspectives on American Political Ideals and Institutions

Voices of Diversity
Perspectives on American Political Ideals and Institutions

Pat Andrews
West Valley College

DPG
The Dushkin Publishing Group, Inc.
Guilford, Connecticut

This book is printed
on recycled paper

Cover: *Selma March*, James H. Karales
Cover design by Charles Vitelli.

Printed in the United States of America

Library of Congress Catalog Card Number: 94-079177

International Standard Book Number (ISBN): 1-56134-251-3

The Dushkin Publishing Group, Inc., Sluice Dock, Guilford, CT 06437

Preface

This book brings together two kinds of primary sources: the often eloquent words of American women and minority-group members raised in protest at the unfair treatment they confronted in American life; and the responses of government to their grievances. Together, these sources paint a portrait of American society and government that is both ever changing and ever commited to the ideals upon which the nation was founded.

Collected in chapters 2, 4, 6, and 8 are the voices of many people who were long excluded. Their speeches, letters, essays, articles, and books tell us how they suffered firsthand the nation's failure to live up to its ideals of equal treatment and civil rights for all. Often filled with frustration and pain, their words describe their struggle to be heard.

The documents in chapters 1, 3, 5, 7, and 9—laws, constitutional amendments, presidential proclamations, and other official acts—stand as a powerful testament to the effective role that these and other voices have played in forging a more inclusive democracy. Together, the two types of sources demonstrate to students how enduring the nation's commitment has been to the fundamental ideal of equality, and how minority groups and women have helped to shape the continuing evolution of democratic principles.

The majority of readings demonstrate the persistence of women, African Americans, Native Americans, and Mexican Americans in their opposition to the status quo. These readings are balanced against many of the official responses to their opposition. Instructors and students alike will readily identify additional groups struggling to bring to the nation's attention the gap between the reality they experience and the principles upon which the United States was founded.

An appropriate adjunct to introductory courses in American history or political science, *Voices of Diversity: Perspectives on American Political Ideals and Institutions* is also one of the few collections of primary sources available to instructors for use in the many courses on multiculturalism now being offered. The readings begin with the founding of the United

States in 1776 and conclude with recent federal and state legislation addressing minority-group concerns. Most documents are included in their entirety rather than relying on brief excerpts to convey their messages. Each chapter provides an introductory overview of the historic period covered, and each reading begins with a summary of its author's background and intent and ends with several study questions.

Without the help of many people, I would not have been able to complete this book. At The Dushkin Publishing Group, my appreciation goes to Irv Rockwood, publisher, for his continuing belief in this project, and my grateful respect goes to Catherine Leonard, whose substantial contributions of organization, writing, and editing have vastly improved the text. My thanks as well to my niece, Patricia Andrews, for her production work; to Mark Page for his research and questions; to the librarians at West Valley College for locating some elusive information on authors; to Liz Ansnes for her support and suggestions; and to the early reviewers, whose constructive criticism helped to render this volume a better product. Those reviewers included Robert W. Behrman, Marshall University; Michael Bellesiles, Emory University; Carl D. Cavalli, Memphis State University; Dale A. Hathaway, Butler University; Kennith G. Hunter, Lamar University; Sharon G. Whitney, Luther College; and Jay Zarowitz, Muskegon Community College.

Finally, I want to acknowledge my life's real treasures—my daughter, Lisa, and granddaughters, Danielle and Jennifer, for the endless joy they bring me; my friend Robert Mora, for the humor he brings to our daily experiences; my parents for their unwavering belief in me; and my son, Christopher, a kindred spirit. Walker and Samantha also deserve credit for providing me with feline companionship during the long nights when I worked on this book.

Pat Andrews

Contents

Chapter 7: All Persons Shall Be Entitled: 167
Extending the Ideal of Equality

Chapter 8: The New Politics: Redefining Democracy 205

Chapter 9: One Nation, Many Peoples: The Essence   254
of a Democratic Society

Introduction

This book pays tribute to the profound impact that diverse peoples in the United States have had upon American society and politics. In it, you will meet some of the women, African Americans, Native Americans, Mexican Americans, and other minority-group members whose eloquent words of appeal have influenced the nation's development. Despite the fame of some of their writings, such as Dr. Martin Luther King Jr.'s "I Have a Dream" speech or Betty Friedan's *The Feminine Mystique,* many of these readings will not be familiar to you. For example, surprisingly few people know that as far back as 1776, Abigail Adams, wife of one U.S. president and mother of another, warned of a fomenting rebellion from women who were controlled by male "tyrants."

Mrs. Adams's words were not heeded quickly. It has taken scores of years for the grievances of many different peoples in the United States to be heard. They raised their voices to protest the gap between the reality they experienced and the ideals articulated in other famous documents you will read here—the Declaration of Independence and the Constitution of the United States.

Nevertheless, theirs and many other voices have been heard. Along with their expressions of outrage and protest, this book contains the official responses of the nation, in the form of constitutional amendments, state and federal laws, and other actions that have slowly but surely broadened the definitions of equality and civil rights to their present degree of inclusiveness.

In *Voices of Diversity: Perspectives on American Political Ideals and Institutions,* you'll read the actual words people spoke, rather than the reports or interpretations of historians and political scientists. You can judge for yourself the effectiveness of each protest, and the contribution each reading has made to the evolution of American civil rights and equality. You will also see snapshots of the nation as it was during various times in its history and witness representative government in action through the American political process. Most of all, I hope this book will enhance your understanding of the vital role of pluralism in the United States.

P. A.

1

We the People:
The Ideals Are Established

From the European colonists who first settled in the New World to the men who drafted the Constitution more than 150 years later, the majority of early Americans pledged allegiance to three basic ideals for their new nation: individual liberty, equality, and representative self-government.

The immigrants had come to America seeking religious and personal freedom, or civil liberties.

Most settlers also sought to minimize social rank and create equal opportunity for all, a philosophy made all the more appropriate, even essential, by the enormous amounts of labor required to clear, plant, and build on miles of wilderness land.

The principle of republican self-government was embodied from the very beginning at Jamestown, in the colony's first representative assembly in 1619. The Mayflower Compact of 1620 was a social contract based on the consent of the governed, and New England town meetings have since then featured aspects of direct democracy. The Fundamental Orders of Connecticut in 1639 provided for majority rule, and the First and Second Continental Congresses served as representative bodies for the colonies.

What were the origins of these ideals that took such firm root in American soil?

The mood of Europe played a key role. With the Age of Enlightenment, writers and thinkers began to view human nature with cautious optimism and give credence to the individual's ability to reason. England granted a Bill of Rights to its citizens, and English philosopher John Locke (1632–1704) contributed much to the belief in natural rights, self-government, and the concept of a social contract. He called these ideas

1

self-evident truths. His *Two Treatises of Civil Government,* 1690, were particularly influential.

When Englishmen settled the New World, with its abundant land, plentiful resources, and independence from Old World values, America became rich ground in which to sow seeds of freedom and self-rule.

Following the French and Indian War, a 7-year struggle for colonial supremacy in North America that ended in 1763, England levied a series of taxes on the colonies to help pay off the war debt and imposed rules about westward expansion and economic development.

Americans resisted such policies and demanded representation in government decision making, claiming "rights of Englishmen." Fundamental disagreements erupted. Americans insisted that self-government was a right; the British said it was a privilege. The British asserted that Americans had *virtual representation* by Englishmen in Parliament. Americans called for *actual representation* by colonial emissaries. Some American colonists defiantly formed secret organizations in opposition, while others led protests and boycotts. Repeal of most taxes led to a period of calm until, in 1773, a new tax was levied on tea, a staple purchase by colonists. Resistance was immediate and widespread. When the Sons of Liberty dumped a load of tea overboard in rebellion, Britain cracked down, closing the Port of Boston and banning public meetings.

Americans called the First Continental Congress in the autumn of 1774 to produce a list of grievances to submit to the king. That statement of grievances became in addition a statement of rights, setting out the demands of the colonists. The Congress also recommended that a second Continental Congress convene in May 1775.

The Declaration of Independence, written by Thomas Jefferson in June of 1776, represented a national spirit of unity and purpose. Adopted by the second Continental Congress, the document referred for the first time to the United States of America and expressed a statement of democratic principles.

> We hold these truths to be self-evident, that all men are created equal, that they are endowed by their Creator with certain unalienable rights. . . . That . . . governments are instituted among men, deriving their just powers from the consent of the governed.

The First Continental Congress drafted the Articles of Confederation for the new nation later that summer, but the war for independence took precedence. The articles, submitted to the states the following year, were not ratified until 1781. Americans' faith lay primarily in state governments, and the articles granted the federal government very little power.

Within a few years, however, it became evident that a stronger, more centralized system was necessary; states were wrangling with each other over issues relating to money, commerce, and territory and had no place to go to resolve such differences. In 1787, therefore, delegates from all states except Rhode Island convened to consider their form of government. The Constitution of the United States that they ultimately drafted united the former states into a "more perfect union" by establishing a federal republic, divided in power between a national government and state governments. The system was representative of the people through a bicameral Congress, one half of which was directly elected. The Constitution established the authority of the United States with a system of laws outlining what government could and could not do, along with a blueprint for the institutions necessary to execute its power. The document is a collective expression of values, a guiding set of beliefs, with the ideals of the Declaration of Independence interwoven into its fabric.

Soon after the Constitution was ratified by the states, the framers added the Bill of Rights to satisfy some skeptics who were apprehensive about the added power of the federal government. The first 10 amendments to the Constitution reinforced the limits to authority over individual rights, such as speech, the press, and the right to practice one's religion. This "sensible expedient," as James Madison called it, became the linchpin of American democracy.

The principles of liberty, equality, and republican self-government have endured and continue to evolve. People from around the world study the American founding documents and apply these principles in pursuit of their own democracies.

Reading **1**

Thomas Jefferson, 1776

The Declaration of Independence

The Declaration of Independence was written by Thomas Jefferson (1743–1826) and adopted by the Second Continental Congress. A set of grievances was laid out in the Declaration in reaction to a long history of "injuries and usurpations" by the English king upon the colonists. Jefferson, like Locke and other Enlightenment thinkers before him, asserted that government derived its power from "the consent of the governed" and was responsible for protecting the "unalienable rights" of men. Those who helped to inspire the American Revolution believed that the rights of the colonists had not been represented and that it had therefore become necessary to "dissolve the political bands" which tied them to the mother country. This reading sets forth a fundamental principle of democracy, that power is derived from the consent of the governed. The Declaration does not exclude anyone.

The Declaration of Independence

The unanimous Declaration of the Thirteen United States of America

PREAMBLE

When, in the course of human events, it becomes necessary for one people to dissolve the political bands which have connected them with another, and to assume, among the powers of the earth, the separate and equal station to which the laws of nature and of nature's God entitle them, a decent respect to the opinions of mankind requires that they should declare the causes which impel them to the separation.

New Principles of Government

We hold these truths to be self-evident; that all men are created equal, that they are endowed by their Creator with certain unalienable rights, that among these are life, liberty, and the pursuit of happiness.

That, to secure these rights, governments are instituted among men, deriving their just powers from the consent of the governed;

That whenever any form of government becomes destructive of these ends, it is the right of the people to alter or to abolish it, and to institute new government, laying its foundation on such principles, and organizing its powers in such form, as to them shall seem most likely to effect their safety and happiness. Prudence, indeed, will dictate that governments long established should not be changed for light and transient causes; and accordingly all experience hath shown that mankind are more disposed to suffer while evils are sufferable, than to right themselves by abolishing the forms to which they are accustomed. But when a long train of abuses and usurpations, pursuing invariably the same object, evinces a design to reduce them under absolute despotism, it is their right, it is their duty, to throw off such government, and to provide new guards for their future security.

Reasons for Separation

Such has been the patient sufference of these colonies; and such is now the necessity which constrains them to alter their former systems of government. The history of the present king of Great Britain is a history of repeated injuries and usurpations, all having in direct object the establishment of an absolute tyranny over these states. To prove this, let facts be submitted to a candid world.

He has refused his assent to laws the most wholesome and necessary for the public good.

He has forbidden his governors to pass laws of immediate and pressing importance unless suspended in their operation till his assent should be obtained; and when so suspended, he has utterly neglected to attend to them.

He has refused to pass other laws for the accommodation of large districts of people, unless those people would relinquish the right of representation in the legislature, a right inestimable to them, and formidable to tyrants only.

He has called together legislative bodies at places unusual, uncomfortable, and distant from the depository of their public records, for the sole purpose of fatiguing them into compliance with his measures.

He has dissolved representative houses repeatedly, for opposing, with manly firmness, his invasions on the rights of people.

He has refused, for a long time after such dissolutions, to cause others to be elected; whereby the legislative powers, incapable of annihilation, have returned to the people at large for their exercise; the state remaining, in the mean time, exposed to all the dangers of invasion from without and convulsions within.

He has endeavored to prevent the population of these states; for that purpose obstructing the laws of naturalization of foreigners, refusing to pass others to encourage their migration hither, and raising the conditions of new appropriations of lands.

He has obstructed the administration of justice, by refusing his assent to laws for establishing judiciary powers.

He has made judges dependent on his will alone for the tenure of their offices, and the amount and payment of their salaries.

He has erected a multitude of new offices, and sent hither swarms of officers to harass our people and eat out their substance.

He has kept among us, in times of peace, standing armies, without the consent of our legislature.

He has affected to render the military independent of, and superior to, the civil power.

He has combined with others to subject us to a jurisdiction foreign to our constitution and unacknowledged by our laws, giving his assent to their acts of pretended legislation:

For quartering large bodies of armed troops among us;

For protecting them, by a mock trial, from punishment for any murders which they should commit on the inhabitants of these states;

For cutting off our trade with all parts of the world;

For imposing taxes on us without our consent;

For depriving us, in many cases, of the benefits of trial by jury;

For transporting us beyond seas, to be tried for pretended offenses;

For abolishing the free system of English laws in a neighboring province, establishing therein an arbitrary government, and enlarging its boundaries, so as to render it at once an example and fit instrument for introducing the same absolute rule into these colonies;

For taking away our charters, abolishing our most valuable laws, and altering, fundamentally, the forms of our governments;

For suspending our own legislatures, and declaring themselves invested with power to legislate for us in all cases whatsoever.

He has abdicated government here, by declaring us out of his protection and waging war against us.

He has plundered our seas, ravaged our coasts, burned our towns, and destroyed the lives of our people.

He is at this time transporting large armies of foreign mercenaries to complete the works of death, desolation, and tyranny already begun with circumstances of cruelty and perfidy scarcely paralleled in the most barbarous ages and totally unworthy the head of a civilized nation.

He has constrained our fellow citizens, taken captive on the high seas, to bear arms against their country, to become the executioners of their friends and brethren, or to fall themselves by their hands.

He has excited domestic insurrections among us, and has endeavored to bring on the inhabitants of our frontiers the merciless Indian savages, whose known rule of warfare is an undistinguished destruction of all ages, sexes, and conditions.

In every stage of these oppressions we have petitioned for redress in the most humble terms; our repeated petitions have been answered only by repeated injury. A prince whose character is thus marked by every act which may define a tyrant is unfit to be the ruler of a free people.

Nor have we been wanting in attention to our British brethren. We have warned them, from time to time, of attempts by their legislature to extend an unwarrantable jurisdiction over us. We have reminded them of the circumstances of our emigration and settlement here. We have appealed to their native justice and magnanimity; and we have conjured them, by the ties of our common kindred, to disavow these usurpations, which would inevitably interrupt our connections and correspondence. They, too, have been deaf to the voice of justice and of consanguinity. We must, therefore, acquiesce in the necessity which denounces our separation, and hold them, as we hold the rest of mankind, enemies in war, in peace, friends.

We, therefore, the representatives of the United States of America, in General Congress assembled, appealing to the Supreme Judge of the world for the rectitude of our intentions, do, in the name and by authority of the good people of these colonies, solemnly publish and declare, that these united colonies are, and of right ought to be, free and independent states; that they are absolved from all allegiance to the British crown, and that all political connection between them and the state of Great Britain is, and ought to be, totally dissolved; and that, as free and independent states, they have full power to levy war, conclude peace, contract alliances, establish commerce, and do all other acts and things which independent states may of a right do. And, for the support of this declaration, with a firm reliance on the protection of Divine Providence, we mutually pledge to each other our lives, our fortunes, and our sacred honor.

Questions for Review and Reflection

1. When does it become necessary for one group to dissolve a political connection with another?
2. What are these "self-evident" truths of which Jefferson speaks?
3. John Locke had earlier termed the basic rights as "life, liberty, and property." Jefferson changed this to "life, liberty, and the pursuit of happiness." Why do you think Jefferson made this change?
4. Where do governments derive their just power to govern?
5. How does Jefferson justify rebellion from England?
6. When does a people have the right to abolish the government? When do they have the duty?
7. In your opinion, what are the three most serious charges against the king of England? Would Jefferson agree with you? Why?
8. Why do the "United Colonies" have the right to be "FREE AND INDEPENDENT STATES"?
9. How does Jefferson call upon God at the end of the document?

Reading 2

John Adams, 1776

Thoughts on Government

Advocate for independence, delegate to the First and Second Continental Congresses, and the country's second president,

John Adams (1735-1826) believed in representative democracy. Adams made a strong case for *republicanism*, which is an indirect democracy where the people are represented by elected officials. "The first necessary step, then, is to depute power from the many to a few of the most wise and good. . . ." Adams believed that a republic should represent the interests, concerns, and wishes of the people. In his thoughts, he wrote that "the greatest care should be employed in constituting this republican assembly. . . . It should think, feel, reason and act like [the people]."

Which people and what form of representation was left unsaid.

We ought to consider what is the end of government, before we determine which is the best form. Upon this point all speculative politicians will agree, that the happiness of society is the end of government, as all divines and moral philosophers will agree that the happiness of the individual is the end of man. From this principle it will follow, that the form of government which communicates ease, comfort, security, or, in one word, happiness, to the greatest number of persons, and in the greatest degree, is the best. . . .

Fear is the foundation of most governments; but it is so sordid and brutal a passion, and renders men ill whose breasts it predominates so stupid and miserable, that Americans will not be likely to approve of any political institution which is founded on it.

Honor is truly sacred, but holds a lower rank in the scale of moral excellence than virtue. Indeed, the former is but a part of the latter, and consequently has not equal pretensions to support a frame of government productive of human happiness.

The foundation of every government is some principle or passion in the minds of the people. The noblest principles and most generous affections in our nature, then, have the fairest chance to support the noblest and most generous models of government. . . .

As good government is an empire of laws, how shall your laws be made? In a large society, inhabiting an extensive country, it is impossible that the whole should assemble to make laws. The first necessary step, then, is to depute power from the many to a few of the most wise and good. But by what rules shall you choose your representatives? Agree upon the number and qualifications of persons who shall have the benefit of choosing, or annex this privilege to the inhabitants of a certain extent of ground.

The principal difficulty lies, and the greatest care should be employed, in constituting this representative assembly. It should be in miniature an exact portrait of the people at large. It should think, feel, reason, and act like them.

That it may be the interest of this assembly to do strict justice at all times, it should be an equal representation, or, in other words, equal interests among the people should have equal interests in it. Great care should be taken to effect this, and to prevent unfair, partial, and corrupt elections. Such regulations, however, may be better made in times of greater tranquillity than the present; they will spring up themselves naturally, when all the powers of government come to be in the hands of the people's friends. At present, it will be safest to proceed in all established modes, to which the people have been familiarized by habit.

A representation of the people in one assembly being obtained, a question arises, whether all the powers of government, legislative, executive, and judicial, shall be left in this body? I think a people cannot be long free, nor ever happy, whose government is in one assembly. . . .

The dignity and stability of government in all its branches, the morals of the people, and every blessing of society depend so much upon an upright and skilful administration of justice, that the judicial power ought to be distinct from both the legislative and executive, and independent upon both, that so it may be a check upon both, as both should be checks upon that. The judges, therefore, should be always men of learning and experience in the laws, of exemplary morals, great patience, calmness, coolness, and attention. Their minds should not be distracted with jarring interests; they should not be dependent upon any man, or body of men. To these ends, they should hold estates for life in their offices; or, in other words, their commissions should be during good behavior, and their salaries ascertained and established by law. For misbehavior, the grand inquest of the colony, the house of representatives, should impeach them before the governor and council, where they should have time and opportunity to make their defence; but, if convicted, should be removed from their offices, and subjected to such other punishment as shall be thought proper. . . .

A constitution founded on these principles introduces knowledge among the people, and inspires them with a conscious dignity becoming freemen; a general emulation takes place, which causes good humor, sociability, good manners, and good morals to be general. That elevation of sentiment inspired by such a government, makes the common people brave and enterprising. That ambition which is inspired by it makes them sober, industrious, and frugal. You will find among them some elegance, perhaps, but more solidity; a little pleasure, but a great deal of business; some politeness, but more civility. . . .

If the colonies should assume governments separately, they should be left entirely to their own choice of the forms; and if a continental constitution should be formed, it should be a congress, containing a fair and adequate representation of the colonies, and its authority should sacredly be confined to these cases, namely, war, trade, disputes between colony and colony, the post-office, and the unappropriated lands of the crown, as they used to be called.

These colonies, under such forms of government, and in such a union, would be unconquerable by all the monarchies of Europe.

You and I, my dear friend, have been sent into life at a time when the greatest lawgivers of antiquity would have wished to live. How few of the human race have ever enjoyed an opportunity of making an election of government, more than of air, soil, or climate, for themselves or their children! When, before the present epoch, had three millions of people full power and a fair opportunity to form and establish the wisest and happiest government that human wisdom can contrive? I hope you will avail yourself and your country of that extensive learning and indefatigable industry which you possess, to assist her in the formation of the happiest governments and the best character of a great people.

Questions for Review and Reflection

1. On what point do all "speculative politicians" agree, according to Adams?
2. Why does Adams believe that the best government is one that offers "comfort, security, or, in one word, happiness"?
3. According to Adams, what is the foundation of most governments?
4. In what way is this article an argument for the republican form of democratic government?
5. Why does Adams believe that "the greatest lawgivers of antiquity" would have wished to live in Adams's day?
6. On what principles does Adams believe a constitution should be founded?
7. Describe Adams's philosophy on checks and balances in the government.
8. According to Adams, what are the best principles on which to found a government?

Reading 3

Benjamin Franklin, 1784

Letter to Europeans Seeking a New Life in America

Benjamin Franklin (1706-1790) was both a statesman and a scientist who had served in multiple capacities on behalf of the revolution. He helped to draft the Declaration of Independence, gave counsel at the Constitutional Convention, and served as ambassador to France, America's chief ally, during crucial periods of early American history.

Many Europeans who contemplated a move to America wrote to Franklin asking about life in the New World. Franklin's response was to create a pamphlet, "Information for Those Who Would Remove to America," which was first published in London and Dublin, with later printings in Italy and Germany. In this essay, Franklin captured America's egalitarian spirit in his response.

He explained that no newly arriving immigrant to America was going to be granted any privilege or position based upon birth, but only upon performance and merit. People had no rights based on who they were, but all had an equal right to earn a share in the bounties of the new country.

Many persons in Europe, having directly or by letters, expressed to the writer, who is well acquainted with North America, their desire of transporting and establishing themselves in that country; but who appear to have formed, through ignorance, mistaken ideas and expectations of what is to be obtained there; he thinks it may be useful, and prevent inconvenient, expensive, and fruitless removals and voyages of improper persons, if he gives some clearer and truer notions of that part of the world, than appear to have hitherto prevailed.

He finds it is imagined by numbers, that the inhabitants of North America are rich, capable of rewarding, and disposed to reward, all sorts of ingenuity; that they are at the same time ignorant of all the sciences, and, consequently, that strangers, possessing talents in the belles-lettres, fine arts, etc., must be highly esteemed, and so well paid, as to become easily rich themselves; that there are also abundance of profitable offices to be disposed of, which the natives are not qualified to fill; and that having few persons of family among them, strangers of birth must be greatly respected, and of course easily obtain the best of those offices, which will make all their fortunes; that the governments too, to encourage emigration from Europe, not only pay the expense of personal transportation, but give land gratis to strangers, with Negroes to work for them, utensils of husbandry, and stocks of cattle. These are all wild imaginations; and those who go to America with expectations founded upon them, will surely find themselves disappointed.

The truth is, that though there are in that country few people so miserable as the poor of Europe, there are also very few that in Europe would be called rich; it is rather a general happy mediocrity that prevails. There are few great proprietors of the soil, and few tenants; most people cultivate their own lands, or follow some handicraft or merchandise; very few rich enough to live idly upon their rents or incomes, or to pay the highest prices given in Europe for painting, statues, architecture, and the other works of art, that are more curious than useful. Hence the natural geniuses that have arisen in America with such talents have uniformly quitted that country for Europe, where they can be more suitably rewarded. It is true that letters and mathematical knowledge are in esteem there, but they are at the same time more common than is apprehended; there being already existing nine colleges or universities, viz. four in New England, and one in each of the provinces of New York, New Jersey, Pennsylvania, Maryland, and Virginia, all furnished with learned professors; besides a number of smaller academies; these educate many of their youth in the languages, and those sciences that qualify men for the professions of divinity, law, or physic. Strangers are by no means excluded from exercising these professions; and the quick increase of inhabitants everywhere gives them a chance of employ[ment], which they have in common with the natives. Of civil offices, or employments, there are few; no superfluous ones, as in Europe; and it is a rule established in some of the States, that no office should be so profitable as to make it desirable. . . .

The almost general mediocrity of fortune that prevails in America obliging its people to follow some business for subsistence, those vices that arise usually from idleness are in a great measure prevented. Industry and constant employment are great preservatives of the morals and virtue of a nation. Hence bad examples to youth are more rare in America, which must be a comfortable consideration to parents. To this may be truly added, that serious religion, under its various denominations, is not only tolerated, but respected and practised. Atheism is unknown there; infidelity rare and secret; so that persons may live to a great age in that country, without having their piety shocked by meeting with either an atheist or an infidel. And the Divine Being seems to have manifested his approbation of the mutual forbearance and kindness with which the different sects treat each other, by the remarkable prosperity with which He has been pleased to favor the whole country.

⟨Q⟩uestions for Review and Reflection

1. What is Franklin's "clearer and truer notion" of America?
2. Franklin speaks of preventing "improper persons" from coming to America by describing the characteristics of the New World. Who might he be describing?
3. What are the "natural geniuses" that have arisen in the New World?
4. Why is the American model a much better example for youth than the European model?

Reading 4

Thomas Jefferson, 1787

Letter to James Madison

Thomas Jefferson (1743-1826), author of the Declaration of Independence, scholar, statesman and America's third president, wrote to James Madison at the conclusion of the Constitutional Convention. He enumerated all that he liked about the draft of the new Constitution, but he wrote, "I will now add what I do not like. First the omission of a Bill of Rights. . . . [It is] what the people are entitled to against every government on earth . . . and what no just government should refuse."

Jefferson felt that a clear "declaration of rights" was essential to protect individuals from majorities as well as from the great potential for power of the new central government. Protecting citizens from the abuse of government goes all the way back to the Magna Carta of 1215, which guaranteed the privileged class some protection from arbitrary authority by the monarch.

I like much the general idea of framing a government which should go on of itself peaceably, without needing continual recurrence to the state legislatures. I like the organization of the government into Legislative, Judiciary and Executive. I like the power given the Legislature to levy taxes; and for that reason solely approve of the greater house being chosen by the people directly. For tho' I think a house chosen by them will be, very illy qualified to legislate for the Union, for foreign nations &c. yet this evil does not weigh against the good of preserving inviolate the fundamental principle that the people are not to be taxed but by representatives chosen immediately by themselves. I am captivated by the compromise of the opposite claims of the great and little states, of the latter to equal, and the former to proportional influence. I am much pleased too with the substitution of the method of voting by persons, instead of that of voting by states: and I like the negative given to the Executive with a third of either house, though I should have liked it better had the Judiciary been associated for that purpose, or invested with a similar and separate power. There are other good things of less moment. I will now add what I do not like. First the omission of a bill of rights providing clearly and without the aid of sophisms for freedom of religion, freedom of the press, protection against standing armies, restriction against monopolies, the eternal and unremitting force of the habeas corpus laws, and trials by jury in all matters of fact triable by the laws of the land and not by the law of Nations. To say, as Mr. Wilson does that a bill of rights was not necessary because all is reserved in the case of the general government which is not given, while in the particular ones all is given which is not reserved might do for the Audience to whom it was addressed, but is surely gratis dictum, opposed by strong inferences from the body of the instrument, as well as from the omission of the clause of our present confederation which had declared that in express terms. It was a hard conclusion to say because there has been no uniformity among the states as to the cases triable by jury, because some have been so incautious as to abandon this mode of trial, therefore the more prudent states shall be reduced to the same level of calamity. It would have been much more just and wise to have concluded the other way that as most of the states had judiciously preserved this palladium, those who had wandered should be brought back to it, and to have established general right instead of general wrong. Let me add that a bill of rights is what the people are entitled to against every government on earth, general or particular, and what no just government should refuse, or rest on inference. . . . I have thus told you freely what I like and dislike: merely as a matter of curiosity for I know your own judgment has been formed on all these points after having heard every thing which could be urged on them. I own I am not a friend to a very energetic government. It is always oppressive. The late rebellion in Massachusetts has given more alarm than I think it should have done. Calculate that one rebellion in 13 states in the course of 11 years, is but one for each state in a century and a half. No country should be so long without one. Nor will any degree of power in the hands of government prevent insurrections. France with all its despotism, and two or three hundred thousand men always in arms has had three insurrections in the three years I have been here in every one of which greater numbers were engaged than in Massachusetts and a great deal more blood was spilt. . . . After all, it is my principle that the will of the Majority should always prevail. If they approve the proposed Convention in all its parts, I shall concur in it cheerfully, in hopes that they will amend it whenever they shall find it works wrong. . . .

|Q| uestions for Review and Reflection

1. What logic does Jefferson employ to argue for a Bill of Rights?
2. Why is a Bill of Rights a political necessity, in Jefferson's opinion?
3. What three divisions does Jefferson like to see in a government? Which powers does he relegate to each?

4. In which house, in Jefferson's opinion, should the power to impose taxes exist? Why?
5. What is the primary fault with the proposed Constitution? What would remedy its deficiency?

Reading 5

Constitutional Convention, 1789

The Constitution of the United States

The United States Constitution is the oldest working constitution in the world. This blueprint of government establishes the framework within which American democracy functions.

The Constitution defines the powers and limits of American government, describes the institutions that will serve the people, and establishes a supreme law of the land. Within this framework, only very general principles were established, with the specifics left to the decisions of future generations. Mindful of how much the nation would change over time, Jefferson wrote, "The Constitution belongs to the living. Laws and institutions must go hand in hand with the progress of the human mind," and suggested that revisions might be necessary every 20 years. "The example of changing a constitution, by assembling the wise men of the state, instead of assembling armies, will be worth as much to the world as the former examples we had given them." Indeed, Jefferson's words were prophetic for America, if not for the entire world. It is the very process of changing the specifics of the Constitution in response to changing needs that has made it such an enduring foundation of democratic government.

America became a federal system that divided power between the national government and existing state governments. National power was distributed among the legislative, judicial, and executive branches served by representatives of differing constituencies with distinct terms. Each branch was given the power to halt the actions of another branch in order to prevent the accumulation of too much power. This structure was meant to be more effective than the Articles of Confederation without becoming tyrannical.

Over time, the separation of powers with checks and balances proved beneficial to many dissenting groups. African Americans achieved some progress in the courts and later in Congress. Women made gains in Congress and later in the courts. Latinos have effected change by becoming active in local government.

The protection of individual liberty followed the completion of the Constitution. Its blueprint provided the means for democracy to progress because of its underlying principles and flexibility. The text is reprinted here without the constitutional amendments, many of which will be included in later readings. To date, the Constitution has been amended 27 times, most recently in 1992, to establish a waiting period before congressional salary increases can be implemented.

The Constitution of the United States

Preamble

We the People of the United States, in Order to form a more perfect Union, establish Justice, insure domestic Tranquility, provide for the common defence, promote the general Welfare, and secure the Blessings of Liberty to ourselves and our Posterity, do ordain and establish this Constitution for the United States of America.

ARTICLE I
Congress

Section I. All legislative Powers herein granted shall be vested in a Congress of the United States, which shall consist of a Senate and House of Representatives.

House of Representatives

Section 2. The House of Representatives shall be composed of Members chosen every second Year by the People of the several States, and the Electors in each State shall have the Qualifications requisite for Electors of the most numerous Branch of the State Legislature.

No Person shall be a Representative who shall not have attained to the Age of twenty five Years, and been seven Years a Citizen of the United States, and who shall not, when elected, be an Inhabitant of that State in which he shall be chosen.

Representatives and direct Taxes shall be apportioned among the several States which may be included within this Union, according to their respective Numbers, which shall be determined by adding to the whole Number of free Persons, including those bound to Service for a Term of Years, and excluding Indians not taxed, three fifths of all other Persons. The actual Enumeration shall be made within three Years after the first Meeting of the Congress of the United States, and within every subsequent Term of ten Years, in such Manner as they shall by Law direct. The Number of Representatives shall not exceed one for every thirty Thousand, but each State shall have at Least one Representative; and until such enumeration shall be made, the State of New Hampshire shall be entitled to chuse three, Massachusetts eight, Rhode-Island and Providence Plantations one, Connecticut five, New-York six, New Jersey four, Pennsylvania eight, Delaware one, Maryland six, Virginia ten, North Carolina five, South Carolina five, and Georgia three.

When vacancies happen in the Representation from any State, the Executive Authority thereof shall issue Writs of Election to fill such Vacancies.

The House of Representatives shall chuse their Speaker and other Officers; and shall have the sole Power of Impeachment.

Senate

Section 3. The Senate of the United States shall be composed of two Senators from each State, chosen by the Legislature thereof, for six Years; and each Senator shall have one Vote.

Immediately after they shall be assembled in Consequence of the first Election, they shall be divided as equally as may be into three Classes. The Seats of the Senators of the first Class shall be vacated at the Expiration of the second Year, of the second Class at the Expiration of the fourth Year, and of the third Class at the Expiration of the sixth Year, so that one third may be chosen every second Year; and if Vacancies happen by Resignation, or otherwise, during the Recess of the Legislature of any State, the Executive thereof may make temporary Appointments until the next Meeting of the Legislature, which shall then fill such Vacancies.

No Person shall be a Senator who shall not have attained to the Age of thirty Years, and been nine Years a Citizen of the United States, and who shall not, when elected, be an Inhabitant of that State for which he shall be chosen.

The Vice President of the United States shall be President of the Senate, but shall have no Vote, unless they be equally divided.

The Senate shall chuse their other Officers, and also a President pro tempore, in the Absence of the Vice President, or when he shall exercise the Office of President of the United States.

The Senate shall have the sole Power to try all Impeachments. When sitting for that Purpose, they shall be on Oath of Affirmation. When the President of the United States is tried, the Chief Justice shall preside: And no Person shall be convicted without the Concurrence of two thirds of the Members present.

Judgment in Cases of Impeachment shall not extend further than to removal from Office, and disqualification to hold and enjoy any Office of honor, Trust or Profit under the United States: but the Party convicted shall nevertheless be liable and subject to Indictment, Trial, Judgment and Punishment, according to Law.

Congressional Elections, Prerogatives, and Procedures

Section 4. The Times, Places and Manner of holding Elections for Senators and Representatives, shall be prescribed in each State by the Legislature thereof; but the Congress may at any time by Law make or alter such Regulations, except as to the Places of chusing Senators.

The Congress shall assemble at least once in every Year, and such Meeting shall be on the first Monday in December, unless they shall by Law appoint a different Day.

Section 5. Each House shall be the Judge of the Elections, Returns and Qualifications of its own Members, and a Majority of each shall constitute a Quorum to do Business; but a smaller Number may adjourn from day to day, and may be authorized to compel the Attendance of absent Members, in such Manner, and under such Penalties as each House may provide.

Each House may determine the Rules of its Proceedings, punish its Members for disorderly Behaviour, and, with the Concurrence of two thirds, expel a Member.

Each House shall keep a Journal of its Proceedings, and from time to time publish the same, excepting such Parts as may in their Judgment require Secrecy; and the Yeas and Nays of the Members of either House on any question shall, at the Desire of one fifth of those Present, be entered on the Journal.

Neither House, during the Session of Congress, shall, without the Consent of the other, adjourn for more than three days, nor to any other Place than that in which the two Houses shall be sitting.

Section 6. The Senators and Representatives shall receive a Compensation for their Services, to be ascertained by Law, and paid out of the Treasury of the United States. They shall in all Cases, except Treason, Felony and Breach of the Peace, be privileged from Arrest during their Attendance at the Session of their respective Houses, and in going to and returning from the same; and for any Speech or Debate in either House, they shall not be questioned in any other Place.

No Senator or Representative shall, during the Time for which he was elected, be appointed to any civil Office under the Authority of the United States, which shall have been created, or the Emoluments whereof shall have been encreased during such time; and no Person holding any Office under the United States, shall be a Member of either House during his Continuance in Office.

Section 7. All Bills for raising Revenue shall originate in the House of Representatives; but the Senate may propose or concur with Amendments as on other Bills.

Every Bill which shall have passed the House of Representatives and the Senate, shall, before it become a Law, be presented to the President of the United States; If he approve he shall sign it, but if not he shall return it, with his Objections to that House in which it shall have originated, who shall enter the Objections at large on their Journal, and proceed to reconsider it. If after such Reconsideration two thirds of that House shall agree to pass the Bill, it shall be sent, together with the Objections, to the other House, by which it shall likewise be reconsidered, and if approved by two thirds of that House, It shall become a Law. But in all such Cases the Votes of both Houses shall be determined by yeas and Nays, and the Names of the Persons voting for and against the Bill shall be entered on the Journal of each House respectively. If any Bill shall not be returned by the President within ten Days (Sundays excepted) after it shall have been presented to him, the Same shall be a Law, in like Manner as if he had signed it, unless the Congress by their Adjournment prevent its Return, in which Case it shall not be a Law.

Every Order, Resolution, or Vote to which the Concurrence of the Senate and House of Representatives may be necessary (except on a question of Adjournment) shall be presented to the President of the United States; and before the Same shall take Effect, shall be approved by him, or being disapproved by him, shall be repassed by two thirds of the Senate and House of Representatives, according to the Rules and Limitations prescribed in the Case of a Bill.

Congressional Powers

Section 8. The Congress shall have Power To lay and collect Taxes, Duties, Imposts and Excises, to pay the Debts and provide for the common Defence and general Welfare of the United States; but all Duties, Imposts and Excises shall be uniform throughout the United States;

To borrow Money on the credit of the United States;

To regulate Commerce with foreign Nations, and among the several States, and with the Indian Tribes;

To establish an uniform Rule of Naturalization, and uniform Laws on the subject of Bankruptcies throughout the United States;

To coin Money, regulate the Value thereof, and of foreign Coin, and fix the Standard of Weights and Measures;

To provide for the Punishment of counterfeiting the Securities and current Coin of the United States;

To establish Post Offices and post Roads;

To promote the Progress of Science and useful Arts, by securing for limited Times to Authors and Inventors the exclusive Right to their respective Writings and Discoveries;

To constitute Tribunals inferior to the supreme Court;

To define and punish Piracies and Felonies committed on the high Seas, and Offences against the Law of Nations;

To declare War, grant Letters of Marque and Reprisal, and make Rules concerning Captures on Land and Water;

To raise and support Armies, but no Appropriation of Money to that Use shall be for a longer Term than two Years;

To provide and maintain a Navy;

To make Rules for the Government and Regulation of the land and naval Forces;

To provide for calling forth the Militia to execute the Laws of the Union, suppress Insurrections and repel Invasions;

To provide for organizing, arming, and disciplining, the Militia, and for governing such Part of them as may be employed in the Service of the United States, reserving to the States respectively, the Appointment of the Officers, and the Authority of training the Militia according to the discipline prescribed by Congress;

To exercise exclusive Legislation in all Cases whatsoever, over such District (not exceeding ten Miles square) as may, by Cession of particular States, and the Acceptance of Congress, become the Seat of the Government of the United States, and to exercise like Authority over all Places purchased by the Consent of the Legislature of the State in which the Same shall be, for the Erection of Forts, Magazines, Arsenals, dock-Yards, and other needful Buildings;—And

To make all Laws which shall be necessary and proper for carrying into Execution the foregoing Powers, and all other Powers vested by this Constitution in the Government of the United States, or in any Department or Officer thereof.

Limitations on Congressional Power

Section 9. The Migration or Importation of such Persons as any of the States now existing shall think proper to admit, shall not be prohibited by the Congress prior to the year one thousand eight hundred and eight, but a Tax or duty may be imposed on such Importation, not exceeding ten dollars for each Person.

The Privilege of the Writ of Habeas Corpus shall not be suspended, unless when in Cases of Rebellion or Invasion the public Safety may require it.

No Bill of Attainder or ex post facto Law shall be passed.

No Capitation, or other direct, Tax shall be laid, unless in Proportion to the Census or Enumeration herein before directed to be taken.

No Tax or Duty shall be laid on Articles exported from any State.

No Preference shall be given by any Regulation of Commerce or Revenue to the Ports of one State over those of another; nor shall Vessels bound to, or from, one State, be obliged to enter, clear, or pay Duties in another.

No Money shall be drawn from the Treasury, but in Consequence of Appropriations made by Law; and a regular Statement and Account of the Receipts and Expenditures of all public Money shall be published from time to time.

No Title of Nobility shall be granted by the United States: And no Person holding any Office of Profit or Trust under them, shall, without the Consent of the Congress, accept of any present, Emolument, Office, or Title, of any kind whatever, from any King, Prince, or foreign State.

Limitations on Powers of State

Section 10. No State shall enter into any Treaty, Alliance, or Confederation; grant Letters of Marque and Reprisal; coin Money; emit Bills of Credit; make any Thing but gold and silver Coin a Tender in Payment of Debts; pass any Bill of Attainder, ex post facto Law, or Law impairing the Obligation of Contracts, or grant any Title of Nobility.

No State shall, without the Consent of the Congress, lay any Imposts or Duties on Imports or Exports, except what may be absolutely necessary for executing its inspection Laws: and the net Produce of all Duties and Imposts, laid by any State on Imports or Exports, shall be for the Use of the Treasury of the United States; and all such Laws shall be subject to the Revision and Controul of the Congress.

No State shall, without the Consent of Congress, lay any Duty of Tonnage, keep Troops, or Ships of War in time of Peace, enter into any Agreement or Compact with another State, or with a foreign Power, or engage in War, unless actually invaded, or in such imminent Danger as will not admit of delay.

ARTICLE II
The President

Electing the President

Section 1. The executive Power shall be vested in a President of the United States of America. He shall hold his Office during the Term of four Years, and, together with the Vice President, chosen for the same Term, be elected, as follows:

Each State shall appoint, in such Manner as the Legislature thereof may direct, a Number of Electors, equal to the whole Number of Senators and Representatives to which the State may be entitled in the Congress: but no Senator or Representative, or Person holding an Office of Trust or Profit under the United States, shall be appointed an Elector.

The Electors shall meet in their respective States, and vote by Ballot for two Persons, of whom one at least shall not be an Inhabitant of the same State with themselves. And they shall make a List of all the Persons voted for, and of the Number of Votes for each; which List they shall sign and certify, and transmit sealed to the Seat of the Government of the United States, directed to the President of the Senate. The President of the Senate shall, in the Presence of the Senate and House of Representatives, open all the Certificates, and the Votes shall then be counted. The Person having the greatest Number of Votes shall be the President, if such Number be a Majority of the whole Number of Electors appointed; and if there be more than one who have such Majority, and have an equal Number of Votes, then the House of Representatives shall immediately chuse by Ballot one of them for President; and if no Person have a Majority, then from the five highest on the List the said House shall in like Manner chuse the President. But in chusing the President, the Votes shall be taken by States, the Representation from each State having one Vote; A Quorum for this Purpose shall consist of a Member or Members from two thirds of the States, and a Majority of all the States shall be necessary to a Choice. In every Case, after the Choice of the President, the person having the greatest Number of Votes of the Electors shall be the Vice President. But if there should remain two or more who have equal Votes, the Senate shall chuse from them by Ballot the Vice President.

The Congress may determine the Time of chusing the Electors, and the Day on which they shall give their Votes; which Day shall be the same throughout the United States.

No Person except a natural born Citizen, or a Citizen of the United States, at the time of the Adoption of this Constitution, shall be eligible to the Office of President; neither shall any Person be eligible to that Office who shall not have attained to the Age of thirty five Years, and been fourteen Years a Resident within the United States.

In Case of the Removal of the President from Office, or of his Death, Resignation, or Inability to discharge the Powers and Duties of the said Office, the Same shall devolve on the Vice President, and the Congress may by Law provide for the Case of Removal, Death, Resignation or Inability, both of the President and Vice President, declaring what Officer shall then act as President, and such Officer shall act accordingly, until the Disability be removed, or a President shall be elected.

The President shall, at stated Times, receive for his Services, a Compensation, which shall neither be encreased nor diminished during the Period for which he shall have been elected, and he shall not receive within that Period any other Emolument from the United States, or any of them.

Before he enter on the Execution of his Office, he shall take the following Oath or Affirmation:—"I do solemnly swear (or affirm) that I will faithfully execute the Office of President of the United States, and will to the best of my Ability, preserve, protect and defend the Constitution of the United States."

Powers and Duties of the President

Section 2. The President shall be Commander in Chief of the Army and Navy of the United States, and of the Militia of the several States, when called into the actual Service of the United States; he may require the Opinion, in writing, of the principal Officer in each of the executive Departments, upon any Subject relating to the Duties of their respective Offices, and he shall have Power to grant Reprieves and Pardons for Offences against the United States, except in Cases of Impeachment.

He shall have Power, by and with the Advice and Consent of the Senate, to make Treaties, provided two thirds of the Senators present concur; and he shall nominate, and by and with the Advice and Consent of the Senate, shall appoint Ambassadors, other public Ministers and Consuls, Judges of the supreme Court, and all other Officers of the United States, whose Appointments are not herein otherwise provided for, and which shall be established by Law: but the Congress may by Law vest the Appointment of such inferior Officers, as they think proper, in the President alone, in the Courts of Law, or in the Heads of Departments.

The President shall have Power to fill up all Vacancies that may happen during the Recess of the Senate, by granting Commissions which shall expire at the End of their next Session.

Section 3. He shall from time to time give to the Congress Information of the State of the Union, and recommend to their Consideration such Measures as he shall judge necessary and expedient; he may, on extraordinary Occasions, convene both Houses, or either of them, and in Case of Disagreement between them, with Respect to the Time of Adjournment, he may adjourn them to such Time as he shall think proper; he shall receive Ambassadors and other public Ministers; he shall take Care that the Laws be faithfully executed, and shall Commission all of the Officers of the United States.

Section 4. The President, Vice President and all civil Officers of the United States, shall be removed from Office on Impeachment for, and Conviction of, Treason, Bribery, or other high Crimes and Misdemeanors.

ARTICLE III
Federal Judiciary

Section 1. The judicial Power of the United States, shall be vested in one supreme Court, and in such inferior Courts as the Congress may from time to time ordain and establish. The Judges, both of the supreme and inferior Courts, shall hold their Offices during good Behaviour, and shall, at stated Times, receive for their Services, a Compensation, which shall not be diminished during their Continuance in Office.

Section 2. The judicial Power shall extend to all Cases, in Law and Equity, arising under this Constitution, the Laws of the United States, and Treaties made, or which shall be made, under their Authority;—to all Cases affecting Ambassadors, other public Ministers and Consuls; —to all Cases of admiralty and maritime Jurisdiction;—to Controversies to which the United States shall be a Party;—to Controversies between two or more States;—between a State and Citizens of another State;—between Citizens of different States,—between Citizens of the same State claiming Lands under Grants of different States, and between a State, or the Citizens thereof, and foreign States, Citizens or Subjects.

In all Cases affecting Ambassadors, other public Ministers and Consuls, and those in which a State shall be Party, the supreme Court shall have original Jurisdiction. In all the other Cases before mentioned, the supreme Court shall have appellate Jurisdiction, both as to Law and Fact, with such Exceptions, and under such Regulations as the Congress shall make.

The Trial of all Crimes, except in Cases of Impeachment, shall be by Jury; and such Trial shall be held in the State where the said Crimes shall have been committed; but when not committed within any State, the Trial shall be at such Place or Places as the Congress may by Law have directed.

Section 3. Treason against the United States, shall consist only in levying War against them, or in adhering to their enemies, giving them Aid and Comfort. No Person shall be convicted of Treason unless on the Testimony of two Witnesses to the same overt Act, or on Confession in open Court.

The Congress shall have Power to declare the Punishment of Treason, but no Attainder of Treason shall work Corruption of Blood, or Forfeiture except during the Life of the Person attainted.

ARTICLE IV
Relations among the States

Section 1. Full Faith and Credit shall be given in each State to the public Acts, Records, and judicial Proceedings of every other State. And the Congress may by general Laws prescribe the Manner in which such Acts, Records, and Proceedings shall be proved, and the Effect thereof.

Section 2 The Citizens of each State shall be entitled to all Privileges and Immunities of Citizens in the several States.

A Person charged in any State with Treason, Felony, or other Crime, who shall flee from Justice, and be found in another State, shall on Demand of the executive Authority of the State from which he fled, be delivered up, to be removed to the State having Jurisdiction of the Crime.

No Person held to Service or Labour in one State, under the Laws thereof, escaping into another, shall, in Consequence of any Law or Regulation therein, be discharged from such Service or Labour, but shall be delivered up on Claim of the Party to whom such Service or Labour may be due.

Section 3. New States may be admitted by the Congress into this Union; but no new State shall be formed or erected within the Jurisdiction of any other State; nor any State be formed by the Junction of two or more States, or Parts of States, without the Consent of the Legislatures of the States concerned as well as of the Congress.

The Congress shall have Power to dispose of and make all needful Rules and Regulations respecting the Territory or other Property belonging to the United States; and nothing in this Constitution shall be so construed as to Prejudice any Claims of the United States, or of any particular State.

Section 4. The United States shall guarantee to every State in this Union a Republican Form of Government, and shall protect each of them against Invasion; and on Application of the Legislature, or of the Executive (when the Legislature cannot be convened) against domestic Violence.

ARTICLE V
Amending Procedures

The Congress, whenever two thirds of both Houses shall deem it necessary, shall propose Amendments to this Constitution, or, on the Application of the

Legislatures of two thirds of the several States, shall call a Convention for proposing Amendments, which, in either Case, shall be valid to all Intents and Purposes, as Part of this Constitution, when ratified by the Legislatures of three fourths of the several States, or by Conventions in three fourths thereof, as the one or the other Mode of Ratification may be proposed by the Congress; Provided that no Amendment which may be made prior to the Year One thousand eight hundred and eight shall in any Manner affect the first and fourth Clauses in the Ninth Section of the first Article; and that no State, without its Consent, shall be deprived of its equal Suffrage in the Senate.

ARTICLE VI
Supremacy Clause

All Debts contracted and Engagements entered into, before the Adoption of this Constitution, shall be as valid against the United States under this Constitution, as under the Confederation.

The Constitution, and the Laws of the United States which shall be made in Pursuance thereof; and all Treaties made, or which shall be made, under the Authority of the United States, shall be the supreme Law of the Land; and the Judges in every State shall be bound thereby, any Thing in the Constitution or Laws of any State to the Contrary notwithstanding.

The Senators and Representatives before mentioned, and the Members of the several State Legislatures, and all executive and judicial Officers, both of the United States and of the several States, shall be bound by Oath or Affirmation, to support this Constitution; but no religious Test shall ever be required as a Qualification to any Office or public Trust under the United States.

ARTICLE VII
Ratifying the Constitution

The Ratification of the Conventions of nine States, shall be sufficient for the Establishment of this Constitution between the States so ratifying the Same.

Done in Convention by the Unanimous Consent of the States present the Seventeenth Day of September in the Year of our Lord one thousand seven hundred and Eighty seven and of the Independence of the United States of America the Twelfth IN WITNESS whereof We have hereunto subscribed our Names,

G°· Washington	Presidᵗ. and deputy from Virginia.

New Hampshire	John Langdon, Nicholas Gilman.
Massachusetts	Nathaniel Gorham, Rufus King.
Connecticut	Wm. Saml. Johnson, Roger Sherman.

New York	Alexander Hamilton.
New Jersey	Wil: Livingston, David Brearley, Wm. Paterson, Jona: Dayton.
Pennsylvania	B Franklin, Thomas Mifflin, Robt Morris, Geo. Clymer, Thos. FitzSimons, Jared Ingersoll, James Wilson, Gouv Morris.
Delaware	Geo: Read, Gunning Bedford jun, John Dickinson, Richard Bassett, Jaco: Broom.
Maryland	James McHenry, Dan of St Thos. Jenifer, Danl Carroll.
Virginia	John Blair—, James Madison Jr.
North Carolina	Wm. Blount, Rich'd Dobbs Spaight, Hu Williamson.
South Carolina	J. Rutledge, Charles Cotesworth Pinckney, Charles Pinckney, Pierce Butler.
Georgia	William Few, Abr Baldwin.
	Attest: William Jackson, Secretary.

 uestions for Review and Reflection

According to the United States Constitution and its preamble:
1. Are we creating a Union of states or of people?
2. What kinds of power does the federal government have?
3. What kinds of actions are restricted?
4. How many states did it take to make the Constitution an operating document?
5. Locate some of the checks and balances that are prescribed in the Constitution.

Reading **6**

United States Congress, 1791

The Bill of Rights

The first 10 amendments were added to the Constitution by James Madison during the first Congress of the new government under the Constitution of the United States. These 10 amendments collectively are a "declaration of rights." Liberties such as freedom of the press, of speech, and of the practice of religion are guaranteed, as is "due process," a legal set of procedures to which all persons are entitled when the full weight of government authority is brought to bear.

These kinds of constitutional protections serve as a bulwark against authority and defend minority rights. The Ninth and Tenth Amendments granted certain powers to states and individuals and limited federal powers to those outlined in the Constitution. With the Fourteenth Amendment, states were required to adhere to these rights except for the provisions located in the Second, Third, Seventh, and Tenth Amendments.

Amendments

[The first 10 Amendments, known as the Bill of Rights, were ratified on December 15, 1791.]

AMENDMENT I

No Religious Establishment; Freedom of Religion, Speech, Press, and Assembly
    Congress shall make no law respecting an establishment of religion, or prohibiting the free exercise thereof; or abridging the freedom of speech, or of the press, or the right of the people peaceably to assemble, and to petition the Government for a redress of grievances.

AMENDMENT II
Right to Bear Arms

A well regulated Militia, being necessary to the security of a free State, the right of the people to keep and bear Arms, shall not be infringed.

AMENDMENT III
Quartering of Soldiers

No Soldier shall in time of peace be quartered in any house, without the consent of the Owner, nor in time of war, but in a manner to be prescribed by law.

AMENDMENT IV
Searches and Seizures

The right of the people to be secure in their persons, houses, papers, and effects, against unreasonable searches and seizures, shall not be violated, and no Warrants shall issue, but upon probable cause, supported by Oath or affirmation, and particularly describing the place to be searched and the persons or things to be seized.

AMENDMENT V
Grand Jury Indictments, Double Jeopardy, Self-Incrimination, Due Process, and Just Compensation

No person shall be held to answer for a capital, or otherwise infamous crime, unless on a presentiment or indictment of a Grand Jury, except in cases arising in the land or naval forces, or in the Militia, when in actual service in time of War or public danger, nor shall any person be subject for the same offence to be twice put in jeopardy of life or limb; nor shall be compelled in any criminal case to be a witness against himself, nor be deprived of life, liberty, or property, without due process of law; nor shall private property be taken for public use without just compensation.

AMENDMENT VI
Fair Trials

In all criminal prosecutions, the accused shall enjoy the right to a speedy and public trial, by an impartial jury of the State and district wherein the crime shall have been committed, which district shall have been previously ascertained by law, and to be informed of the nature and cause of the accusation; to be confronted with the witnesses against him; to have compusory process for obtaining witnesses in his favor, and to have the Assistance of Counsel for his defence.

AMENDMENT VII
Jury Trials

In Suits at common law, where the value in controversy shall exceed twenty dollars, the right of trial by jury shall be preserved, and no fact tried by a jury, shall be otherwise re-examined in any Court of the United States, than according to the rules of the common law.

AMENDMENT VIII
No Excessive Bail or Cruel and Unusual Punishment

Excessive bail shall not be required, nor excessive fines imposed, nor cruel and unusual punishments inflicted.

AMENDMENT IX
Not an Exhaustive List of Rights

The enumeration in the Constitution, of certain rights, shall not be construed to deny or disparage others retained by the people.

AMENDMENT X
Reserved Powers

The powers not delegated to the United States by the Constitution, nor prohibited by it to the States, are reserved to the States respectively, or to the people.

Questions for Review and Reflection

1. Distinguish between those rights which might be termed as "unalienable" from other rights in the Bill of Rights.
2. What is the emphasis of the original first 10 amendments?
3. Where does the right of privacy exist in the Bill of Rights?
4. What might be included in "due process"?
5. Analyze the language found in the Bill of Rights to determine what approach it took toward government authority.
6. Interpret the Tenth Amendment in terms of the kinds of power retained by the states.

2

A Government Defect: Early Critical Voices

America grew rapidly. Settlement spread westward from the original colonies, and the federal government purchased Louisiana from France in 1803. In the spirit of "manifest destiny," Texas was annexed in 1845 and Oregon the following year. War with Mexico added the territories of California and New Mexico, so that by 1848 the nation extended from the Atlantic to the Pacific Oceans.

Transportation networks sprang up to service such a vast area. Roads, bridges, railroads, and canals were built with private and public funds. Steamboats and clipper ships provided the means to carry freight and passengers.

Machinery revolutionized farming, making large profits possible. Industrial development advanced rapidly through inventions and the introduction of the factory system.

New England and the mid-Atlantic states industrialized significantly. The South remained agricultural, with large-scale crops of tobacco, sugar, rice, and "king cotton." The West consisted primarily of small farming. These regional differences brought about periodic sectional conflict throughout the first half of the nineteenth century over tariffs, internal improvements, territorial expansion, slave labor, and other issues. Evolving political parties debated how government ought to resolve the disagreements. Many Americans were excluded from the debate, however. The Constitution spoke of "the people," but embraced only certain kinds.

Women were citizens of the country only arguably, since they could not vote or participate in government. Once married, a woman became a member of a household with a single voice represented by its head. Women were often denied rights to property, to business ownership, employment, or educational opportunities, even to serve on a jury. Marriage and divorce laws, as well as issues of child custody, were decided by men. Almost from the beginning, women had begun calling for their voices to be recognized, as did Abigail Adams in Reading 1. Many who worked in the antislavery campaign began to compare their own condition with that of slaves. Having no voice in government and having to swear obedience to their husbands in the marriage contract, some acknowledged a similarity of status. Their antislavery associations became antecedents to a women's movement. In 1848, well before the Civil War, a group of women wrote their own declaration of rights, asserted that "all men and women are created equal," and called for the immediate franchise for women (see Reading 5).

Beginning in 1619, African Americans had been brought to America as indentured servants. Many free blacks had even been allowed to vote. When the cotton gin triggered a demand for mass labor, black servants became slaves owned by their masters. The Constitution, with its $3/5$ compromise, allowed states to count every five slaves as equal to three free persons for purposes of representation in Congress. Further, it legitimized the institution of slavery by allowing such people to be imported until 1808. The Missouri Compromise of 1820 and the Compromise of 1850, discussed in more detail in Chapter 3, offered the opportunity for the expansion of slavery. African Americans created organizations and societies that demanded an immediate end to slavery and a guarantee of political rights for all blacks. They submitted petitions to state legislatures, to the courts, and even to Congress, seeking a redress of grievances. They networked at conventions, published newspapers, sought white support through public meetings, and bought freedom for slaves when they could.

Native American tribes were defined as separate nations. Treaties determined their relationship to the federal government and their territorial rights. Nevertheless, expansion soon forced Indians off their land in violation of treaties in order to make room for settlement. The federal government stood by and witnessed the slaughter of Indians by greedy white settlers who were hungry for the land their states had grabbed despite the treaty guarantees. Pressured by Georgians' demands for Cherokee territory, Congress in 1830 enacted the Indian Removal Act, which appropriated a half-million dollars to force the evacuation of eastern tribes to lands west of the Mississippi. Native Americans challenged a government that allowed Indians to lose lands in direct violation of federal treaty obligations and questioned whether the federal government held supremacy over state governments, since federal laws could not be enforced. A notable challenge is that of the Cherokees in Reading 3.

Chinese immigrants came to California during the Gold Rush of the late 1840s to mine and were also recruited as "coolie" labor for large construction projects. They kept mainly to themselves and organized their own community institutions. Their success caused resentment; their settlements brought about fear of their alien cultural practices. Eventually, California denied them citizenship, and the United States suspended Chinese immigration. Chinese-Americans asked to remain in America and for their new nation to maintain an unrestricted immigration policy.

Excluded from participation in the democratic process, all these groups claimed such treatment was a defect in government They sought fulfillment of the democratic ideals outlined in the Declaration of Independence, the Constitution, and the Bill of Rights. Their dissenting voices rang out loudly and forcefully, demanding change.

Reading 1

Abigail Adams, 1776

Letter to John Adams

"Mrs. President" might be an epithet for Hillary Clinton; in fact, this was a reference to Mrs. John Adams, Abigail, wife of America's second president. Considered intellectually equal by her husband, Abigail (1744-1818) was self-educated, politically sage, and well-versed in current events.

As wife to one president and mother to another, Abigail understood her traditional role. Still, she was outspoken on the subject of equality of the sexes and the need for women to be represented. Enduring long separations caused by the Revolution, John and Abigail relied on letter writing. It was in this correspondence that many of her ideas were advanced. Here she exhorted her husband to "remember the ladies" as he worked on a blueprint for government. She warned of a fomenting rebellion from women who were controlled by "tyrants."

John replied that he found her advice unnecessary and assured her that men "knew better than to repeal our Masculine system," since women, he revealed, were only controlled in theory but in practice were in full charge. Her letter signaled a warning that women would not long suffer a lack of representation.

Braintree March 31, 1776

—I long to hear that you have declared an independancy—and by the way in the new Code of Laws which I suppose it will be necessary for you to make I desire you would Remember the Ladies, and be more generous and favourable to them than your ancestors. Do not put such unlimited power into the hands of the Husbands. Remember all Men would be tyrants if they could. If perticular care and attention is not paid to the Laidies we are determined to foment a Rebelion, and will not hold ourselves bound by any Laws in which we have no voice, or Representation.

That your Sex are Naturally Tyrannical is a Truth so thoroughly established as to admit of no dispute, but such of you as wish to be happy willingly give up the harsh title of Master for the more tender and endearing one of Friend. Why then, not put it out of the power of the vicious and the Lawless to use us with cruelty and indignity with impunity. Men of Sense in all Ages abhor those customs which treat us as the vassals of your Sex. Regard us then as Beings placed by providence under your protection and in imitation of the Supreme Being make use of that power only for our happiness.

Questions for Review and Reflection

1. Who does Abigail Adams want included in the proposed new "Code of Laws"?
2. By comparison, did Adams's ancestors treat women better than her contemporaries?
3. How does Adams draw on the philosophy contained in the Declaration of Independence in her argument?
4. Under what circumstances would Adams support a rebellion?
5. Which sex is "naturally Tyrannical"? In what way?
6. How is this letter the Declaration of Women's Independence?
7. How does Adams evoke the "Supreme Being"?

Reading 2

Manumitted Slaves of North Carolina, 1797

Petition to Redress Set of Grievances

Hunted by dogs or jailed or beaten, runaway slaves were at the mercy of southern slaveholders even if they had been liberated by their owners. Manumission, a legal release from servitude, had been practiced by some masters, but it had produced so many freed blacks that North Carolina enacted laws to curtail the practice. A state statute of 1778 assigned "countenance and authority in violently seizing, imprisoning, and selling into slavery, such as had been so emancipated." As a result, bands of whites roamed the southern landscape ferreting out blacks lucky enough to have been let go.

Four of these "fugitives" petitioned the House of Representatives for a redress of grievances on behalf of all manumitted slaves on the run. Their appeal pointed to a "governmental defect" that allowed slavery in the first place. They avowed that "we are all human," and asked that they be allowed to represent the multitudes held unconstitutionally. In a 50–33 vote, the House refused to accept the petition. This reading sets forth one method utilized by American Negroes to challenge a system that did not recognize their right to representation.

To the President, Senate, and House of Representatives

The Petition and Representation of the under-named Freemen, respectfully showeth:—

That, being of African descent, late inhabitants and natives of North Carolina, to you only, under God, can we apply with any hope of effect, for redress of our Grievances, having been compelled to leave the State wherein we had a right of residence, as freemen liberated under the hand and seal of humane and conscientious masters, the validity of which act of justice, in restoring us to our native right of freedom, was confirmed by judgment of the Superior Court of North Carolina, wherein it was brought to trial; yet, not long after this decision, a law of that State was enacted, under which men of cruel disposition, and void of just principle, received countenance and authority in violently seizing, imprisoning, and selling into slavery, such as had been so emancipated; whereby we were reduced to the necessity of separating from some of our nearest and most tender connexions, and of seeking refuge in such parts of the Union where more regard is paid to the public declaration in favor of liberty and the common right of man, several hundreds, under our circumstances, having in consequence of the said law, been hunted day and night, like beasts of the forest, by armed men with dogs, and made a prey of as free and lawful plunder. . . .

We beseech your impartial attention to our hard condition, not only with respect to our personal sufferings, as freemen, but as a class of that people who, distinguished by color, are therefore with a degrading partiality, considered by many, even of those in eminent stations, as unentitled to that public justice and protection which is the great object of Government. We indulge not a hope, or presume to ask for the interposition of your honorable body, beyond the extent of your constitutional power or influence, yet are willing to believe your serious, disinterested, and candid consideration of the premises, under the benign impressions of equity and mercy, producing upright exertion of what is in your power, may not be without some salutary effect, both for our relief as a people, and toward the removal of obstructions to public order and well-being.

If, notwithstanding all that has been publicly avowed as essential principles respecting the extent of human right to freedom; notwithstanding we have had that right restored to us, so far as was in the power of those by whom we were held as slaves, we cannot claim the privilege of representation in your councils, yet we trust we may address you as fellow-men, who, under God, the sovereign Ruler of the Universe, are intrusted with the distribution of justice, for the terror of evil-doers, the encouragement and protection of the innocent, not doubting that you are men of liberal minds, susceptible of benevolent feelings and clear conception of rectitude to a catholic extent, who can admit that black people (servile as their condition generally is throughout this Continent) have natural affections, social and domestic attachments and sensibilities; and that, therefore, we may hope for a share in your sympathetic attention while we represent that the unconstitutional bondage in which multitudes of our fellows in complexion are held, is to us a subject sorrowfully affecting; for we cannot conceive this condition (more especially those who have been emancipated and tasted the sweets of liberty, and again reduced to slavery by kidnappers and man-stealers) to be less afflicting or deplorable than the situation of citizens of the United States, captured and enslaved through the unrighteous policy prevalent in Algiers. We are far from considering all those who retain slaves as wilful oppressors, being well assured that numbers in the State from whence we are exiles, hold their slaves in bondage, not of choice, but possessing them by inheritance, feel their minds burdened under the slavish restraint of legal impediments to doing justice which they are convinced is due to fellow-rationals. May we not be allowed to consider this stretch of power, morally and politically, a Governmental defect, if not a direct violation of the declared fundamental principles of the

Constitution; and finally, is not some remedy for an evil of such magnitude highly worthy of the deep inquiry and unfeigned zeal of the supreme Legislative body of a free and enlightened people? Submitting our cause to God, and humbly craving your best aid and influence, as you may be favored and directed by that wisdom which is from above, wherewith that you may be eminently dignified and rendered conspicuously, in the view of nations, a blessing to the people you represent, is the sincere prayer of your petitioners.

JACOB NICHOLSON,
JUPITER NICHOLSON, his mark,
JOB ALBERT, his mark,
THOMAS PRITCHET, his mark.

Questions for Review and Reflection

1. What was confirmed by the Superior Court of North Carolina? What changed?
2. What was the petitioners' objection to a recent North Carolina law? How did they respond?
3. Why did it become necessary for the petitioners to leave the state? In what other parts of the Union might the petitioners seek refuge?
4. What legislative remedy were the petitioners seeking?
5. Why couldn't the petitioners claim the privilege of representation in the state's legislature?
6. What is the petitioners' opinion of a majority of slaveholders? What might explain their attitude?
7. What constitutional principle does the petition evoke?
8. How often do the petitioners invoke the Deity in their appeal? Do you think the Representatives were receptive to this tactic?

Reading 3

The Cherokee Nation, 1830

Appeal to the People of the United States

From the late 1600s on, treaty making between colonial and U.S. governments and Indian tribes was used to transfer property rights in an orderly fashion and to avoid bloodshed. The Cherokee nation had a 1791 treaty with the U.S.—only one of many signed over the years–that designated their territory. But gold was discovered, and Georgia passed a law to gain control over Cherokee land.

The Cherokees appealed to the federal government to uphold the treaty as the supreme law of the land, superseding any state law. Instead, Congress enacted the Indian Removal Act of 1830, which provided resettlement funds to move the Indians further west. The tribe then appealed to the people of the United States to have the government honor its treaty obligations. "[I]t never occurred to us . . . that without even a pretended compact, and against our vehement and unanimous protestations, we should be delivered over to the discretion of those, who had declared by a legislative act, that they wanted the Cherokee lands and would have them."

The Supreme Court ruled in favor of the Cherokees, but President Andrew Jackson refused to enforce the decision. Instead, during 1838 the tribe was evicted from their homes and marched to Oklahoma. Their "Trail of Tears" caused great hardship and loss of life.

More than a year ago we were officially given to understand by the secretary of war, that the president could not protect us against the laws of Georgia. This information was entirely unexpected; as it went upon the principle, that treaties made between the United States and the Cherokee nation have no power to withstand the legislation of separate states; and of course, that they have no efficacy whatever, but leave our people to the mercy of the neighboring whites, whose supposed interests would be promoted by our expulsion, or extermination. It would be impossible to describe the sorrow, which affected our minds on learning that the chief magistrate of the United States had come to this conclusion, that all his illustrious predecessors had held intercourse with us on principles which could not be sustained; that they had made promises of vital importance to us, which could not be fulfilled—promises made hundreds of times in almost every conceivable manner,—often in the form of solemn treaties, sometimes in letters written by the chief magistrate with his own hand, very often in letters written by the secretary of war under his direction, sometimes orally by the president and the secretary to our chiefs, and frequently and always, both orally and in writing by the agent of the United States residing among us, whose most important business it was, to see the guaranty of the United States faithfully executed. . . .

Finding that relief could not be obtained from the chief magistrate, and not doubting that our claim to protection was just, we made our application to Congress. During four long months our delegation waited, at the doors of the national legislature of the United States, and the people at home, in the most painful suspense, to learn in what manner our application would be answered; and, now that Congress has adjourned, on the very day before the date fixed by Georgia for the extension of her oppressive laws over the greater part of our country, the distressing intelligence has been received that we have received no answer at all; and no department of the government has assured us, that we are to receive the desired protection. But just at the close of the session, an act was passed, by which an half a million of dollars was appropriated towards effecting a removal of Indians; and we have great reason to fear that the influence of this act will be brought to bear most injuriously upon us. The passage of this act was certainly understood by the representatives of Georgia as abandoning us to the oppressive and cruel measures of the state, and as sanctioning the opinion that treaties with Indians do not restrain state legislation. We are informed by those, who are competent to judge, that the recent act does not admit of such construction; but that the passage of it, under the actual circumstances of the controversy, will be considered as sanctioning the pretensions of Georgia, there is too much reason to fear.

Thus have we realized, with heavy hearts, that our supplication has not been heard; that the protection heretofore experienced is now to be withheld; that the guaranty, in consequence of which our fathers laid aside their arms and ceded the best portions of their country, means nothing; and that we must either emigrate to an unknown region and leave the pleasant land to which we have the strongest attachment, or submit to the legislation of a state, which has already made our people outlaws, and enacted that any Cherokee, who shall endeavor to prevent the selling of his country, shall be imprisoned in the penitentiary of Georgia not less than four years. To our countrymen this has been melancholy intelligence, and with the most bitter disappointment has it been received.

But in the midst of our sorrows, we do not forget our obligations to our friends and benefactors. It was with sensations of inexpressible joy that we have learned that the voice of thousands, in many parts of the United States, has been raised in our behalf, and numerous memorials offered in our favor, in both houses of Congress. To those numerous friends, who have thus sympathized with us in our low estate, we tender our grateful acknowledgements. In pleading our cause, they have pleaded the cause of the poor and defenceless throughout the world. Our special thanks are due, however, to those honorable men, who so ably and eloquently asserted our rights, in both branches of the national legislature. Their efforts will be appreciated wherever the merits of this question shall be known; and we cannot but think, that they have secured for themselves a permanent reputation among the disinterested advocates of humanity, equal rights, justice, and good faith. We even cherish the hope, that these efforts, seconded and followed by others of a similar character, will yet be available, so far as to mitigate our sufferings, if not to effect our entire deliverance. . . .

We wish to remain on the land of our fathers. We have a perfect and original right to remain without interruption or molestation. The treaties with us, and laws of the United States made in pursuance of treaties, guaranty our residency and our privileges, and secure us against intruders. Our only request is, that these treaties may be fulfilled, and these laws executed. . . .

It is under a sense of the most pungent feelings that we make this, perhaps our last appeal to the good people of the United States. It cannot be that the community we are addressing, remarkable for its intelligence and religious sensibilities, and pre-eminent for its devotion to the rights of man, will lay aside this appeal, without considering that we stand in need of its sympathy and commiseration. We know that to the Christian and to the philanthropist the voice of our multiplied sorrows and fiery trials will not appear as an idle tale. In our own land, on our own soil, and in our own dwellings, which we reared for our wives and for our little ones, when there was peace on our mountains and in our valleys, we are encountering troubles which cannot but try our very souls. But shall we, on account of these troubles, forsake our beloved country? Shall we be compelled by a civilized and Christian people, with whom we have lived in perfect peace for the last forty years, and for whom we have willingly bled in war, to bid a final adieu to our homes, our farms, our streams and our beautiful forests? No. We are still firm. We intend still to cling, with our wonted affection, to the land which gave us birth, and which, every day of our lives, brings to us new and stronger ties of attachment. We appeal to the judge of all the earth, who will finally award us justice, and to the good sense of the American people, whether we are intruders upon the land of others. Our consciences bear us witness that we are the invaders of no man's rights—we have robbed no man of his territory—we have usurped no man's authority, nor have we deprived any one of his unalienable privileges. How then shall we indirectly confess the right of another people to our land by leaving it forever? On the soil which contains the ashes of our beloved men we wish to live—on this soil we wish to die.

Questions for Review and Reflection

1. What two choices did the federal government give the Cherokees?
2. Was the Cherokees' faith in earlier treaties justified? What was their reaction to learning that they had negotiated on "principles which could not be sustained"?
3. This appeal was addressed to the American people, but how might it also be considered an appeal to the international community?

Reading 4

Sarah Grimké, 1837

Letters on Equality of the Sexes

As members of a slave-owning South Carolina aristocracy, Sarah Grimké (1792–1873) and her sister, Angelina, observed firsthand the effects of the slavery system. From an early age, they abhorred the institution, and they freed their family's slaves immediately upon their father's death.

Both went north and began speaking on the abolitionist lecture circuit, Sarah in the late 1820s and Angelina a few years later. The sisters joined forces with William Lloyd Garrison, publisher of the abolitionist newspaper *The Liberator,* who ultimately married Angelina Grimké. That they were women who spoke in public was not always acceptable, as is evident in Grimké's second letter. Despite their probable support of abolition, the Congregational ministers of Massachusetts opined that "her character becomes unnatural when woman assumes the place and tone of man as a public reformer." And in the face of such bias, what the Grimkés had begun as a campaign to abolish slavery turned into the seminal crusade for women's rights. Grimké reacted to her critics with a defense of women as equals possessed of mighty power "in opposition to a corrupt public opinion." Though other women, like Abigail Adams in Reading 1, had expressed their concerns privately, the Grimké sisters have been credited with the start of the women's movement as a public issue in America. Sarah's letters, excerpted here, were written to Mary Parker, president of the Boston Female Anti-Slavery Society.

Amesbury, 7th Mo. 11th, 1837.

My Dear Friend,—In attempting to comply with thy request to give my views on the Province of Woman, I feel that I am venturing on nearly untrodden ground, and that I shall advance arguments in opposition to a corrupt public opinion, and to the perverted interpretation of Holy Writ, which has so universally obtained. But I am in search of truth; and no obstacle shall prevent my prosecuting that search, because I believe the welfare of the world will be materially advanced by every new discovery we make of the designs of

Jehovah in the creation of woman. It is impossible that we can answer the purpose of our being, unless we understand that purpose. It is impossible that we should fulfill our duties, unless we comprehend them; or live up to our privileges, unless we know what they are. . . .

We must first view woman at the period of her creation. 'And God said, Let us make man in our own image, after our likeness; and let them have dominion over the fish of the sea, and over the fowl of the air, and over the cattle, and over all the earth, and over every creeping thing that creepeth upon the earth. So God created man in his own image, in the image of God created he him, male and female created he them.' In all this sublime description of the creation of man, (which is a generic term including man and woman,) there is not one particle of difference intimated as existing between them. They were both made in the image of God; dominion was given to both over every other creature, but not over each other. Created in perfect equality, they were expected to exercise the viceregence intrusted to them by their Maker, in harmony and love. . . .

Here then I plant myself. God created us equal;—he created us free agents;—he is our Lawgiver, our King and our Judge, and to him alone is woman bound to be in subjection, and to him alone is she accountable for the use of those talents with which her Heavenly Father has entrusted her. . . .

Thine for the oppressed in the bonds of womanhood,

Sarah M. Grimké
Haverhill, 7th Mo. 17, 1837.

Dear Friend,—When I last addressed thee, I had not seen the Pastoral Letter of the General Association [of Congregational Ministers of Massachusetts]. It has since fallen into my hands, and I must digress from my intention of exhibiting the condition of women in different parts of the world, in order to make some remarks on this extraordinary document. I am persuaded that when the minds of men and women become emancipated from the thraldom of superstition and 'traditions of men,' the sentiments contained in the Pastoral Letter will be recurred to with as much astonishment as the opinions of Cotton Mather and other distinguished men of his day, on the subject of witchcraft; nor will it be deemed less wonderful, that a body of divines should gravely assemble and endeavor to prove that woman has no right to 'open her mouth for the dumb,' than it now is that judges should have sat on the trials of witches, and solemnly condemned nineteen persons and one dog to death for witchcraft.

But to the letter. It says, 'We invite your attention to the dangers which at present seem to threaten the FEMALE CHARACTER with widespread and permanent injury.' I rejoice that they have called the attention of my sex to this subject, because I believe if woman investigates it, she will soon discover that danger is impending, though from a totally different source from that which the Association apprehends,—danger from those who, having long held the reins of *usurped* authority, are unwilling to permit us to fill that sphere which God created us to move in, and who have entered into league to crush the immortal mind of woman. I rejoice, because I am persuaded that the rights of women, like the rights of slaves, need only be examined to be understood and asserted, even by some of those, who are now endeavoring to smother the irrepressible desire for mental and spiritual freedom which glows in the breast of many, who hardly dare to speak their sentiments.

'The appropriate duties and influence of women are clearly stated in the New Testament. Those duties are unobtrusive and private, but the sources of *mighty power.* When the mild, *dependent,* softening influence of woman upon the sternness of man's opinions is fully exercised, society feels the effects of it in a thousand ways.' No one can desire more earnestly than I do, that woman may move exactly in the sphere which her Creator has assigned her; and I believe her having been displaced from that sphere has introduced confusion into the world. It is, therefore, of vast importance to herself and to all the rational creation, that she should ascertain what are her duties and her privileges as a responsible and immortal being.

The New Testament has been referred to, and I am willing to abide by its decisions, but must enter my protest against the false translation of some passages by the MEN who did that work, and against the perverted interpretation by the MEN who undertook to write commentaries thereon. I am inclined to think, when we are admitted to the honor of studying Greek and Hebrew, we shall produce some various readings of the Bible a little different from those we now have.

The Lord Jesus defines the duties of his followers in his Sermon on the Mount. He lays down grand principles by which they should be governed, without any reference to sex or condition:—'Ye are the light of the world. A city that is set on a hill cannot be hid. Neither do men light a candle and put it under a bushel, but on a candlestick, and it giveth light unto all that are in the house. Let your light so shine before men, that they may see your good works, and glorify your Father which is in Heaven.' I follow him through all his precepts, and find him giving the same directions to women as to men, never even referring to the distinction now so strenuously insisted upon between masculine and feminine virtues: this is one of the anti-christian 'traditions of men' which are taught instead of the 'commandments of God.' Men and women were CREATED EQUAL; they are both moral and account-able beings, and whatever is *right* for man to do, is *right* for woman.

But the influence of woman, says the Association, is to be private and unobtrusive; her light is not to shine before man like that of her brethren; but she is passively to let the lords of the creation, as they call themselves, put the bushel over it, lest peradventure it might appear that the world has been benefitted by the rays of *her* candle. So that her quenched light, according to their judgment, will be of more use than if it were set on the candlestick. 'Her influence is the source of mighty power.' This has ever been the flattering language of man since he laid aside the whip as a means to keep woman in subjection. He spares her body; but the war he has waged against her mind, her heart, and her soul, has been no less destructive to her as a moral being. How monstrous, how anti-christian, is the doctrine that woman is to be dependent on man! Where, in all the sacred Scriptures, is this taught? Alas! she has too well learned the lesson which MAN has labored to teach her. She has surrendered her dearest RIGHTS, and been satisfied with the privileges which man has assumed to grant her; she has been amused with the show of power, whilst man has absorbed all the reality into himself. He has adorned the creature whom God gave him as a companion, with baubles and gewgaws, turned her attention to personal attractions, offered incense to her vanity, and made her the instrument of his selfish gratification, a plaything to please his eye and amuse his hours of leisure. 'Rule by obedience and by submission sway,' or in other words, study to be a hypocrite, pretend to submit, but gain your point, has been the code of household morality which woman has been taught. The poet has sung, in sickly strains, the loveliness of woman's dependence upon man, and now we find it reechoed by those who profess to teach the religion of the Bible. God says, 'Cease ye from man whose breath is in his nostrils, for wherein is he to be accounted of?' Man says, depend upon me. God says, 'HE will teach us of his ways.' Man says, believe it not, I am to be your teacher. This doctrine of dependence upon man is utterly at variance with the doctrine of the Bible. In that book I find nothing like the softness of woman, nor the sternness of man: both are equally commanded to bring forth the fruits of the Spirit, love, meekness, gentleness, etc.

But we are told, 'the power of woman is in her dependence, flowing from a consciousness of that weakness which God has given her for her protection.' If physical weakness is alluded to, I cheerfully concede the superiority; if brute force is what my brethren are claiming, I am willing to let them have all the honor they desire; but if they mean to intimate, that mental or moral weakness belongs to woman, more than to man, I utterly disclaim the charge. Our powers of mind have been crushed, as far as man could do it, our sense of morality has been impaired by his interpretation of our duties; but no where does God say that he made any distinction between us, as moral and intelligent beings.

Sarah M. Grimké

Questions for Review and Reflection

1. What are the "new discoveries" concerning Jehovah's creation of women, according to Grimké? What argument does Grimké make to include women in the biblical phrase, "God created man in his own image"?

2. What is Grimké's attitude about the pastoral letter of the General Association of Congregational Ministers of Massachusetts? According to this document, what are the dangers to the "female character"?
3. How is the doctrine of dependence upon men at variance with the doctrine of the Bible? Who is responsible for this variance? How did it come about?

Reading 5

Seneca Falls Convention, 1848

Declaration of Sentiments

Drawn by a local newspaper ad, several hundred people assembled in a small New York town for this first meeting for women's rights. A declaration, modeled on the Declaration of Independence, was drawn up. There was a long list of grievances itemizing the "injuries and usurpations" visited on women by men. Whether single or married, women had no power over matters of property, children, employment, divorce, or taxes, to name only a few.

"We hold these truths to be self-evident: that all men and women are created equal: that they are endowed by their Creator with certain inalienable rights," their declaration stated. They insisted on the immediate extension to females of all the rights and privileges of any American citizen. This is one of the most significant documents of the women's rights movement. The writers' tactic of employing the language of the earlier declaration served to enhance their position on an "inalienable right" to representation.

Declaration of Sentiments

When, in the course of human events, it becomes necessary for one portion of the family of man to assume among the people of the earth a position different from that which they have hitherto occupied, but one to which the laws of nature and of nature's God entitle them, a decent respect to the opinions of mankind requires that they should declare the causes that impel them to such a course.

We hold these truths to be self-evident: that all men and women are created equal; that they are endowed by their Creator with certain inalienable rights, that among these are life, liberty, and the pursuit of happiness; that to secure these rights governments are instituted, deriving their just powers from the consent of the governed. Whenever any form of government becomes destructive of these ends, it is the right of those who suffer from it to refuse allegiance to it, and to insist upon the institution of a new government, laying its foundation on such principles, and organizing its powers in such form as to them shall seem most likely to effect their safety and happiness. Prudence, indeed, will dictate that governments long established should not be changed for light and transient causes; and accordingly, all experience hath shown that mankind are more disposed to suffer, while evils are sufferable, than to right themselves by abolishing the forms to which they were accustomed. But when a long train of abuses and usurpations, pursuing invariably the same object evinces a design to reduce them under absolute despotism, it is their duty to throw off such government, and to provide new guards for their future security. Such has been the patient sufferance of the women under this government, and such is now the necessity which constrains them to demand the equal station to which they are entitled.

The history of mankind is a history of repeated injuries and usurpations on the part of man toward woman, having in direct object the establishment of an absolute tyranny over her. To prove this, let facts be submitted to a candid world.

He has never permitted her to exercise her inalienable right to the elective franchise.

He has compelled her to submit to laws, in the formation of which she had no voice.

He has withheld from her the rights which are given to the most ignorant and degraded men—both natives and foreigners.

Having deprived her of this right of a citizen, the elective franchise, thereby leaving her without representation in the halls of legislation, he has oppressed her on all sides.

He has made her, if married, in the eye of the law, civilly dead.

He has taken from her all right in property, even to the wages she earns.

He has made her, morally, an irresponsible being, as she can commit many crimes with impunity, provided they be done in the presence of her husband. In the covenant of marriage, she is compelled to promise obedience to her husband, he becoming, to all intents and purposes, her master—the law giving him power to deprive her of her liberty, and to administer chastisement.

He has so framed the laws of divorce, as to what shall be the proper causes of divorce; in case of separation, to whom the guardianship of the children shall be given; as to be wholly regardless of the happiness of woman—the law, in all cases, going upon a false supposition of the supremacy of man, and giving all power into his hands.

After depriving her of all rights as a married woman, if single and the owner of property, he has taxed her to support a government which recognizes her only when her property can be made profitable to it.

He has monopolized nearly all the profitable employments, and from those she is permitted to follow, she receives but a scanty remuneration.

He closes against her all the avenues to wealth and distinction, which he considers most honorable to himself. As a teacher of theology, medicine, or law, she is not known.

He has denied her the facilities for obtaining a thorough education—all colleges being closed against her.

He allows her in Church, as well as State, but a subordinate position, claiming Apostolic authority for her exclusion from the ministry, and, with some exception, from any public participation in the affairs of the Church.

He has created a false public sentiment, by giving to the world a different code of morals for men and women, by which moral delinquencies which exclude women from society, are not only tolerated but deemed of little account in man.

He has usurped the prerogative of Jehovah himself, claiming it as his right to assign for her a sphere of action, when that belongs to her conscience and to her God.

He has endeavored, in every way that he could, to destroy her confidence in her own powers, to lessen her self-respect, and to make her willing to lead a dependent and abject life.

Now, in view of this entire disfranchisement of one-half the people of this country, their social and religious degradation,—in view of the unjust laws above mentioned, and because women do feel themselves aggrieved, oppressed, and fraudulently deprived of their most sacred rights, we insist that they have immediate admission to all the rights and privileges which belong to them as citizens of the United States.

In entering upon the great work before us, we anticipate no small amount of misconception, misrepresentation, and ridicule; but we shall use every instrumentality within our powers to effect our object. We shall employ agents, circulate tracts, petition the state and national legislatures, and endeavor to enlist the pulpit and the press in our behalf. We hope this Convention will be followed by a series of Conventions, embracing every part of the country.

Firmly relying upon the final triumph of the Right and the True, we do this day affix our signatures to this declaration.

Lucretia Mott
Harriet Cady Eaton
Margaret Pryor
Elizabeth Cady Stanton
Eunice Newton Foote
Mary Ann McClintock

[Q]uestions for Review and Reflection

1. In what way does the Seneca Falls movement draw upon and expand Jefferson's understanding of natural rights? Is this effective? How is this similar to the Constitution and the Declaration of Independence?
2. What has history demonstrated concerning the relationships between men and women? What examples do the authors cite in their argument concerning men's treatment of women?
3. In what way did marriage infringe upon a woman's rights in the 1840s? Is this a fair argument?
4. What remedy does the Seneca Falls movement seek?
5. Does the Seneca Falls movement expect favorable or unfavorable public reception of their group's goals and attitudes?

Reading 6

William Wells Brown, 1849

Letter to Enoch Price

William Wells Brown (1814–1884) was a fugitive slave from Kentucky who had become prominent in the antislavery movement. He made speeches, wrote letters that were published in abolitionist newspapers, and participated for a time in the underground railroad, helping others to escape to freedom. He eventually traveled to Europe and attempted to rally antislavery support. He wrote this letter to his ex-master from London after having served as a delegate to the World Peace Conference in 1849. He challenged a country that had been founded on the principle of liberty for all men but refused citizenship and the right to vote to a native like himself. This letter, reprinted in the abolitionist newspaper *The Liberator,* is only one example of the efforts of many Negro activists who worked specifically for the vote for all blacks in America.

The subject to which I wish to call your attention is one with which you are intimately connected, namely, Chattel Slavery in the United States. The institution of slavery has been branded as infamous by the good and wise throughout the world. It is regarded as an offence in the sight of God, and opposed to the best interests of man. Whatever in its proper tendency and general effect destroys, abridges, or renders insecure, human welfare, is opposed to the spirit and genius of Christianity. There is a proverb, that no man can bind a chain upon the limb of his neighbor, without inevitable fate fastening the other end around his own body. This has been signally verified by the slaveholders of America. While they have been degrading the colored man, by enslaving him, they have become degraded themselves; in withholding education from the minds of their slaves, they have kept their own children in comparative ignorance. The immoralities which have been found to follow in the train of slavery in all countries and all ages, are to be seen in their worst forms in the Slave States of America. This is attributable to the degree of ignorance which is deemed necessary to keep the enslaved in their chains. It is a fact admitted by the American slaveholders themselves, that their slaves are in a worse state of heathenism than any other heathen in the civilized world. . . .

Sir, you are a slaveholder, and by the laws of God and of nature, your slaves, like yourself, are entitled to "life, liberty, and the pursuit of happiness," and you have no right whatever to deprive them of these inestimable blessings which you claim for yourself. Your slaves have the same right to develop their moral and intellectual faculties that you have; but you are keeping them in a state of ignorance and degradation; and if a single ray of light breaks forth, and penetrates to their souls, it is in despite of your efforts to keep their minds obscured in mental darkness.

You profess to be a Christian, and yet you are one of those who have done more to bring contempt upon Christianity in the United States, by connecting that religion with slavery, than all other causes combined. Were it not for slavery, the United States would be what they have long professed to be, but are not, the "land of the free, and the home of the brave." The millions in Europe, who are struggling for political and religious liberty, have looked in vain to the United States for sympathy. The Americans, busily engaged in spreading slavery over new territory, and thereby forging chains for the limbs of unborn millions, are not in the position to sympathise with the oppressed in other countries. America has her Red Republicans, as well as her black slaves; their hands are crimsoned with the blood of their victims. If the atrocities recently practised upon defenceless women in Austria make the blood run cold through the veins of the humane and good throughout the civilized world, the acts committed daily upon the slave women of America should not only cause the blood to chill, but to stop its circulation.

In behalf of your slaves, I ask you, in the name of the God whom you profess to worship, to take the chains from their limbs, and to let them go free. It is a duty that you owe to God, to the slave, and to the world. You are a husband:—I ask you then to treat the wives of your slaves as you would have your own companion dealt with. You are a father:—I ask you, therefore, to treat the children of your slaves as you would have your own legitimate offspring treated. . . . When you look upon your own parents, sisters and brothers, and feel thankful that you are kept in safety together, think of him who now addresses you, and remember how you, with others, tore from him a beloved mother, an affectionate sister, and three dear brothers, and sold them to the slave trader, to be carried to the far South, there to be worked upon a cotton, sugar or rice plantation, where, if still living, they are now wearing the galling chains of slavery. By your professed love of America, I conjure you to use your influence for the abolition of an institution which has done a thousand times more to blacken the character of the American people, and to render the name of their boasted free republic more odious to the ears of the friends of human freedom throughout the world, than all their other faults combined. I will not yield to you in affection for America, but I hate her institution of slavery. I love her, because I am identified with her enslaved millions by every tie that should bind man to his fellow-man. The United States has disfranchised me, and declared that I am not a citizen, but a chattel: her Constitution dooms me to be your slave.

Questions for Review and Reflection

1. According to William Wells Brown, what rights do slaves have?
2. What is the condition of slavery elsewhere in the world?
3. How does slavery "blacken" the American landscape?
4. How does a slaveholder bring contempt upon Christianity?

Reading 7

Norman Assing, 1852

Letter to Governor Bigler

Slaves were not the only group denied the full promise of American democracy because of their color. Asian-Americans suffered prohibitions as well. Norman Assing, a Chinese merchant and self-described community leader in California, complained to the state's governor in 1852 about a proposed restriction on Chinese immigration. Assing called a republic "reprehensible" that admitted "no asylum to any other than the pale face." Fleeing famine and political upheaval in their homeland, Chinese immigrants had initially been welcomed as cheap labor. They went to work mining for gold, farming, and performing construction work. The number of Chinese who emigrated to California for the Gold Rush of the 1840s was small compared to the size of the Asian force that came to build America's railroads 20 years later. But even the Gold Rush immigrants created a white backlash against those Chinese who decided to make their homes in America. Assing described himself as a republican and wrote that he could not believe that "the framers of your declaration of rights ever suggested the propriety of establishing an aristocracy of skin."

Despite the protests of Assing and others, by the 1880s, immigration laws were passed to exclude Chinese from further entry into the United States for at least ten years. Assing's letter, which was reprinted in the *Daily Alta,* a California newspaper, spoke directly to the issue of diversity and democracy.

To His Excellency Gov. Bigler

Sir:—I am a Chinaman, a republican, and a lover of free institutions; am much attached to the principles of the Government of the United States, and therefore take the liberty of addressing you as the chief of the government of this state. . . .

I am not much acquainted with your logic, that by excluding population from this state you enhance its wealth. I always have considered that population was wealth; particularly a population of producers, of men who by the labor of their hands or intellect, enrich the warehouses or the granaries of the country with the products of nature and art. You are deeply convinced you say "that to enhance the prosperity and to preserve the tranquility of this state, Asiatic immigration must be checked." This, your Excellency, is but one step towards a retrograde movement of the government, which, on reflection, you will discover; and which the citizens of this country ought never to tolerate. It was one of the principal causes of quarrel between you (when colonies) and England; when the latter pressed laws against emigration, you looked for immigration; it came, and immigration made *you what you are*—your nation what it is. It transferred you at once from childhood to manhood, and made you great and respectable throughout the nations of the earth. I am sure your Excellency cannot, if you would, prevent your being called, the descendant of an immigrant, for I am sure you do not boast of being a descendant of the red men. But your further logic is more reprehensible. You argue that this is a republic of a particular race—that the Constitution of the United States admits of no asylum to any other than the pale face. This proposition is false in the extreme; and you know it. The declaration of your independence, and all the acts of your government, your people, and your history, are against you. . . .

It is true, you have degraded the negro because of your holding him in involuntary servitude, and because for the sake of union in some of your states such was tolerated. And amongst this class you would endeavor to place us; and no doubt it would be pleasing to some would-be freemen to mark the brand of servitude upon us. But we would beg to remind you that when your nation was a wilderness, . . . we exercised most of the arts and virtues of civilized life; that we are possessed of a language and literature, and that men skilled in science and the arts are numerous amongst us; that the productions of our manufactories, our sail and work-shops, form no small share of the commerce of the world; and that for centuries colleges, schools, charitable institutions, asylums and hospitals, have been as common as in your own land. That our people cannot be reproved for their idleness, and that your historians have given them due credit for the variety and richness of their works of art, and for their simplicity of manners, and particularly their industry. And we beg to remark, that so far as the history of our race in California goes, it stamps with the test of truth the fact that we are not the degraded race you would make us. We came amongst you as mechanics or traders, and following every honorable business of life. You do not find us pursuing occupations of a degrading character, except you consider labor degrading, which I am sure you do not; and if our countrymen save the proceeds of their industry from the tavern and the gambling house, to spend it in the purchase of farms or town lots or on their families, surely you will admit that even these are virtues. You say "you desire to see no change in the generous policy of this Government as far as regards Europeans." It is out of your power to say, however, in what way or to whom the doctrines of the Constitution shall apply. You have no more right to propose a measure for checking immigration, than you have to assume the right of sending a message to the Legislature on the subject. As far as regards the color and complexion of our race, we are perfectly aware that our population have been a little more tanned than yours.

Your Excellency will discover, however, that we are as much allied to the *African* race or the red man as you are yourself, and that as far as the aristocracy of *skin* is concerned, ours might compare with many of the European races; nor do we consider that your Excellency, as a Democrat, will make us believe that the framers of your declaration of rights ever suggested the propriety of establishing an aristocracy of *skin*.

uestions for Review and Reflection

1. What is Governor Bigler's apparent rationale for halting Asian immigration?
2. What similarities does Assing see between the current situation and the quarrel between the American colonies and England?

3. How did immigration transform America at once from childhood to manhood, in Assing's opinion?

4. In what way do the Declaration of Independence, acts of Congress, and American history diminish the governor's argument?

5. What comparison does Assing draw between the relatively new American culture and the ancient culture of China? Why does he make this argument?

6. What fault does Assing find with Western historians?

7. What argument does Assing make to support his belief that it is not right for Americans to check immigration in the manner suggested by the governor?

8. What similarities does Assing see between his people's plight and that of the red and black races?

9. What is this "aristocracy of skin" of which Assing speaks?

The Nation Divides and Reunites:
Addressing the Slavery Issue

Issues that were destined to explode into civil war dominated the period between 1820 and 1870, and the powers of Congress were used to resolve conflicts. Primary among the problems was slavery, and congressional legislation seemed to be the solution.

In 1820, Congress enacted the Missouri Compromise, which was designed to maintain a balance of power between free states and slave states by admitting one of each. It also stipulated that slavery would not expand into the remaining Louisiana territories. Congress followed with the Compromise of 1850, which allowed California in as a free state, allowed the New Mexico/Utah territory to decide the issue of slavery by popular sovereignty, and enacted a strict fugitive slave law to force the return of slaves who had found sanctuary in the North. But in 1854, Congress also entitled the new territories of Kansas and Nebraska (part of the Louisiana territory) to use popular sovereignty to answer the question of slavery. The Kansas-Nebraska Act effectively repealed the Missouri Compromise of 1820, which had explicitly denied such a possibility. Outraged by this legislation, some Northerners chose to ignore the fugitive slave provisions of the Compromise of 1850.

Further confounding the issue, the Supreme Court, in its *Dred Scott* decision of 1857, declared that Mr. Scott had no legal standing in a federal court because he was a slave, and therefore not a citizen of the United States. Further, the court ruled that Congress had no authority to abolish slavery; rather, it had a duty to protect private property, not limit it. By this reasoning, the Court found the Missouri Compromise unconstitutional.

Slavery, popular sovereignty, the *Dred Scott* decision, federal ver
sus state power—all fueled the national crisis. Abraham Lincoln engaged
in some famous debates over these issues when he ran for Congress
from Illinois in 1858. He opposed slavery on many grounds but was
willing to tolerate it where it existed. He lost that election to Stephen
A. Douglas, but in 1860 he was nominated for president by the newly
formed Republican Party, which pledged to stop further expansion of
slavery.

Lincoln was elected, and shortly thereafter, the South seceded from
the Union. With an imbalance weighted toward free states already in the
Congress, and with a new Republican president who had won only a sectional victory (his name had not even appeared on any Southern ballot),
many in the South felt their way of life was doomed unless they separated
from such a Union.

Lincoln's Emancipation Proclamation, written in 1862 and signed as
an Executive Order on January 1, 1863, is often characterized as the end
of slavery in the United States. In reality, it was an attempt to bring
rebellious Southern states into line by freeing slaves in those areas. This
Northern Republican strategy was designed both to undermine the plantation economy and to commandeer freed slaves into the Union Army. It
created the impression that in pursuing the Civil War, the North was fighting against slavery. Slaves in Confederate states occupied by Union troops,
and those in border states loyal to the Union, were not affected. Not only
did the proclamation fail to resolve the overall question of slavery, but
some members of Congress felt that the president had no right under the
Constitution to repeal laws of individual states.

Nor, as we know, did the proclamation succeed in quelling the Confederate rebellion. The Civil War continued, ending in defeat for the South.
With the Union preserved, Congress turned its attention to resolving the
slavery issue.

The framers had given the power to amend the Constitution to Congress and the states, outlining the process in Article V. Accordingly, Congress decided to initiate the changes that became known as the Civil War
Amendments, all of which were later ratified by the states.

The Thirteenth Amendment freed all slaves throughout the nation,
rendering the questions raised by the Emancipation Proclamation moot,
since Article V stated that such amendments "shall be valid to all intents
and purposes, as part of this Constitution."

The Fourteenth Amendment defined citizenship and made previous
slaves citizens of the United States and of the state wherein they resided.
They were entitled to all the privileges of citizens; no state could deprive
citizens of life, liberty, or property without due process of law, nor of the
equal protection of the laws. Congress was clear in its intent and cemented
those rights through amendment rather than legislation.

Finally, the Fifteenth Amendment extended the right to vote to all citizens, without regard to race, color, or previous condition of servitude, an extension of federal power over the states.

Ratification of these amendments was a condition of return to the Union. Southern states balked, raised a defense of slavery again, but resignedly ratified the changes.

These Civil War Amendments specifically gave new authority to the Congress with the enabling clause at the end of each, which stated that, "The Congress shall have power to enforce this article by appropriate legislation." In a sense, then, the Civil War changed the Constitution in significant ways.

In his famous Gettysburg Address, President Lincoln spoke of the "new nation, conceived in liberty, and dedicated to the proposition that all men are created equal." As Garry Wills said in his 1993 book, *Lincoln at Gettysburg,* "For most people now, the Declaration [of Independence] means what Lincoln told us it means, as a way of correcting the Constitution itself without overthrowing it. It is this correction of the spirit, this intellectual revolution, that makes attempts to go back beyond Lincoln to some earlier version so feckless. The proponents of states' rights may have arguments, but they have lost their force, in courts as well as in the popular mind. By accepting the Gettysburg Address, its concept of a single people dedicated to the proposition [of equality], we have been changed. Because of it, we live in a different America." The "government of the people, by the people, for the people" had changed its definition of "people" and allowed a much broader interpretation of the Constitution. In the bargain, the federal government won for itself sweeping new power.

Reading 1

John Quincy Adams, 1820

Diaries

Slavery was a hotly contested issue that called for regular negotiation and compromise. The dispute was not only a moral one; because each slave counted as three-fifths of a citizen for congressional representation, slave states had a political advantage. And, Northern states' production costs, boosted by wages, were higher than those of states using slave labor. With the introduction of Eli Whitney's cotton gin, mills in New England became ever more dependent on supplies of Southern cotton,

fueling cotton growers' hunger for land. Striking a balance between competing interests was the solution Congress reached
by admitting an equal number of free and slave states to the
Union. This seemed to work until Missouri applied for admission as a slave state, which would have disrupted the balance.
John Quincy Adams, son of the nation's second president,
served as secretary of state under President James Monroe during the bitter debates over the Missouri Compromise of 1820.
Maine was eventually let in as a free state to balance the admission of Missouri as a slave state, but the compromise denied
further expansion of slavery into the western territories.

In his diary, John Q. Adams (1767-1848) wrote that he
believed this was all that "could be effected under the present
Constitution." He raised the issue of limits to constitutional
authority and asked whether a new constitution would be necessary to relieve the country of slavery. One diary entry was
strikingly prophetic: "If the Union must be dissolved, slavery
is precisely the question upon which it ought to break."

Feb. 11, 1820 . . . We attended an evening party at Mr. Calhoun's, and
heard of nothing but the Missouri question and Mr. [Federalist Rufus] King's
[antislavery] speeches. The slave-holders cannot hear of them without being
seized with cramps. They call them seditious and inflammatory, when their
greatest real defect is their timidity. Never since human sentiments and human
conduct were influenced by human speech was there a theme for eloquence
like the free side of this question now before Congress of this Union. By what
fatality does it happen that all the most eloquent orators of the body are on
its slavish side? There is a great mass of cool judgment and plain sense on
the side of freedom and humanity, but the ardent spirits and passions are on
the side of oppression. Oh, if but one man could arise with a genius capable
of comprehending, a heart capable of supporting, and an utterance capable
of communicating those eternal truths that belong to this question, to lay bare
in all its nakedness that outrage upon the goodness of God, human slavery,
now is the time, and this is the occasion, upon which such a man would
perform the duties of an angel upon earth!

March 3, 1820—When I came this day to my office, I found there a
note requesting me to call at one o'clock at the President's house. It was then
one, and I immediately went over. He expected that the two bills, for the
admission of Maine, and to enable Missouri to make a Constitution, would
have been brought to him for his signature, and he had summoned all the
members of the Administration to ask their opinions in writing, to be deposited
in the Department of State, upon two questions: 1, whether Congress had a

Constitutional right to prohibit slavery in a Territory: and 2, whether the eighth section of the Missouri bill (which interdicts slavery forever in the Territory north of thirty-six and a half latitude) was applicable only to the Territorial State, or could extend to it after it should become a State.

As to the first question, it was unanimously agreed that Congress have the power to prohibit slavery in the Territories. . . . I had no doubt of the right of Congress to interdict slavery in the Territories, and urged that the power contained in the term "dispose of" included the authority to do everything that could be done with it as mere property, and that the additional words, authorizing needful rules and regulations respecting it, must have reference to persons connected with it, or could have no meaning at all. As to the force of the term needful, I observed, it was relative, and must always be supposed to have reference to some end. Needful to what end? Needful in the Constitution of the United States to any of the ends for which that compact was formed. Those ends are declared in its preamble: to establish justice, for example. What can be more needful for the establishment of justice than the interdiction of slavery where it does not exist? . . .

After this meeting, I walked home with Calhoun, who said that the principles which I had avowed were just and noble: but that in the Southern country, whenever they were mentioned, they were always understood as applying only to white men. Domestic labor was confined to the blacks, and such was the prejudice, that if he, who was the most popular man in his district, were to keep a white servant in his house, his character and reputation would be irretrievably ruined.

I said that this confounding of the ideas of servitude and labor was one of the bad effects of slavery: but he thought it attended with many excellent consequences. It did not apply to all kinds of labor—not, for example, to farming. He himself had often held the plough: so had his father. Manufacturing and mechanical labor was not degrading. It was only manual labor—the proper work of slaves. No white person could descend to that. And it was the best guarantee to equality among the whites. It produced an unvarying level among them. It not only did not excite, but did not even admit of inequalities, by which one white man could domineer over another.

I told Calhoun I could not see things in the same light. It is, in truth, all perverted sentiment—mistaking labor for slavery and dominion for freedom. The discussion of this Missouri question has betrayed the secret of their souls. In the abstract they admit that slavery is an evil, they disclaim all participation in the introduction of it, and cast it all upon the shoulders of our old Grandam Britain. But when probed to the quick upon it, they show at the bottom of their souls pride and vainglory in their condition of masterdom. They fancy themselves more generous and noble-hearted than the plain freemen who labor for subsistence. They look down upon the simplicity of a Yankee's manners, because he has no habits of overbearing like theirs and cannot treat negroes like dogs. It is among the evils of slavery that it taints the very sources of moral principle. It establishes false estimates of virtue and vice: for what can be more false and heartless than this doctrine which makes the first and holiest rights of humanity to depend upon the color of the skin? . . .

I have favored this Missouri compromise, believing it to be all that could be effected under the present Constitution, and from extreme unwillingness to put the Union at hazard. But perhaps it would have been a wiser as well as a bolder course to have persisted in the restriction upon Missouri, till it should have terminated in a convention of the States to revise and amend the Constitution. This would have produced a new Union of thirteen or fourteen States unpolluted with slavery, with a great and glorious object to effect, namely that of rallying to their standard the other States by the universal emancipation of their slaves. If the Union must be dissolved, slavery is precisely the question upon which it ought to break. For the present, however, this contest is laid asleep.

Nov. 29, 1820—I returned Mr. Baldwin's visit, and had a long conversation with him on the subject of the Missouri question of the present session. . . . If slavery be the destined sword in the hand of the destroying angel which is to sever the ties of this Union, the same sword will cut in sunder the bonds of slavery itself. A dissolution of the Union for the cause of slavery would be followed by a servile war in the slave-holding States, combined with a war between the two severed portions of the Union. It seems to me that its result must be the extirpation of slavery from this whole continent; and, calamitous and desolating as this course of events in its progress must be, so glorious would be its final issue, that, as God shall judge me, I dare not say that it is not to be desired.

Questions for Review and Reflection

1. According to Adams, what were President Monroe's two chief concerns involving the enabling legislation for Missouri and Maine? How were these questions answered?
2. What irony might Adams have seen in the fact that the greatest orators for their cause were from the slaveholding South?
3. By what manner of reasoning did the South argue that the institution of slavery created a more equal society?
4. Why did Adams favor the Missouri Compromise? What did he believe might happen if compromise on the inclusion of free and slave states into the Union weren't resolved?

Reading 2

Abraham Lincoln, 1854

Fragments on Slavery

History remembers Abraham Lincoln (1809–1865) in part because of his association with the issue of slavery. Early on, as a member of the Illinois legislature, Lincoln spoke out against slavery. He was willing to tolerate it where the practice existed, perhaps because he believed that if slavery were confined to those states, it would eventually die off.

The Kansas-Nebraska Act of May 1854 was a wake-up call. This act permitted these new territories to decide by popular sovereignty whether to be admitted as slave or free states, contravening the Missouri Compromise, which had denied further expansion of slavery. Northerners saw this as a betrayal.

Lincoln attacked the whole system on the grounds that it contradicted all the basic principles of democracy. "Most governments have been based, practically, on the denial of equal rights of men . . . ; *ours* began, by affirming those rights." He felt slavery discredited the country in the eyes of the rest of the world because America preached one set of principles and practiced another.

The ant, who has toiled and dragged a crumb to his nest, will furiously defend the fruit of his labor, against whatever robber assails him. So plain, that the most dumb and stupid slave that ever toiled for a master, does constantly know that he is wronged. So plain that no one, high or low, ever does mistake it, except in a plainly selfish way; for although volume upon volume is written to prove slavery a very good thing, we never hear of the man who wishes to take the good of it, by being a slave himself.

Most governments have been based, practically, on the denial of equal rights of men, as I have, in part, stated them; *ours* began, by affirming those rights. They said, some men are too ignorant, and vicious, to share in government. Possibly so, said we; and, by your system, you would always keep them ignorant, and vicious. We proposed to give *all* a chance, and we expected the weak to grow stronger, the ignorant, wiser; and all better, and happier together. . . .

If A. can prove, however conclusively, that he may, of right enslave B.—why may not B. match the same argument and prove equally, that he may enslave A.? . . .

You say A. is white, and B. is black. Is it color, then; the lighter, having the right to enslave the darker? Take care. By this rule, you are to be slave to the first man you meet, with fairer skin than you own.

You do not mean color exactly?—You mean the whites are intellectually the superiors of the blacks, and therefore have the right to enslave them? Take care again. By this rule, you are to be slave to the first man you meet, with an intellect superior to your own.

But, say you, it is a question of interest; and, if you can make it your *interest,* you have the right to enslave another. Very well. And if he can make it his interest, he has the right to enslave you.

Questions for Review and Reflection

1. What was the point Lincoln sought to make by employing the parable of the ant? How does this relate to the concept of slavery?
2. According to Lincoln, what is the one thing that all people know, even the least intelligent slave? What does this reveal about Lincoln's view of human nature?
3. What is the logic behind Lincoln's example of the slave reversing roles with the master?
4. What is the fault in logic that claims the lighter skin has the right to enslave the darker?
5. What is wrong in basing the distinction solely upon intellect and intelligence?

Reading 3

United States Congress, 1865

Thirteenth Amendment

The slavery issue became more and more hotly contested as the 1850s ended. In President Lincoln's 1861 inaugural address, he promised not to interfere with slavery where it existed, but he took a strong position against expansion of the practice. He warned Confederate states that he would uphold his oath of office and defend the Constitution of the United States against secession.

When war had broken out, Lincoln drafted the Emancipation Proclamation, which declared freedom for the slaves in rebelling states (but did not affect those in occupied territories.) Two years later, in the wake of Southern defeat, the Thirteenth Amendment abolished forever the institution of slavery everywhere in the country. Through presidential leadership and congressional action, America finally brought to an end the practice that had caused so much tragedy for its people.

Amendment XIII

Section 1. Neither slavery nor involuntary servitude, except as a punishment for crime whereof the party shall have been duly convicted, shall exist within the United States, or any place subject to their jurisdiction.

Section 2. Congress shall have power to enforce this article by appropriate legislation.

Questions for Review and Reflection

1. Define involuntary servitude.
2. Do you feel that involuntary servitude could include being drafted into the armed services?

Reading 4

United States Congress, 1868

Fourteenth Amendment

One of the most significant amendments for all American citizens has been the Fourteenth Amendment. Through this change, principles not previously considered possible became a part of the Constitution. National citizenship was defined. Due process and equal protection were guaranteed. By granting *national* protection for individual rights, this amendment changed the relationship between federal and state governments.

Produced by the 39th Congress during the period of 1865–1867, the amendment was ratified when congressional leaders threatened to prevent Southern states from returning to Congress after the war unless they passed it. As a result, millions of people became citizens entitled to all the rights that such status provided.

Important as it was to spell out the privileges of citizenship in the Constitution, their existence as an ideal was no guarantee they would be available in practice. As we will see in later chapters, ratification of the Fourteenth Amendment was only a first step. In fact, the United States was not ready in 1868 for political integration, and still less so for social integration. Lincoln himself had said during his 1858 debates with Stephen Douglas, "There is a physical difference between the white and black races which I believe will for ever forbid the two races living together on terms of political or social equality." The conviction that African Americans were inherently inferior stubbornly endured, and conservative federal courts strove to protect states' rights. Decades of struggle were necessary before the amendment began to fulfill its promise of equal representation and protection.

Amendment XIV

Section 1. All persons born or naturalized in the United States and subject to the jurisdiction thereof, are citizens of the United States and of the State wherein they reside. No State shall make or enforce any law which shall abridge the privileges or immunities of citizens of the United States; nor shall any State deprive any person of life, liberty, or property, without due process of law; nor deny to any person within its jurisdiction the equal protection of the laws.

Section 2. Representatives shall be apportioned among the several States according to their respective numbers, counting the whole number of persons in each State, excluding Indians not taxed. But when the right to vote at any election for the choice of electors for President and Vice President of the United States, Representatives in Congress, the Executive and Judicial officers of a State, or the members of the Legislature thereof, is denied to any of the male inhabitants of such State, being twenty-one years of age, and citizens of the United States, or in any way abridged, except for participation in rebellion, or other crime, the basis of representation therein shall be reduced in the proportion which the number of such male citizens shall bear to the whole number of male citizens twenty-one years of age in such State.

Section 3. No person shall be a Senator or Representative in Congress, or elector of President and Vice President, or hold any office, civil or military, under the United States, or under any State, who, having previously taken an oath, as a, member of Congress, or as an officer of the United States, or as a member of any State legislature, or as an executive or judicial officer of any State, to support the Constitution of the United States, shall have engaged in insurrection or rebellion against the same, or given aid or comfort to the enemies thereof. But Congress may by a vote of two-thirds of each House, remove such disability.

Section 4. The validity of the public debt of the United States, authorized by law, including debts incurred for payment of pensions and bounties for services in suppressing insurrection or rebellion, shall not be questioned. But neither the United States nor any State shall assume or pay any debt or obligation incurred in aid of insurrection or rebellion against the United States, or any claim for the loss or emancipation of any slave; but all such debts, obligations and claims shall be held illegal and void.

Section 5. The Congress shall have power to enforce, by appropriate legislation, the provisions of this article.

Questions for Review and Reflection

According to the Fourteenth Amendment:
1. Who is a citizen?
2. How does the language differ from the three-fifths clause of the original Constitution?
3. How does citizenship status change the relationship between the federal government and state governments?

Reading 5

United States Congress, 1870

Fifteenth Amendment

Not covered in the Fourteenth Amendment was the issue of political rights for the newly freed slaves. Republicans quickly realized their need for black votes, as demonstrated in the 1866 elections, and introduced this amendment, which guaranteed that the right to vote would not be denied based on race, color, or previous condition of servitude. Since voting regulations had previously belonged to the states, this was a national limit on their power that still further changed their relationship to the federal government. The enforcement power written into the Fifteenth Amendment gave legislative authority to Congress. The Fifteenth Amendment established the intent of Congress to guarantee the right to vote.

In practice, however, this guarantee proved as elusive as those of the Fourteenth Amendment. State and local governments erected a wide variety of barriers to universal voting rights, such as requiring proof of property ownership, levying poll taxes, demanding answers to obscure legal questions in so-called literacy tests, and limiting voters to those whose grandfathers were entitled to vote. In fact, nearly a century passed before Congress finally provided the means, in the Voting Rights Act of 1965, to guarantee that right to African Americans, who had been continuously denied the franchise for so many years.

Amendment XV

Section 1. The right of citizens of the United States to vote shall not be denied or abridged by the United States or by any State on account of race, color, or previous condition of servitude.

Section 2. The Congress shall have power to enforce this article by appropriate legislation.

Questions for Review and Reflection

1. What is the significance of Section 2 of the Fifteenth Amendment? How does this apply to the Voting Rights Act 100 years later?
2. Could the Fifteenth Amendment apply to women? Was that the intent when it was written?

The Rights of Life: Securing Basic Liberty

Threnation focused on industrialization and expansion after the Civil War. Rapid advances took place in communications and transportation. Technology brought about endless inventions, new sources of energy, mass production of consumer goods, and a higher standard of living. Factories grew quickly; migrants from the farm and immigrants from Europe flocked to the cities for work on the assembly lines. Refrigerators, sewing machines, clothes, canned goods, and much more were now available to large numbers of Americans.

But such rapid change also brought problems. Cities were overcrowded. Public services, such as water, garbage pickup, and police and fire protection, were inadequate. The construction of housing, schools, parks, and hospitals did not keep up with growth. People worked long hours for subsistence wages, often in unsafe conditions. They came home to crime, disease, and poverty.

Against this backdrop, excluded groups continued to agitate for full participation in American democracy. While the Civil War Amendments had established constitutional guarantees for African Americans, the only freedom they truly won was that from slavery. Guarantees to citizenship, to equality, and to the vote were never fully implemented. Millions of people, free to pursue their own course in life, had not the means to do so—they had no education, few skills, and no support from the federal government for implementation of the rights and equality expressed in the Fourteenth and Fifteenth Amendments. Attempts during Reconstruction to force Southern states to extend equal treatment to freed slaves were short-lived and ultimately futile.

Nearly 30 years after the passage of the Fourteenth Amendment, African Americans confronted still another obstacle in their struggle for equality. In its famous Plessy v. Ferguson decision in 1896, the Supreme Court permitted discriminatory practices by ruling that "separate but equal" facilities met the amendment's equal protection guarantee. Throughout the South, segregation was installed as public policy. White supremacy was fully revived, and blacks were consigned to a second-class citizenship. Sharecropping, tenant farming, or domestic work were the few opportunities available; such work kept black Americans in service to their former masters.

The National Association for the Advancement of Colored People was established early in the twentieth century to combat discrimination, to work toward political and social equality, and to secure the blessings of liberty by appealing to the judicial system.

Women had long been organizers in crusades for social change. They had worked actively in the abolitionist movement and effectively organized to bring about Prohibition. Now they turned their organizational skills to dealing with both the good and the bad effects of industrialization and urbanization. Some women formed literary clubs that served as a substitute for formal education. Such groups offered enriching cultural and literary events. Often, those same clubs became civic-minded and adopted agendas for reform in the cities by addressing political issues, such as child labor, pure foods and drugs, and access to housing, education, and health care. For some women, freedom had to include reproductive rights and contraception, and these became political issues. For others, suffrage remained a high priority. Many women had felt excluded by the language of the Fourteenth Amendment, which specifically referred to "male inhabitants" in reference to the right to vote. It would be several decades before women secured the blessing of liberty through the franchise.

Industrialization also fueled the westward movement. Five transcontinental railroads were built to support a national marketplace for goods. Among those who went west were miners, farmers, and settlers looking for a new way of life. Their path ran head on into Native Americans. Sioux, Cheyenne, Apache, Comanche, and Nez Percé were a few of the many tribes that stood in the way of white expansion. Indian tribes were treated as non-American aliens, and relations with them continued to be organized by treaty. Territories were defined and boundaries established. Armed conflict erupted when respect was not paid to treaty obligations, and these battles often decimated the tribal forces. In fact, these wars, along with disease and the slaughter of buffalo, amounted nearly to genocide. Several million Indians had lived in what is now the United States when white traders first arrived. But between 1890 and 1910, the total Native American population fell to 250,000. Missionaries endeavored to educate and Christianize Native Americans in order to assimilate them into the American way of life. But Native Americans had never wanted to become a part of the United States or to adopt the American lifestyle. All they sought was a chance to preserve their cultures on traditional Indian land.

Indians were forced to succumb, especially by means of the Dawes Act of 1887, an allotment plan to distribute reservation land in 160-acre plots to Indian families for the purpose of promoting property ownership, a farm existence, and more rapid assimilation.

American citizenship was granted to Indians born in the United States in 1924, but discrimination and exploitation continued unabated. The Indian Reorganization Act of 1934 authorized a return to the tribal system on reservation lands, promoted economic development, provided for educational facilities, and outlined procedures for elections and constitutional self-government. But budgetary constraints created by the Depression and World War II prevented this plan from ever being fully implemented.

The role of the federal government in the lives of all Americans changed during the period of 1880 to 1944. Early on, government was generous in granting land and subsidies to big business for purposes of development but generally remained committed to a policy of laissez-faire, or "hands-off," in public affairs.

However, the excesses of big business precipitated Progressive Era calls for government regulation of monopoly and protection for labor, farmers, and small business owners.

When the Great Depression of 1929 battered the country, it hurt a large segment of American society through unemployment, business losses, home foreclosures, and bank failures. President Franklin D. Roosevelt proposed a plan to use the full force of government to furnish relief, recovery, and reform. He expanded the federal role to include the social and economic well-being of the nation.

His New Deal introduced Social Security, unemployment insurance, fair labor standards, and assistance to farmers and other workers.

Throughout these decades, the meaning of the principle of liberty evolved from its earlier definition of "freedom from" into a concept that included "freedom to." Government came to be expected to supply the means by which the blessings of liberty could be achieved.

Reading **1**

Red Cloud, 1870

Speech at Cooper Institute

Red Cloud (1822-1909), Oglala Chief of the Teton Sioux tribe, renowned horsemen of the Great Plains, met with the "great white father," President Grant, to complain about having been deceived by interpreters during a treaty negotiation with the U.S. government in 1867. The treaty had designated boundaries for a great Sioux Nation—all of what is now South Dakota—and provided for "unceded Indian territory." Later, the U.S. government violated some provisions of the treaty and claimed back part of the territory. Eventually, the Sioux were confined to a small site as dependents of the government.

Red Cloud embarked on what he called a Peace Crusade. "All I want is right and justice," he said, first to "the great white father," and later at New York City's Cooper Union, to a meeting of the Indian Peace Commission established to mediate disputes between the Indians and the U.S. Government.

Red Cloud's concerns epitomized the concerns of many of the Indian tribes forced off their lands into territories further west. They wanted the authority of the U.S. government to honor and enforce the commitments and obligations of treaties.

My brethren and my friends who are here before me this day, God Almighty has made us all, and He is here to bless what I have to say to you today. The Good Spirit made us both. He gave you lands and He gave us lands; He gave us these lands; you came in here, and we respected you as brothers. God Almighty made you but made you all white and clothed you; when He made us He made us with red skins and poor; now you have come.

When you first came we were very many, and you were few; now you are many, and we are getting very few, and we are poor. You do not know who appears before you today to speak. I am a representative of the original American race, the first people of this continent. We are good and not bad. The reports that you hear concerning us are all on one side. We are always well disposed to them. You are here told that we are traders and thieves, and it is not so. We have given you nearly all our lands, and if we had any more land to give we would be very glad to give it. We have nothing more. We are driven into a very little land, and we want you now, as our dear friends, to help us with the government of the United States. . . .

In 1868 men came out and brought papers. We are ignorant and do not read papers, and they did not tell us right what was in these papers. We wanted them to take away their forts, leave our country, . . . not make war, and give our traders something. They said we had bound ourselves to trade on the Missouri, and we said, no, we did not want that. The interpreters deceived us. When I went to Washington I saw the Great Father. The Great Father showed me what the treaties were; he showed me all these points and showed me that the interpreters had deceived me and did not let me know what the right side of the treaty was. All I want is right and justice. . . . I represent the Sioux Nation; they will be governed by what I say and what I represent. . . .

I have sent a great many words to the Great Father, but I don't know that they ever reach the Great Father. They were drowned on the way, therefore I was a little offended with it. The words I told the Great Father lately would never come to him, so I thought I would come and tell you myself.

And I am going to leave you today, and I am going back to my home. I want to tell the people that we cannot trust his agents and superintendents. I don't want strange people that we know nothing about. I am very glad that we have come here and found you and that we can understand one another. I don't want any more such men sent out there, who are so poor that when they come out there their first thoughts are how they can fill their own pockets.

We want preserves in our reserves. We want honest men, and we want you to help to keep us in the lands that belong to us so that we may not be a prey to those who are viciously disposed. I am going back home. I am very glad that you have listened to me, and I wish you good-bye and give you an affectionate farewell.

Q uestions for Review and Reflection

1. Do you think that Red Cloud's argument about the Indians being the "original American race" was effective? Why or why not?
2. How was deception used by the federal government to secure the Teton Sioux's cooperation?
3. Originally, what were the Teton Sioux seeking in their dealings with the federal government? What are their new goals, according to Red Cloud?
4. How does Red Cloud refer to the President of the United States? To the Supreme Being?
5. What are Red Cloud's recommendations to his people? Are they practical?

Reading 2

Victoria Woodhull, 1871

Testimony before Congress

Following the Civil War, local governments began, piecemeal, to grant some rights to women. Individual states dropped legal restrictions that prevented women from owning property or making contracts. Education became more accessible. But the franchise remained out of reach.

Victoria Woodhull (1838–1927) was a successful business-woman who ran a brokerage house in New York. She also published a weekly newsletter, *The Woodhull Reader,* in which she posited that women already had the vote by the constitutional guarantees of the Fourteenth Amendment.

Although the House Judiciary Committee had decided against enfranchising women under the Fourteenth Amendment, Congress held hearings on this issue in 1871, and Woodhull was called to testify. She stunned her audience with a comparison of women's grievances to those of the colonists who had revolted against "taxation without representation." She enumerated all the taxes she paid, asserting that government had "departed from the principles of the Constitution" when it excluded a taxpayer from the political process.

I trust you will pardon me the expression when I say that I do not comprehend how there can exist an honest and perfect appreciation of the fundamental propositions upon which the superstructure of our government is based, and, at the same time, an honest hostility to the legitimate deductions of them, therefore I appear before you to expound as best I may the law involved by these propositions and to point out the inconsistencies of those who evince hostility to such deductions.

I come before you, to declare that my sex are entitled to the inalienable right to life, liberty and the pursuit of happiness. The first two I cannot be deprived of except for cause and by due process of law; but upon the last, a right is usurped to place restrictions so general as to include the whole of my sex, and for which no reasons of public good can be assigned. I ask the right to pursue happiness by having a voice in that government to which I am accountable. I have not forfeited that right, still I am denied. Was assumed arbitrary authority ever more arbitrarily exercised? In practice, then, our laws are false to the principles which we profess. I have the right to life, to liberty, unless I forfeit it by an infringement upon others' rights, in which case the State becomes the arbiter and deprives me of them for the public good. I also have the right to pursue happiness, unless I forfeit it in the same way, and am denied it accordingly. It cannot be said, with any justice, that my pursuit of happiness in voting for any man for office, would be an infringement of one of his rights as a citizen or as an individual. I hold, then, that in denying me this right without my having forfeited it, that departure is made from the principles of the Constitution, and also from the true principles of government, for I am denied a right born with me, and which is inalienable. Nor can it be objected that women had no part in organizing this government. They were not denied. To-day we seek a voice in government and *are* denied. There are *thousands* of male citizens in the country who seldom or never vote. They are not denied: they pursue happiness by not voting. Could it be assumed, because this body of citizens do not choose to exercise the right to vote, that they could be *permanently* denied the exercise thereof? *If* not, *neither* should it be assumed to deny women, who wish to vote, the right to do so.

And were it true that a majority of women do not wish to vote, it would be *no* reason why those who do, should be denied. If a right exist, and only *one in a million* desires to exercise it, *no* government should deny its enjoyment to that one. If the thousands of men who do not choose to vote should send their petitions to Congress, asking them to prevent others who do vote from so doing, would they listen to them? I went before Congress, to ask for myself and others of my sex, who wish to pursue our happiness by participating in government, protection in such pursuit, and I was told Congress has not the necessary power.

If there are women who do not desire to have a voice in the laws to which they are accountable, and which they must contribute to support, let them speak for themselves; but they should not assume to speak for me, or for those whom I represent. . . .

In the records of the early days of the Republic, there are found *numerous* authorities bearing directly upon this point, such as, "that by the law of nature no man has a right to impose laws more than to levy taxes upon another; that the free man pays no taxes, as the freeman submits to no law but such as emanate from the body in which he is represented." If the freeman pays no taxes without representation, how is it that the free woman is compelled to do so? Not long since I was notified by a United States officer that if I did not pay a certain tax the government had imposed upon me, my property would be levied upon and sold for that purpose. Is *this* tyranny, or can men find some *other* word to take the place of that used by our fathers so freely, and by Congress, not so long ago as to be forgotten, with such powerful effect? Has oppression become less odious, that in these days twenty of the forty millions of people who compose the sovereign people of this country must *quietly* submit to what has been, in all ages of representative government, denounced as *tyranny*?

But let us hear more of the principles which actuated our fathers: "All men having sufficient evidence of permanent common interest with, and attachment to, the community, have the right of suffrage, and cannot be taxed or deprived of their property for public uses without their own consent or that of their representatives so elected, nor bound by any law to which they have not in like manner assented for the public good."—*Virginia Bill of Rights,* Jan. 12, 1776.

So it appears that our fathers declared that *no one* should be bound by *any* law in the making of which he had no voice. *How* would this principle operate to-day should I refuse to pay the taxes levied against me without my consent and in direct opposition to my wishes? Would I be justified in declaring that I would not pay? I might be *justified,* but I do not think I should escape the tyranny. . . .

If freedom consists in having an *actual share* in appointing those who frame the laws, are not the women of this country in absolute *bondage,* and can government, in the face of the XV. Amendment, assume to deny them the right to vote, being in this "condition of servitude?" According to Franklin we are absolutely enslaved, for there *are* "governors set over us by other men," and we are "subject to the laws" they make. Is *not* Franklin good authority in matters of freedom? Again, rehearsing the arguments that have emanated from Congress and applying them to the present case, we learn that "It is idle to show that, in certain instances, the fathers failed to apply the sublime principles which they declared. Their failure can be *no* apology for those on whom the duty is now cast." Shall it be an apology *now?* Shall the omission of others to do justice keep the government from measuring it to those who now cry out for it? I went before Congress like Richelieu to his king asking for justice. Will they deny it as he did until the exigencies of the case compel them?

I *am* subject to tyranny! I am taxed in every conceivable way. For publishing a paper I must pay—for engaging in banking and brokerage business I must pay—of what it is my fortune to acquire each year I must turn over a certain per cent.—I must pay high prices for tea, coffee and sugar: to *all* these must I submit, that *men's* government may be maintained, a government in the administration of which I am denied a voice, and from its edicts there is no appeal. I must submit to a heavy advance upon the first cost of *nearly everything I wear* in order that industries in which I have no interest may exist at my expense. I am compelled to pay extravagant rates of fare wherever I travel, because the franchises, extended to gigantic corporations, enable them to *sap* the vitality of the country, to make their *managers money kings,* by means of which they boast of being able to control not only legislators but even a State judiciary.

To be compelled to submit to *these* extortions that *such* ends may be gained, upon *any* pretext or under *any* circumstances, is bad enough; but to be compelled to submit to them, and also denied the right to cast my vote *against* them, is a tyranny *more* odious than that which, being rebelled against, gave this country independence.

Questions for Review and Reflection

1. Woodhull uses the phrase "superstructure of a government." To what is she referring?
2. What "inconsistencies" do you think Woodhull is referring to in this testimony?
3. What historic documents does Woodhull draw upon to underscore the legitimacy of her request?
4. What are the rights contained in the U.S. Constitution that Woodhull believes apply to women as well as to men?
5. What is Woodhull seeking in her petition?
6. What irony does Woodhull see in the thousands of males who do not choose to exercise their franchise?
7. How many different arguments for female suffrage can you count in this portion of Woodhull's testimony?
8. What action does Woodhull recommend for women who do not wish to vote?
9. What contradiction does Woodhull see in the definition, of freedom that stresses "self-determination" in regard to the right of women to vote?
10. Can you find Woodhull's "taxation without representation" argument in this testimony? Does it remind you of a similar line of reasoning used by men on an earlier occasion?

Reading 3

Congressman R. H. Cain, 1875

Speech to House of Representatives

With the new political rights guaranteed to freedmen by the Civil War amendments, black voters were encouraged to register to vote and to run for office. Republicans recognized them as potential new allies and in a wave of support for black Americans, Congress passed a series of Civil Rights Acts. The new laws looked beyond political rights to more equitable social treatment.

As a result, many new state and federal officeholders were African Americans. Congressman R. H. Cain (1825-1887) was elected to the U.S. House of Representatives from South Carolina. He had been a minister in one of the largest churches of that state. He fully supported the 1875 Civil Rights Act, which called for the racial integration of public facilities.

"The great principle which underlies our Government, of liberty, of justice, of right, will eventually prevail . . . and we shall enjoy equal rights under the laws," he said on the floor of the House.

Although the bill passed, it was declared unconstitutional in 1883 by the Supreme Court, on the grounds that it covered such private acts as the management of hotels, inns, public transport, and theaters. The Court held that the Fourteenth Amendment could apply only to official acts of state, not to private business decisions.

It is also necessary, Mr. Speaker, that this bill should pass that we may go through the length and breadth of this country without lot or hinderance. I know there are prejudices; but we must expect that these will exist. Let the laws of the country be just; let the laws of the country be equitable; that is all we ask, and we will take our chances under the laws in this land. We do not want the laws of this country to make discriminations between us. Place all citizens upon one broad platform; and if the negro is not qualified to hoe his row in this contest of life, then let him go down. All we ask of this country is to put no barriers between us, to lay no stumbling blocks in our way, to give us freedom to accomplish our destiny, that we may thus acquire all that is necessary to our interest and welfare in this country. Do this, sir, and we shall ask nothing more.

. . . The gentleman from Virginia calls in question the propriety of passing the civil-rights bill. I cannot agree with him, and for this reason; my understanding of human rights, of democracy if you please, is all rights to all men, the government of the people by the people, and for the people's interest, without regard to sections, complexions, or anything else.

Why not pass the civil-rights bill? Are there not five millions of men, women, and children in this country, a larger number than inhabited this country when the fathers made the tea party in Boston harbor, five millions whose rights are as dear and sacred to them, humble though they be, as are the rights of the thirty-odd millions of white people in this land? I am at a loss to understand the philosophy which these gentlemen have learned; how they can abrogate to themselves all rights, all liberty, all law, all government, all progress, all science, all arts, all literature, and deny them to other men formed of God equally as they are formed, clothed with the same humanity, and endowed with the same intellectual powers, but robbed by their connivance of the means of development. I say I am at a loss to understand how they can deny to us these privileges and claim them for themselves.

The civil-rights bill simply declares this: that there shall be no discriminations between citizens of this land so far as the laws of the land are concerned. I can find no fault with that. The great living principle of the American Government is that all men are free. We admit from every land and every nationality men to come here and under the folds of that noble flag repose in peace and protection. We assume that, whatever education his mind may have received, each man may aspire to and acquire all the rights of citizenship. Yet because, forsooth, God Almighty made the face of the negro black, these gentlemen would deny him that right though he be a man. Born on your soil, reared here amid the toils and sorrows and griefs of the land, producing by his long years of toil the products which have made your country great, earnestly laboring to develop the resources of this land, docile though outraged, yet when the gentlemen who held them in bondage—sir, I will not repeat the dark scenes that transpired under the benign influence and direction of that class of men. . . .

I regard it as essential to the peace of the country that there shall be no discrimination between citizens; and the civil-rights bill I regard as a just and righteous measure which this Government must adopt in order to guarantee to all citizens equal rights.

And, Mr. Speaker, I am astonished that there is an apparent disposition in some quarters to give this question the go-by. "O," gentlemen say, "you will stir up strife in the country"—"bad blood," the gentleman from Virginia said. Well, I think there has been a good deal of "bad blood" in the South already. It seems to me that a few years ago they had some "bad blood" in the South—very bad blood. And if any one will read the transactions in the South during the last few months, he will find that the "bad blood" has not all got out of the South—bad blood stirred up, not by the northern people, but by the southern people themselves.

Now, I do not think there is so much bad blood between the blacks and whites. The gentleman tells us in the next breath that they have the best laborers in the country. Well, if the labor is so good why do you not treat your laborers well? If they are the best class of laborers, if they do so much, why not guarantee to them their rights? If they are good laborers, if they produce your corn and your rice, if they give you such grand products, is it not proper and just that you should accord to them the rights that belong to them in common with other men?

The gentleman said that the slaves lived better than their masters. That is susceptible of grave doubt. I think there is a great difference between hog and hominy in the log cabin and all the luxuries of life in the richly-carpeted mansion. It seems to me there is a great difference when one class bear all the labor and produce all the crops, while the other class ride in their carriages, do all the buying and selling, and pocket all the money. . . .

But, sir, I have no fear for the future. I believe the time will come when the sense of justice of this nation, when the enlightenment of this century, when the wisdom of our legislators, when the good feeling of the whole people will complete this grand work by lifting up out of degradation a race of men which has served long and faithfully by placing it, so far as the laws are concerned, upon an equal footing with all other classes. I have faith in this country. My ideas are progressive. I recognize the fact that there has been a constant progress in the development of ideas in this country. The great principle which underlies our Government, of liberty, of justice, of right, will eventually prevail in this land and we shall enjoy equal rights under the laws. I regret exceedingly gentlemen talk of social equality. That seems to be their great bugaboo. O, if you put colored men upon an equality before the law they will want social equality! I do not believe a word of it. Do you suppose I would introduce into my family a class of white men I see in this country? Do you suppose for one moment I would do it? No, sir; There are men even who have positions upon this floor, and for whom I have respect, but of whom I should be careful how I introduced them into my family. I should be afraid indeed their old habits acquired beyond Mason and Dixon's line might return. No, Mr. Speaker, it is a damnable prejudice, the result of the old cursed system of slavery. It is that which brought about this prejudice and has caused it to overshadow the whole land. Slavery has left the poison still in their minds. Slavery and its effects have nearly expired. It is, to be sure, in its last dying throes. The rude hand of war opened a cavern into which ran much of the bad blood spoken of. The stamp of Phil Sheridan's gallant troopers let much more of it out. Before this Congress closes it will pass the civil-rights bill, giving equal rights and protection to all classes throughout the country. Then indeed, thank God, the last vestige of that old barbarism will have disappeared, and peace shall spread her wings over a united, prosperous, and happy people.

Questions for Review and Reflection

1. What famous documents does Cain draw upon to support his argument? What additions does he make to these documents in his argument?
2. How does Cain characterize and summarize the scope and nature of the Civil Rights Act?
3. What does Cain regard as "essential" for a peaceful society in America? How would the civil rights bill accomplish this?

4. Cain argues that there has been "constant progress" in the development of "ideas" in America. What are these "ideas," and how have they progressed?
5. What distinction does Cain draw between political equality and "social equality"?
6. What is Cain's attitude toward prejudice? How might he have put this attitude into practice in his own life?

Reading 4

Chief Joseph, April 1879

"An Indian's View of Indian Affairs"

The nineteenth century witnessed the slow wearing down of Indian resistance to white encroachment onto tribal lands. Gold was discovered in the Black Hills of the Dakotas, which caused a rash of speculators into the territories and last-ditch efforts on the part of various tribes to defend what remained of their independence.

In 1877, Chief Joseph of the Nez Percés (1840–1904) led his people on a 1,000-mile escape attempt rather than submit to an order to get off tribal lands to make way for white settlement.

He eventually surrendered in October 1877, after many months of retreat, and was sent to Indian territory in Oklahoma. Defeated and tired, Chief Joseph pleaded only for an equal chance for his tribe to be free to lead a quiet life. "I know that my race must change. We cannot hold our own with the white man as they are. We only ask an even chance." He spoke for members of most remaining tribes in this article, which appeared in the *North American Review.*

My friends, I have been asked to show you my heart. I am glad to have a chance to do so. I want the white people to understand my people. Some of you think an Indian is like a wild animal. This is a great mistake. I will tell you about our people, and then you can judge whether an Indian is a man or not. I believe much trouble and blood would be saved if we opened our hearts more. I will tell you in my way how the Indian sees things. The white man has more words to tell you how they look to him, but it does not require many words to speak the truth. What I have to say will come from my heart, and I will speak with a straight tongue. Ah-cum-kin-i-ma-me-hut (the Great Spirit) is looking at me, and will hear me.

My name is In-mut-too-yah-lat-lat (Thunder-traveling-over-the-mountains). I am chief of the Wal-lam-wat-kin band of Chute-pa-lu, or Nez Percés (nose-pierced Indians). I was born in eastern Oregon, thirty-eight winters ago. My father was chief before me. When a young man he was called Joseph by Mr. Spalding, a missionary. He died a few years ago. There was no stain on his hands of the blood of a white man. He left a good name on the earth. He advised me well for my people.

Our fathers gave us many laws, which they had learned from their fathers. These laws were good. They told us to treat all men as they treated us; that we should never be the first to break a bargain; that it was a disgrace to tell a lie; that we should speak only the truth; that it was a shame for one man to take from another his wife, or his property, without paying for it. We were taught to believe that the Great Spirit sees and hears everything, and that He never forgets; that hereafter He will give every man a spirit-home according to his deserts; if he has been a good man, he will have a good home; if he has been a bad man, he will have a bad home. This I believe, and all my people believe the same.

The first white men of your people who came to our country were named Lewis and Clarke. They also brought many things that our people had never seen. They talked straight, and our people gave them a great feast, as a proof that their hearts were friendly. These men were very kind. They made presents to our chiefs and our people made presents to them. We had a great many horses of which we gave them what they needed, and they gave us guns and tobacco in return. All the Nez Percés made friends with Lewis and Clarke, and agreed to let them pass through their country, and never to make war on white men. This promise the Nez Percés have never broken. . . .

Next there came a white officer who invited all the Nez Percés to a treaty council. After the council was opened he made known his heart. He said there were a great many white people in the country, and many more would come; that he wanted the land marked out so that the Indians and white men could be separated. If they were to live in peace it was necessary, he said, that the Indians should have a country set apart for them, and in that country they must stay. My father, who represented his band, refused to have anything to do with the council, because he wished to be a free man. He claimed that no man owned any part of the earth, and a man could not sell what was not his own. . . .

For a short time we lived quietly. But this could not last. White men had found gold in the mountains around the land of the winding water. They stole a great many horses from us, and we could not get them back because we were Indians. . . . We could have avenged our wrongs many times, but we did not. Whenever the Government has asked us to help them against other Indians we have never refused. When the white men were few and we were strong we could have killed them off, but the Nez Percés wished to live at peace. . . .

Year after year we have been threatened, but no war was made upon my people until General Howard came to our country two years ago and told us that he was the white war-chief of all that country. He said: "I have a great many soldiers at my back. I am going to bring them up here, and then I will talk to you again. I will not let white men laugh at me the next time I come. The country belongs to the Government, and I intend to make you go upon the reservation." . . .

Again I counseled peace, and I thought the danger was past. We had not complied with General Howard's order because we could not, but we intended to do so as soon as possible. I was leaving the council to kill beef for my family when news came that a young man whose father had been killed had gone out with several hot-blooded young braves and killed four white men. . . .

Words do not pay for my dead people. They do not pay for my country, now overrun by white men. They do not protect my father's grave. They do not pay for my horses and cattle. Good words will not give me back my children. Good words will not make good the promise of your War Chief, General Miles [of reservation land in Idaho]. Good words will not give my people good health and stop them from dying. Good words will not get my people a home where they can live in peace and take care of themselves. I am tired of talk that comes to nothing. . . .

I know that my race must change. We cannot hold our own with the white men as we are. We only ask an even chance to live as other men live. We ask to be recognized as men. We ask that the same law shall work alike on all men. If the Indian breaks the law, punish him by the law. If the white man breaks the law, punish him also.

Let me be a free man—free to travel, free to stop, free to work, free to trade where I choose, free to choose my own teachers, free to follow the religion of my fathers, free to think and talk and act for myself—and I will obey every law, or submit to the penalty.

Whenever the white man treats the Indian as they treat each other, then we shall have no more wars. We shall be all alike—brothers of one father and one mother, with one sky above us and one country around us, and one government for all. Then the Great Spirit Chief who rules above will smile upon this land, and send rain to wash out the bloody spots made by brothers' hands upon the face of the earth. For this time the Indian race are waiting and praying. I hope that no more groans of wounded men and women will ever go to the ear of the Great Spirit Chief above, and that all people may be one people. . . .

In-mut-too-yah-lat-lat has spoken for his people.

Young Joseph

[Q]uestions for Review and Reflection

1. How does Chief Joseph "humanize" the Nez Percés? Do you think that he understood the nature of American racial prejudice?
2. How are the traditional Nez Percé laws similar in nature and intent to the laws of the American people?
3. Did the American government keep any promises to the Nez Percés?
4. Why does Chief Joseph believe that the Nez Percés must change? What changes do you think that Chief Joseph contemplated?

Reading 5

Frederick Douglass, 1880

Address to Black Convention

Sometimes called the "father of the civil rights movement," Frederick Douglass (1817–1895) was born into slavery. He escaped, educated himself, and became one of the preeminent spokespersons on behalf of abolition and black rights.

As an orator, he rallied large groups to his cause. As publisher of an abolitionist newspaper, *The North Star*, he organized support. As a reformer, he continued well after the Civil War to demand that the United States government live up to the constitutional guarantees awarded to newly freed slaves.

"Our Reconstruction measures were radically defective," he lamented, and said that black citizenship would remain a mockery of the Constitution until government did something to transform African Americans' illiteracy, poverty, and destitution. His joy over the clearly stated principles of the new amendments was tempered by the failure of the government to tend to their full implementation.

How stands the case with the recently-emancipated millions of colored people in our own country? What is their condition to-day? What is their relation to the people who formerly held them slaves? These are important questions, and they are such as trouble the minds of thoughtful men of all colors, at home and abroad. By law, by the Constitution of the United States, slavery has no existence in our country. The legal form has been abolished. By the law and the Constitution, the negro is a man and a citizen, and has all the rights and liberties guaranteed to any other variety of the human family, residing in the United States.

He has a country, a flag, and a government, and may legally claim full and complete protection under the laws. It was the ruling wish, intention, and purpose of the loyal people, after rebellion was suppressed, to have an end to the entire cause of that calamity by forever putting away the system of slavery and all its incidents. In pursuance of this idea, the negro was made free, made a citizen, made eligible to hold office, to be a juryman, a legislator, and a magistrate. To this end, several amendments to the Constitution were proposed, recommended, and adopted. They are now a part of the supreme law of the land, binding alike upon every State and Territory of the United States, North and South. Briefly, this is our legal and theoretical condition. This is our condition on paper and parchment. If only from the national statute book we were left to learn the true condition of the colored race, the result would be altogether creditable to the American people. It would give them a clear title to a place among the most enlightened and liberal nations of the world. We could say of our country, as Curran once said of England, "The spirit of British law makes liberty commensurate with and inseparable from the British soil." Now I say that this eloquent tribute to England, if only we looked into our Constitution, might apply to us. In that instrument we have laid down the law, now and forever, that there shall be no slavery or involuntary servitude in this republic, except for crime.

We have gone still further. We have laid the heavy hand of the Constitution upon the matchless meanness of caste, as well as upon the hell-black crime of slavery. We have declared before all the world that there shall be no denial of rights on account of race, color, or previous condition of servitude. The advantage gained in this respect is immense.

It is a great thing to have the supreme law of the land on the side of justice and liberty. It is the line up to which the nation is destined to march—the law to which the nation's life must ultimately conform. It is a great principle, up to which we may educate the people, and to this extent its value exceeds all speech.

But to-day, in most of the Southern States, the Fourteenth and Fifteenth Amendments are virtually nullified.

The rights which they were intended to guarantee are denied and held in contempt. The citizenship granted in the Fourteenth Amendment is practically a mockery, and the right to vote, provided for in the Fifteenth Amendment, is literally stamped out in face of government. The old master class is today triumphant, and the newly-enfranchised class in a condition but little above that in which they were found before the rebellion.

Do you ask me how, after all that has been done, this state of things has been made possible? I will tell you. Our reconstruction measures were radically defective. They left the former slave completely in the power of the old master, the loyal citizen in the hands of the disloyal rebel against the government. Wise, grand, and comprehensive in scope and design as were the reconstruction measures, high and honorable as were the intentions of the statesmen by whom they were framed and adopted, time and experience, which try all things, have demonstrated that they did not successfully meet the case.

In the hurry and confusion of the hour, and the eager desire to have the Union restored, there was more care for the sublime superstructure of the republic than for the solid foundation upon which it could alone be upheld. To the freedmen was given the machinery of liberty, but there was denied to them the steam to put it in motion. They were given the uniform of soldiers, but no arms; they were called citizens, but left subjects; they were called free, but left almost slaves. The old master class was not deprived of the power of life and death, which was the soul of the relation of master and slave. They could not, of course, sell their former slaves, but they retained the power to starve them to death, and wherever this power is held there is the power of slavery. He who can say to his fellow-man, "You shall serve me or starve," is a master and his subject is a slave. This was seen and felt by Thaddeus Stevens, Charles Sumner, and leading stalwart Republicans; and had their counsels prevailed the terrible evils from which we now suffer would have been averted. The negro to-day would not be on his knees, as he is, abjectly supplicating the old master class to give him leave to toil. Nor would he now be leaving the South as from a doomed city, and seeking a home in the uncongenial North, but tilling his native soil in comparative independence. Though no longer a slave, he is in a thralldom grievous and intolerable, compelled to work for whatever his employer is pleased to pay him, swindled out of his hard earnings by money orders redeemed in stores, compelled to pay the price of an acre of ground for its use during a single year, to pay four times more than a fair price for a pound of bacon and to be kept upon the narrowest margin between life and starvation. Much complaint has been made that the freedmen have shown so little ability to take care of themselves since their emancipation. Men have marvelled that they have made so little progress. I question the justice of this complaint. It is neither reasonable, nor in any sense just. To me the wonder is, not that the freedmen have made so little progress, but, rather, that they have made so much; not that they have been standing still, but that they have been able to stand at all. . . .

We have only to reflect for a moment upon the situation in which these people found themselves when liberated. Consider their ignorance, their poverty, their destitution, and their absolute dependence upon the very class by which they had been held in bondage for centuries, a class whose every sentiment was averse to their freedom, and we shall be prepared to marvel that they have, under the circumstances, done so well.

History does not furnish an example of emancipation under conditions less friendly to the emancipated class than this American example. Liberty came to the freedmen of the United States not in mercy, but in wrath, not by moral choice but by military necessity, not by the generous action of the people among whom they were to live, and whose good-will was essential to the success of the measure, but by strangers, foreigners, invaders, trespassers, aliens, and enemies. The very manner of their emancipation invited to the heads of the freedmen the bitterest hostility of race and class. They were hated because they had been slaves, hated because they were now free, and hated because of those who had freed them. Nothing was to have been expected other than what has happened, and he is a poor student of the human heart who does not see that the old master class would naturally employ every power and means in their reach to make the great measure of emancipation unsuccessful and utterly odious. It was born in the tempest of violence and blood. When the Hebrews were emancipated, they were told to take spoil from the Egyptians. When the serfs of Russia were emancipated they were given three acres of ground upon which they could live and make a living. But not so when our slaves were emancipated. They were sent away empty-handed, without money, without friends and without a foot of land upon which to stand. Old and young, sick and well, were turned loose to the open sky, naked to their enemies. The old slave quarter that had before sheltered them and the fields that had yielded them corn were now denied them. The old master class, in its wrath, said, "Clear out! The Yankees have freed you, now let them feed and shelter you!"

Inhuman as was this treatment, it was the natural result of the bitter resentment felt by the old master class; and, in view of it, the wonder is, not that the colored people of the South have done so little in the way of acquiring a comfortable living, but that they live at all. . . .

Greatness does not come on flowery beds of ease to any people. We must fight to win the prize. No people to whom liberty is given, can hold it as firmly and wear it as grandly as those who wrench their liberty from the iron hand of the tyrant. The hardships and dangers involved in the struggle give strength and toughness to the character, and enable it to stand firm in storm as well as in sunshine.

Questions for Review and Reflection

1. Douglass describes the legal status of black Americans in the early 1880s. What is this status?
2. How does the legal status of black Americans differ from their "real" status? According the Douglass, what have the southern states done to the Fourteenth and Fifteenth Amendments?

3. What defect does Douglass see in Reconstruction legislation? Why did the grand hopes embodied in the Reconstruction laws fail to materialize?
4. Why does Douglass praise the progress of the former slaves, despite their lowly plight?
5. Why do you think Douglass believes that emancipation came not in peace, but in wrath?
6. What is his recommended course of action?

Reading 6

Mary Putnam Jacobi, 1894

Address to New York State Constitutional Convention

Women were often characterized as "the weaker sex." Dr. Mary Putnam Jacobi (1842-1906) did not fit that image. She earned a pharmaceutical degree and then completed her medical degree at Women's Medical College. Later, she gained entrance to Ecole de Médecine in Paris, earning an M.D. from that institution as well. Her medical practice was in New York, where she also wrote and lectured.

Dr. Jacobi argued for full citizenship rights for women at the New York State Constitutional Convention, pointing out the foolhardiness of laws that entitled illiterate, indolent, ignorant men to vote but denied well-educated, wealthy, taxpaying women that same right. She argued that "all the intelligence in the state must be enlisted for its welfare." This reading illustrates the irony of excluding certain groups from voting.

Thus it has happened that women, though unenfranchised, and submitted to the personal sovereignty of the men of their own families and own class, have enjoyed superiority to and even actual supremacy over thousands of men in lower classes. But to-day, for the first time, classes have been indistinguishably fused; all previous lines of cleavage have been consolidated into one great line of demarcation, which makes a political class out of a sex. For the first time, all political right, privilege, and power reposes undisguisedly on the one brutal fact of sex, unsupported, untempered, unalloyed by any attribute of education, any justification of intelligence, any glamour of wealth, any prestige of birth, any insignia of actual power. For the first time, all women, no matter how well born, how well educated, how intelligent, how rich, how serviceable to the State, have been rendered the political inferiors of men, no matter how base-born, how poverty-stricken, how ignorant, how vicious, how brutal. The pauper in the almshouse may vote, the lady who devotes herself to getting that almshouse made habitable may not. The tramp who begs cold victuals in the kitchen may vote; the heiress who feeds him, and endows a university may not. Communities are agitated and Legislatures convulsed to devise means to secure the right of suffrage to the illiterate voter. And the writers, journalists, physicians, teachers, the wives and daughters and the companions of the best educated men in the State, are left in silence; blotted out, swamped, obliterated behind this cloud of often besotted ignorance. . . .

We demand the suffrage as a Right—not in a metaphysical sense,—but because we do fulfil all the essential conditions which the State has proclaimed necessary to qualify for the electorate.

We demand it, on no new principle, but on the double principle which runs through all our institutions, namely: that all the intelligence in the State must be enlisted for its welfare, and that all the weakness in the community must be represented for its own defence. There are women among us of intelligence, of wealth, of leisure, of high character, who only demand the opportunity to serve the State nobly, as they have already shown their ability to promote the welfare of the community in public affairs. And there are other women among us—hard-working, patient, industrious,—who require the suffrage, and the opportunities of the suffrage, and the immense practical education of the suffrage, to enable them to better advance the interests of their own affairs. And there are poor and weak women among us, defenceless except so far as they may be touched by an occasional enthusiasm of philanthropy, who require the status of a definite representation—a medium through which they can make their wants known—which shall do for them, as the suffrage alone has been able to do for other masses of the poor and weak: give them means to defend themselves, enable them to take the initial step in rising out of otherwise easily-forgotten misery. In a community where the definition of a social unit is the person who casts one vote, every one who casts no vote is reckoned as less than a unit,—and hence suffers in the social estimate and in her own. Her power for work is lessened, and its recompense correlatively diminished. . . .

In theory, women are always protected at home. In fact, laws are constantly being required for their special protection. Why is it desirable to leave such legal or social protection to be secured, if at all, by tedious and roundabout methods,—through petitions, and through the efforts of other people, whose warmest enthusiasm can hardly ever equal the energy of those who speak for themselves? Why should not the women have the right to speak for themselves, and by their own mouths to make their own wants known? . . .

We do believe that this special relation of women to children, in which the heart of the world has always felt there was something sacred, serves to impress upon women certain tendencies, to endow them with certain virtues which not only contribute to the charm which their anxious friends fear might be destroyed, but which will render them of special value in public affairs. Their conservatism, their economy, their horror of waste, their interest in personal character, the very simplicity of their judgment, their preoccupation with direct and living issues, are all qualities generated by the special circumstances which have surrounded women, and must continue to surround them. These can not be broken down by the fact of sharing the suffrage, for they lie far deeper than any political condition; they exist in the very nature of things.

A single phrase, often, but none too often repeated, sums up this aspect of the case. To the extent to which women resemble men, they require the same liberties; to the extent to which they differ, they require their own representation, and the State requires their special influence. Under the new, the extremely new régime of universal manhood suffrage, the State has become like a mining camp on the frontier. We claim that it should be re-constituted as a household, where, if man is at the head, for the protection and the defence, woman shall have her equal place as the mother, the daughter, the caretaker, the administrator, the conserver. We do not propose, after all, to change the existing sphere of women. Political status reflects and sanctions social change—it cannot create it. Political activities may become an occupation—but not political rights. How many women would engage in politics were they so empowered—how many would accept office, were they elected, it is impossible to foresee, and it is absolutely useless to discuss. We are not here to seek privileges for a few—but equal opportunity for all.

[Q]uestions for Review and Reflection

1. How does Jacobi compare the past state of women in the middle class and the state of men in the lower classes? What change has occurred?
2. Why does Jacobi argue that it is illogical to bar women from voting simply because of their biology? By implication, what might Jacobi accept as a legitimate way to extend the franchise?
3. According to Jacobi, what special qualities does motherhood bring to a woman that place her in a superior position to vote and influence society for the good?

4. Under universal male suffrage, the government has become like the mining-camp frontier, according to Jacobi. What will female suffrage bring to the body politic?
5. What traditional, "legitimate" sphere of women's activity does Jacobi draw upon to demonstrate that women's suffrage would improve society, rather than detract from it?

Reading 7

Elizabeth Cady Stanton, 1894

"The Solitude of Self"

President of the National Women's Suffrage Association and, according to her colleague, Susan B. Anthony, "the acknowledged leader of Progressive thought," Elizabeth Cady Stanton (1815–1902) was a premier spokesperson on behalf of women's rights. Armed with a fine education, Stanton became a prolific writer in the movement. She married an abolitionist and insisted that they remove the word "obey" from her marriage vows. He strongly supported her efforts on behalf of women; as a state senator in New York, he aided passage of the Married Women's Property Act in that state in 1860. This was a major step forward for women: it entitled widows to inherit property, women to keep their own wages, and mothers to have equal guardianship of their children.

But the vote was the major issue for Stanton. She resented having others represent her and spoke of life as a "solitary voyage" that each of us makes for him- or herself. "Our Republican idea," she exhorted public officials, is "individual citizenship." The text excerpted here is from Stanton's speech before a Senate committee on women's suffrage.

The point I wish plainly to bring before you on this occasion is the individuality of each human soul: our Protestant idea, the right of individual conscience and judgment; our republican idea, individual citizenship. In discussing the rights of woman, we are to consider, first, what belongs to her as an individual, in a world of her own, the arbiter of her own destiny, an imaginary Robinson Crusoe, with her woman, Friday, on a solitary island. Her rights under such circumstances are to use all her faculties for her own safety and happiness. . . .

The strongest reason why we ask for woman a voice in the government under which she lives; in the religion she is asked to believe; equality in social life, where she is the chief factor; a place in the trades and professions, where she may earn her bread, is because of her birthright to self-sovereignty; because as an individual, she must rely on herself. No matter how much women prefer to lean, to be protected and supported, nor how much men desire to have them do so, they must make the voyage of life alone, and for safety in an emergency, they must know something of the laws of navigation. To guide our own craft, we must be captain, pilot, engineer. . . . It matters not whether the solitary voyager is man or woman; nature, having endowed them equally, leaves them to their own skill and judgment in the hour of danger, and, if not equal to the occasion, alike they perish.

To appreciate the importance of fitting every human soul for independent action, think for a moment of the immeasurable solitude of self. We come into the world alone, unlike all who have gone before us, we leave it alone, under circumstances peculiar to ourselves. . . . In youth our most bitter disappointments, our brightest hopes and ambitions, are known only to ourselves. Even our friendship and love we never fully share with another; there is something of every passion, in every situation, we conceal. Even so in our triumphs and our defeats. . . . Alike amid the greatest triumphs and darkest tragedies of life, we walk alone. On the divine heights of human attainment, eulogized and worshipped as a hero or saint, we stand alone. In ignorance, poverty and vice, as a pauper or criminal, alone we starve or steal; alone we suffer the sneers and rebuffs of our fellows. . . . In hours like these we realize the awful solitude of individual life, its pains, its penalties, its responsibilities. . . . Seeing, then, that life must ever be a march and a battle, that each soldier must be equipped for his own protection, it is the height of cruelty to rob the individual of a single natural right. . . .

Inasmuch, then, as woman shares equally the joys and sorrows of time and eternity, is it not the height of presumption in man to propose to represent her at the ballot box and the throne of grace, to do her voting in the state, her praying in the church, and to assume the position of high priest at the family altar? . . . Whatever the theories may be of woman's dependence on man, in the supreme moments of her life, he cannot bear her burdens. Alone she goes to the gates of death to give life to every man that is born into the world; no one can share her fears, no one can mitigate her pangs; and if her sorrow is greater than she can bear, alone she passes beyond the gates into the vast unknown. . . .

When all artificial trammels are removed, and women are recognized as individuals, responsible for their own environments, thoroughly educated for all positions in life they may be called to fill; with all the resources in themselves that liberal thought and broad culture can give; guided by their own conscience and judgment, trained to self-protection, by a healthy development of the muscular system, and skill in the use of weapons and defense; and stimulated to self-support by a knowledge of the business world and the pleasure that pecuniary independence must ever give; when women are trained in this way, they will in a measure be fitted for those hours of solitude that come alike to all, whether prepared or otherwise. As in our extremity we must depend on ourselves, the dictates of wisdom point to complete individual development. . . .

Whatever may be said of man's protecting power in ordinary conditions, amid all the terrible disasters by land and sea, in the supreme moments of danger, alone woman must ever meet the horrors of the situation. . . . In that solemn solitude of self, that links us with the immeasurable and the eternal, each soul lives alone forever. . . . There is a solitude which each and every one of us has always carried with him, more inaccessible than the ice-cold mountains, more profound than the midnight sea: the solitude of self. Our inner being which we call ourself. . . . Such is individual life. Who, I ask you, can take, dare take on himself the rights, the duties, the responsibilities of another human soul?

Questions for Review and Reflection

1. How does Stanton frame her remarks? What point is she trying to make?
2. What is the "Protestant idea" that Stanton draws upon to support her argument?
3. How does Stanton use the image of Robinson Crusoe in her petition?
4. According to Stanton, what is the strongest reason for granting women the franchise?
5. What images of individuality does Stanton draw upon to forward her argument? Are they effective? Why?
6. Why does Stanton discount the argument that women's rights are represented at the ballot box by the men in the family, and thus they do not need the vote?
7. Do you think the legislature was impressed with Stanton's argument?
8. According to Stanton, what happens when women are treated as individuals?

Reading **8**

Booker T. Washington, 1895

Speech at the Atlanta Exposition

Born a slave, Booker T. Washington (1856–1915) acquired an education and eventually became a teacher. He founded the Tuskegee Institute, a vocational school for blacks, and became a leading spokesman for educational and economic opportunities for African Americans.

Washington was a realist. He accepted the segregation that had been established in the South following Reconstruction and urged blacks to get ahead by learning and working hard. He assured people that education and economic power would eventually bring about political and civil liberties.

He sought financial aid from rich industrialists and promised in return that Negroes would make no demands for legal or political rights in exchange for endowments to his school. "The opportunity to earn a dollar in a factory just now is worth infinitely more than the opportunity to spend a dollar in an opera-house." Washington pursued equal rights through economic power rather than political power.

One-third of the population of the South is of the Negro race. No enterprise seeking the material, civil, or moral welfare of this section can disregard this element of our population and reach the highest success. I but convey to you, Mr. President and Directors, the sentiment of the masses of my race when I say that in no way have the value and manhood of the American Negro been more fittingly and generously recognized than by the managers of this magnificent Exposition at every stage of its progress. It is a recognition that will do more to cement the friendship of the two races than any occurrence since the dawn of our freedom.

Our greatest danger is that in the great leap from slavery to freedom we may overlook the fact that the masses of us are to live by the productions of our hands, and fail to keep in mind that we shall prosper in proportion as we learn to dignify and glorify common labour and put brains and skill into the common occupations of life; shall prosper in proportion as we learn to draw the line between the superficial and the substantial, the ornamental gewgaws of life and the useful. No race can prosper till it learns that there is as much dignity in tilling a field as in writing a poem. It is at the bottom of life we must begin, and not at the top. Nor should we permit our grievances to overshadow our opportunities.

To those of the white race who look to the incoming of those of foreign birth and strange tongue and habits for the prosperity of the South, were I permitted I would repeat what I say to my own race, 'Cast down your bucket where you are.' Cast it down among the eight millions of Negroes whose habits you know, whose fidelity and love you have tested in days when to have proved treacherous meant the ruin of your firesides. Cast down your bucket among these people who have, without strikes and labour wars, tilled your fields, cleared your forests, builded your railroads and cities, and brought forth treasures from the bowels of the earth, and helped make possible this magnificent representation of the progress of the South. Casting down your bucket among my people, helping and encouraging them as you are doing on these grounds, and to education of head, hand, and heart, you will find that they will buy your surplus land, make blossom the waste places in your fields, and run your factories. While doing this, you can be sure in the future, as in the past, that you and your families will be surrounded by the most patient, faithful, law-abiding, and unresentful people that the world has seen. As we have proved our loyalty to you in the past, in nursing your children, watching by the sick-bed of your mothers and fathers, and often following them with tear-dimmed eyes to their graves, so in the future, in our humble way, we shall stand by you with a devotion that no foreigner can approach, ready to lay down our lives, if need be, in defence of yours, interlacing our industrial, commercial, civil, and religious life with yours in a way that shall make the interests of both races one. In all things that are purely social we can be as separate as the fingers, yet one as the hand in all things essential to mutual progress. . . .

The wisest among my race understand that the agitation of questions of social equality is the extremest folly, and that progress in the enjoyment of all the privileges that will come to us must be the result of severe and constant struggle rather than of artificial forcing. No race that has anything to contribute to the markets of the world is long in any degree ostracized. It is important and right that all privileges of the law be ours, but it is vastly more important that we be prepared for the exercises of these privileges. The opportunity to earn a dollar in a factory just now is worth infinitely more than the opportunity to spend a dollar in an opera-house.

In conclusion, may I repeat that nothing in thirty years has given us more hope and encouragement, and drawn us so near to you of the white race, as this opportunity offered by the Exposition; and here bending, as it were, over the altar that represents the results of the struggles of your race and mine, both starting practically empty-handed three decades ago, I pledge that in your effort to work out the great and intricate problem which God has laid at the doors of the South, you shall have at all times the patient, sympathetic help of my race; only let this be constantly in mind, that, while from representations in these buildings of the product of field, of forest, of mine, of factory, letters, and art, much good will come, yet far above and beyond material benefits will be that higher good, that, let us pray God, will come, in a blotting out of sectional differences and racial animosities and suspicions, in a determination to administer absolute justice, in a willing obedience among all classes to the mandates of law. This, coupled with our material prosperity, will bring into our beloved South a new heaven and a new earth.

Questions for Review and Reflection

1. For whom does Booker T. Washington claim to be speaking? By what authority does Washington speak for this group?
2. How is the economic plight of Southern blacks obscured by their recent winning of freedom?
3. How does Washington establish the idea that blacks will be "loyal" to the South in the future?
4. In what ways is Washington's philosophy a bid for economic equality, as opposed to a bid for political equality?

Reading 9

Susan B. Anthony, 1897

"The Status of Women"

The legal suit *United States v. Susan B. Anthony* was brought about when Anthony attempted to vote in New York in 1872. Her crime held a penalty of up to three years in prison. Anthony (1820-1906) was quick to point out at her trial that women were denied the right to serve as peers on her jury. She based her legal defense on the Fourteenth Amendment, which said that "all persons" born in the U.S. were citizens. She believed this entitled her to all rights of citizenship, including the vote. She lost her case, continued to work for the Anthony Amendment—"a woman's birthright," she insisted—but did not live to see it happen. This reading, excerpted from an article in the Boston periodical *Arena,* provides a retrospective on the rights women had achieved and accents the need for the right to vote to protect all other rights.

Fifty years ago woman in the United States was without a recognized individuality in any department of life. No provision was made in public or private schools for her education in anything beyond the rudimentary branches. An educated woman was a rarity and was gazed upon with something akin to awe. The women who were known in the world of letters, in the entire country, could be easily counted upon the ten fingers. Margaret Fuller, educated by her father, a Harvard graduate and distinguished lawyer, stood preeminently at the head and challenged the admiration of such men as Emerson, Channing, and Greeley. . . .

Such was the helpless, dependent, fettered condition of woman when the first Woman's Rights Convention was called just forty-nine years ago, at Seneca Falls, N.Y., by Elizabeth Cady Stanton and Lucretia Mott. . . .

While there had been individual demands, from time to time, the first organized body to formulate a declaration of the rights of women was the one which met at Seneca Falls, July 19–20, 1848, and adjourned to meet at Rochester two weeks later. In the Declaration of Sentiments and the Resolutions there framed, every point was covered that, down to the present day, has been contended for by the advocates of equal rights for women. Every inequality of the existing laws and customs was carefully considered and a thorough and complete readjustment demanded. . . .

Now, at the end of half a century, we find that, with few exceptions, all of the demands formulated at this convention have been granted. The great exception is the yielding of political rights, and toward this one point are directed now all the batteries of scorn, of ridicule, of denunciation that formerly poured their fire all along the line. Although not one of the predicted calamities occurred upon the granting of the other demands, the world is asked to believe that all of them will happen if this last stronghold is surrendered.

There is not space to follow the history of the last fifty years and study the methods by which these victories have been gained, but there is not one foot of advanced ground upon which women stand today that has not been obtained through the hard-fought battles of other women. The close of this 19th century finds every trade, vocation, and profession open to women, and every opportunity at their command for preparing themselves to follow these occupations. . . .

The department of politics has been slowest to give admission to women. Suffrage is the pivotal right, and if it could have been secured at the beginning, women would not have been half a century in gaining the privileges enumerated above, for privileges they must be called so long as others may either give or take them away. If women could make the laws or elect those who make them, they would be in the position of sovereigns instead of subjects. Were they the political peers of man, they could command instead of having to beg, petition, and pray. Can it be possible it is for this reason that men have been so determined in their opposition to grant to women political power? . . .

From that little convention at Seneca Falls, with a following of a handful of women scattered through half-a-dozen different states, we have now the great National Association, with headquarters in New York City, and auxiliaries in almost every state in the Union. These state bodies are effecting a thorough system of county and local organizations for the purpose of securing legislation favorable to women, and especially to obtain amendments to their state constitutions. As evidence of the progress of public opinion, more than half of the legislatures in session during the past winter have discussed and voted upon bills for the enfranchisement of women, and in most of them they were adopted by one branch and lost by a very small majority in the other. The legislatures of Washington and South Dakota have submitted woman-suffrage amendments to their electors for 1898, and vigorous campaigns will be made in those states during the next two years.

For a quarter of a century Wyoming has stood as a conspicuous object lesson in woman suffrage, and is now reinforced by the three neighboring states of Colorado, Utah, and Idaho. With this central group, standing on the very crest of the Rocky Mountains, the spirit of justice and freedom for women cannot fail to descend upon all the Western and Northwestern states. No one who makes a careful study of this question can help but believe that, in a very few years, all the states west of the Mississippi River will have enfranchised their women.

While the efforts of each state are concentrated upon its own legislature, all of the states combined in the national organization are directing their energies toward securing a Sixteenth Amendment to the Constitution of the United States. The demands of this body have been received with respectful and encouraging attention from Congress. Hearings have been granted by the committees of both houses, resulting, in a number of instances, in favorable reports. Upon one occasion the question was brought to a discussion in the Senate and received the affirmative vote of one-third of the members.

Until woman has obtained "that right protective of all other rights—the ballot," this agitation must still go on, absorbing the time and the energy of our best and strongest women. Who can measure the advantages that would result if the magnificent abilities of these women could be devoted to the needs of government, society, home, instead of being consumed in the struggle to obtain their birthright of individual freedom? Until this be gained we can never know, we cannot even prophesy, the capacity and power of woman for the uplifting of humanity.

It may be delayed longer than we think; it may be here sooner than we expect; but the day will come when man will recognize woman as his peer, not only at the fireside but in the councils of the nation. Then, and not until then, will there be the perfect comradeship, the ideal union between the sexes that shall result in the highest development of the race. What this shall be we may not attempt to define, but this we know, that only good can come to the individual or to the nation through the rendering of exact justice.

Questions for Review and Reflection

1. According to Anthony, what was different about the Seneca Falls "demands" for real equality and earlier demands for the same?
2. Most of the demands embodied in the Declaration of Sentiments from Seneca Falls were instituted by the end of the century. What was the one notable exception? Why? In what ways is this exception the most important?
3. How would the vote allow women to escape the class of subjects and join the class of sovereigns?
4. Which states considered giving women the franchise in the decades following the Seneca Falls convention? In what part of the country were these states located? What might explain this geographic concentration?
5. Why does Anthony argue that the vote is "that right protective of all other rights"? How might this be considered the central credo of the women's rights movement for Anthony's day?

Reading 10

William E. B. Du Bois, 1903

The Souls of Black Folks

"Separate but equal" was a doctrine established by the Supreme Court in its 1896 *Plessy v. Ferguson* decision that legalized segregation.

Booker T. Washington (see Reading 8) had promised that civil rights would eventually come from economic power, despite the inequalities that resulted from separation of the races. Dr. W. E. B. Du Bois challenged that "old attitude." This scholar and teacher, the first black ever to earn a Ph.D. from Harvard, dared other young black intellectuals to champion self-help by settling for nothing less than absolute political and social equality. He objected to the "passivity" of Washington's tactics and called that plan "belittling."

Dr. Du Bois was instrumental in organizing the Niagara Movement, a civil rights advocacy group and the predecessor of the National Association for the Advancement of Colored People, the oldest and largest nationwide civil rights organization in America.

Mr. Washington represents in Negro thought the old attitude of adjustment and submission; but adjustment at such a peculiar time as to make his programme unique. This is an age of unusual economic development, and Mr. Washington's programme naturally takes an economic cast, becoming a gospel of Work and Money to such an extent as apparently almost completely to overshadow the higher aims of life. Moreover, this is an age when the more advanced races are coming in closer contact with the less developed races, and the race-feeling is therefore intensified; and Mr. Washington's programme practically accepts the alleged inferiority of the Negro races. Again, in our own land, the reaction from the sentiment of war time has given impetus to race-prejudice against Negroes, and Mr. Washington withdraws many of the high demands of Negroes as men and American citizens. In other periods of intensified prejudice all the Negro's tendency to self-assertion has been called forth; at this period a policy of submission is advocated. In the history of nearly all other races and peoples the doctrine preached at such crises has been that manly self-respect is worth more than lands and houses, and that a people who voluntarily surrender such respect, or cease striving for it, are not worth civilizing.

In answer to this, it has been claimed that the Negro can survive only through submission. Mr. Washington distinctly asks that black people give up, at least for the present, three things, —

First, political power,

Second, insistence on civil rights,

Third, higher education of Negro youth,—and concentrate all their energies on industrial education, the accumulation of wealth, and the conciliation of the South. This policy has been courageously and insistently advocated for over fifteen years, and has been triumphant for perhaps ten years. As a result of this tender of the palm-branch, what has been the return? In these years there have occurred:

1. The disfranchisement of the Negro.
2. The legal creation of a distinct status of civil inferiority for the Negro.

3. The steady withdrawal of aid from institutions for the higher training of the Negro.

These movements are not, to be sure, direct results of Mr. Washington's teachings; but his propaganda has, without a shadow of doubt, helped their speedier accomplishment. The question then comes: Is it possible, and probable, that nine millions of men can make effective progress in economic lines if they are deprived of political rights, made a servile caste, and allowed only the most meagre chance for developing their exceptional men? If history and reason give any distinct answer to these questions, it is an emphatic *No.* And Mr. Washington thus faces the triple paradox of his career:

1. He is striving nobly to make Negro artisans business men and property-owners; but it is utterly impossible, under modern competitive methods, for workingmen and property-owners to defend their rights and exist without the right of suffrage.
2. He insists on thrift and self-respect, but at the same time counsels a silent submission to civic inferiority such as is bound to sap the manhood of any race in the long run. . . .

The other class of Negroes who cannot agree with Mr. Washington has hitherto said little aloud. They deprecate the sight of scattered counsels, of internal disagreement; and especially they dislike making their just criticism of a useful and earnest man an excuse for a general discharge of venom from small-minded opponents. Nevertheless, the questions involved are so fundamental and serious that it is difficult to see how men like the Grimkes, Kelly Miller, J. W. E. Bowen, and other representatives of this group, can much longer be silent. Such men feel in conscience bound to ask of this nation three things:

1. The right to vote.
2. Civic equality.
3. The education of youth according to ability. . . .

This group of men honor Mr. Washington for his attitude of conciliation toward the white South; they accept the "Atlanta Compromise" in its broadest interpretation; they recognize, with him, many signs of promise, many men of high purpose and fair judgment, in this section; they know that no easy task has been laid upon a region already tottering under heavy burdens. But, nevertheless, they insist that the way to truth and right lies in straightforward honesty, not in indiscriminate flattery; in praising those of the South who do well and criticising uncompromisingly those who do ill; in taking advantage of the opportunities at hand and urging their fellows to do the same, but at the same time in remembering that only a firm adherence to their higher ideals and aspirations will ever keep those ideals within the realm of possibility.

They do not expect that the free right to vote, to enjoy civic rights, and to be educated, will come in a moment; they do not expect to see the bias and prejudices of years disappear at the blast of a trumpet; but they are absolutely certain that the way for a people to gain their reasonable rights is not by voluntarily throwing them away and insisting that they do not want them; that the way for a people to gain respect is not by continually belittling and ridiculing themselves; that, on the contrary, Negroes must insist continually, in season and out of season, that voting is necessary to modern manhood, that color discrimination is barbarism, and that black boys need education as well as white boys.

In failing thus to state plainly and unequivocally the legitimate demands of their people, even at the cost of opposing an honored leader, the thinking classes of American Negroes would shirk a heavy responsibility,—a responsibility to themselves, a responsibility to the struggling masses, a responsibility to the darker races of men whose future depends so largely on this American experiment, but especially a responsibility to this nation,—this common Fatherland. It is wrong to encourage a man or a people in evil-doing; it is wrong to aid and abet a national crime simply because it is unpopular not to do so. The growing spirit of kindliness and reconciliation between the North and South after the frightful differences of a generation ago ought to be a source of deep congratulation to all, and especially to those whose mistreatment caused the war; but if that reconciliation is to be marked by the industrial slavery and civic death of those same black men, with permanent legislation into a position of inferiority, then those black men, if they are really men, are called upon by every consideration of patriotism and loyalty to oppose such a course by all civilized methods, even though such opposition involves disagreement with Mr. Booker T. Washington. We have no right to sit silently by while the inevitable seeds are sown for a harvest of disaster to our children, black and white. . . .

The black men of America have a duty to perform, a duty stern and delicate,—a forward movement to oppose a part of the work of their greatest leader. So far as Mr. Washington preaches Thrift, Patience, and Industrial Training for the masses, we must hold up his hands and strive with him, rejoicing in his honors and glorying in the strength of this Joshua called of God and of man to lead the headless host. But so far as Mr. Washington apologizes for injustice, North or South, does not rightly value the privilege and duty of voting, belittles the emasculating effects of caste distinctions, and opposes the higher training and ambition of our brighter minds,—so far as he, the South, or the North, does this,—we must unceasingly and firmly oppose them. By every civilized and peaceful method we must strive for the rights which the world accords to men, clinging unwaveringly to those great words which the sons of the Fathers would fain forget: "We hold these truths to be self-evident: That all men are created equal; that they are endowed by their Creator with certain unalienable rights; that among these are life, liberty, and the pursuit of happiness."

Questions for Review and Reflection

1. Compare and contrast Du Bois with Booker T. Washington in terms of philosophy. Which is "right"? Which is "practical"?
2. In what way, according to Du Bois, does Washington speak only for the older generation of black Americans? In what way, by contrast, does Du Bois speak for a new generation?
3. What setbacks in the drive for civil rights did black Americans suffer in the 1890s?
4. What problem does Du Bois have with Washington's philosophy? By contrast, what is Du Bois' recommended course of action?
5. What is the duty of every black American, according to Du Bois?

Reading 11

Margaret Sanger, 1920

Women and the New Race

Margaret Sanger (1883–1966) served 30 days in jail for opening the first birth control clinic in the United States, the antecedent to Planned Parenthood. As a nurse, Sanger had witnessed death due to self-induced abortions. She pledged to offer women safe alternatives and began a crusade for sexual rights. Margaret Sanger went to jail more than once to secure birth control as a means to "basic freedom." She was responding to early twentieth-century society, which still viewed contraception as abnormal and immoral. Women were expected to perform wifely duties of providing sex to their husbands on demand, with little consideration for the reproductive outcome. Abstinence was impractical; withdrawal was unpopular. "Enforced motherhood is the most complete denial of a woman's right to life and liberty," argued Sanger. She devoted her life to a woman's right of control over her reproductive system.

The problem of birth control has arisen directly from the effort of the feminine spirit to free itself from bondage. Woman herself has wrought that bondage through her reproductive powers and while enslaving herself has enslaved the world. The physical suffering to be relieved is chiefly woman's. Hers, too, is the love life that dies first under the blight of too prolific breeding. Within her is wrapped up the future of the race—it is hers to make or mar. All of these considerations point unmistakably to one fact—it is woman's duty as well as her privilege to lay hold of the means of freedom. Whatever men may do, she cannot escape the responsibility. For ages she has been deprived of the opportunity to meet this obligation. She is now emerging from her helplessness. Even as no one can share the suffering of the overburdened mother, so no one can do this work for her. Others may help, but she and she alone can free herself.

The basic freedom of the world is woman's freedom. A free race cannot be born of slave mothers. A woman enchained cannot choose but give a measure of that bondage to her sons and daughters. No woman can call herself free who does not own and control her body. No woman can call herself free until she can choose consciously whether she will or will not be a mother. . . .

With the so-called "free" woman, who chooses a mate in defiance of convention, freedom is largely a question of character and audacity. If she does attain to an unrestricted choice of a mate, she is still in a position to be enslaved through her reproductive powers. Indeed, the pressure of law and custom upon the woman not legally married is likely to make her more of a slave than the woman fortunate enough to marry the man of her choice.

Look at it from any standpoint you will, suggest any solution you will, conventional or unconventional, sanctioned by law or in defiance of law, woman is in the same position, fundamentally, until she is able to determine for herself whether she will be a mother and to fix the number of her offspring. This unavoidable situation is alone enough to make birth control, first of all, a woman's problem. On the very face of the matter, voluntary motherhood is chiefly the concern of the woman. . . .

While it is true that he suffers many evils as the consequence of this situation, she suffers vastly more. While it is true that he should be awakened to the cause of these evils, we know that they come home to her with crushing force every day. It is she who has the long burden of carrying, bearing and rearing the unwanted children. . . .

Conditions, rather than theories, facts, rather than dreams, govern the problem. They place it squarely upon the shoulders of woman. She has learned that whatever the moral responsibility of the man in this direction may be, he does not discharge it. She has learned that, lovable and considerate as the individual husband may be, she has nothing to expect from men in the mass, when they make laws and decree customs. She knows that regardless of what ought to be, the brutal, unavoidable fact is that she will never receive her freedom until she takes it for herself. . . .

Woman must not accept; she must challenge. She must not be awed by that which has been built up around her; she must reverence that within her which struggles for expression. Her eyes must be less upon what is and more clearly upon what should be. She must listen only with a frankly questioning attitude to the dogmatized opinions of man-made society. When she chooses her new, free course of action, it must be in the light of her own opinion—of her own intuition. Only so can she give play to the feminine spirit. Only thus can she free her mate from the bondage which he wrought for himself when he wrought hers. Only thus can she restore to him that of which he robbed himself in restricting her. Only thus can she remake the world.

Questions for Review and Reflection

1. What is basic freedom to Sanger?
2. How do men and women differ on the issue of pregnancy?
3. What is the approach women should take regarding motherhood?

Reading 12

Luther Standing Bear, 1933

Land of the Spotted Eagle

Luther Standing Bear (1868?-1939) was an Oglala Sioux who grew up on the Pine Ridge Reservation in South Dakota. He was one of the many Indian children sent to an assimilation school (part of the Dawes Act of 1887) that was designed to eradicate Indian culture and educate Native Americans in the white man's way.

As a young adult, Luther Standing Bear left the reservation, became a teacher, and later an actor. When he finally returned to Pine Ridge many years later, he found dismal conditions of physical and psychological deterioration.

He denounced assimilation and urged that his people be allowed to live as Indians, raise cattle, practice their own culture, and be left alone. "Regarding the 'civilization' that has been thrust upon me, since the days of reservation, it has not added one whit to my sense of justice; to my reverence for the rights of life; to my love for truth, honesty, and generosity."

His ideas contributed to what Franklin D. Roosevelt hoped would be the "New Deal" for Indians: self-determination, freedom from government control, and self-sufficiency. This reading comes from Luther Standing Bear's 1933 book.

What the Indian Means to America

The feathered and blanketed figure of the American Indian has come to symbolize the American continent. He is the man who through centuries has been moulded and sculped by the same hand that shaped its mountains, forests, and plains, and marked the course of its rivers.

The American Indian is of the soil, whether it be the region of forests, plains, pueblos, or mesas. He fits into the landscape, for the hand that fashioned the continent also fashioned the man for his surroundings. He once grew as naturally as the wild sunflowers; he belongs just as the buffalo belonged.

With a physique that fitted, the man developed fitting skills—crafts which today are called American. And the body had a soul, also formed and moulded by the same master hand of harmony. Out of the Indian approach to existence there came a great freedom—an intense and absorbing love for nature; a respect for life; enriching faith in a Supreme Power; and principles of truth, honesty, generosity, equity, and brotherhood as a guide to mundane relations.

Becoming possessed of a fitting philosophy and art, it was by them that native man perpetuated his identity; stamped it into the history and soul of this country—made land and man one.

By living—struggling, losing, meditating, imbibing, aspiring, achieving— he wrote himself into inerasable evidence—an evidence that can be and often has been ignored, but never totally destroyed. Living—and all the intangible forces that constitute that phenomenon—are brought into being by Spirit, that which no man can alter.

The white man does not understand the Indian for the reason that he does not understand America. He is too far removed from its formative processes. The roots of the tree of his life have not yet grasped the rock and soil. The white man is still troubled with primitive fears; he still has in his consciousness the perils of this frontier continent, some of its fastnesses not yet having yielded to his questing footsteps and inquiring eyes. He shudders still with the memory of the loss of his forefathers upon its scorching deserts and forbidding mountain-tops. The man from Europe is still a foreigner and an alien. And he still hates the man who questioned his path across the continent.

But in the Indian the spirit of the land is still vested; it will be until other men are able to divine and meet its rhythm. Men must be born and reborn to belong. Their bodies must be formed of the dust of their forefathers' bones.

The attempted transformation of the Indian by the white man and the chaos that has resulted are but the fruits of the white man's disobedience of a fundamental and spiritual law. The pressure that has been brought to bear upon the native people, since the cessation of armed conflict, in the attempt to force conformity of custom and habit has caused a reaction more destructive than war, and the injury has not only affected the Indian, but has extended to the white population as well. Tyranny, stupidity, and lack of vision have brought about the situation now alluded to as the 'Indian Problem.'

There is, I insist, no Indian problem as created by the Indian himself. Every problem that exists today in regard to the native population is due to the white man's cast of mind, which is unable, at least reluctant, to seek understanding and achieve adjustment in a new and a significant environment into which it has so recently come. . . .

After subjugation, after dispossession, there was cast the last abuse upon the people who so entirely resented their wrongs and punishments, and that was the stamping and the labeling of them as savages. To make this label stick has been the task of the white race and the greatest salve that it has been able to apply to its sore and troubled conscience now hardened through the habitual practice of injustice.

But all the years of calling the Indian a savage has never made him one; all the denial of his virtues has never taken them from him; and the very resistance he has made to save the things inalienably his has been his saving strength—that which will stand him in need when justice does make its belated appearance and he undertakes rehabilitation.

All sorts of feeble excuses are heard for the continued subjection of the Indian. One of the most common is that he is not yet ready to accept the society of the white man—that he is not yet ready to mingle as a social entity.

This, I maintain, is beside the question. The matter is not one of making-over the external Indian into the likeness of the white race—a process detrimental to both races. Who can say that the white man's way is better for the Indian? Where resides the human judgment with the competence to weigh and value Indian ideals and spiritual concepts, or substitute for them other values?

Then, has the white man's social order been so harmonious and ideal as to merit the respect of the Indian, and for that matter the thinking class of the white race? Is it wise to urge upon the Indian a foreign social form? Let none but the Indian answer!

Rather, let the white brother face about and cast his mental eye upon a new angle of vision. Let him look upon the Indian world as a human world; then let him see to it that human rights be accorded to the Indians. And this for the purpose of retaining for his own order of society a measure of humanity.

The Indian School of Thought

I say again that Indians should teach Indians; that Indians should serve Indians, especially on reservations where the older people remain. There is a definite need of the old for the care and sympathy of the young and they are today perishing for the joys that naturally belong to old Indian people. Old Indians are very close to their progeny. It was their delightful duty to care for and instruct the very young, while in turn they looked forward to being cared for by sons and daughters. These were the privileges and blessings of old age. . . .

Why should not America be cognizant of itself; aware of its identity? In short, why should not America be preserved?

There were ideals and practices in the life of my ancestors that have not been improved upon by the present-day civilization; there were in our culture elements of benefit; and there were influences that would broaden any life. But that almost an entire public needs to be enlightened as to this fact need not be discouraging. For many centuries the human mind labored under the delusion that the world was flat; and thousands of men have believed that the heavens were supported by the strength of an Atlas. The human mind is not yet free from fallacious reasoning; it is not yet an open mind and its deepest recesses are not yet swept free of errors.

But it is now time for a destructive order to be reversed, and it is well to inform other races that the aboriginal culture of America was not devoid of beauty. Furthermore, in denying the Indian his ancestral rights and heritages the white race is but robbing itself. But America can be revived, rejuvenated, by recognizing a native school of thought. The Indian can save America.

Regarding the 'civilization' that has been thrust upon me since the days of reservation, it has not added one whit to my sense of justice; to my reverence for the rights of life; to my love for truth, honesty, and generosity; nor to my faith in Wakan Tanka—God of the Lakotas. For after all the great religions have been preached and expounded, or have been revealed by brilliant scholars, or have been written in books and embellished in fine language with finer covers, man—all man—is still confronted with the Great Mystery.

So if today I had a young mind to direct, to start on the journey of life, and I was faced with the duty of choosing between the natural way of my forefathers and that of the white man's present way of civilization, I would, for its welfare, unhesitatingly set that child's feet in the path of my forefathers. I would raise him to be an Indian!

Questions for Review and Reflection

1. Why does Luther Standing Bear state that the American Indian is of the soil?
2. What are some of the excuses used for the continued subjugation of the Indians?

3. Luther Standing Bear speaks of the attempted "transformation of the Indian" by white men. What do you think the nature of this transformation was? What was his attitude toward this?
4. Can Luther Standing Bear find anything about the American civilization worth incorporating into his way of life?

Reading 13

Ralph Bunche, 1944

The Political Status of the Negro after FDR

Throughout the Depression and World War II, African Americans continued to be relegated to a second-class citizenship. Employment was hard to find, and a policy of "last hired, first fired" prevailed. World events made recruitment into the military an employment option, but the armed forces were segregated, with few promotions offered to black men. The Agricultural Adjustment Act of the New Deal disproportionately evicted black tenant farmers through its policy of paying farmers not to plant. As America prepared to enter World War II, blacks urged, "Don't just get rid of Hitler, but Hitlerism," referring to the racism that continued in the United States.

Grandson of a slave, Dr. Ralph Bunche (1904–1971) received his doctorate in political science from Harvard University. He was a respected diplomat and statesman who earned the Nobel Peace Prize in 1950 for his work in the Arab-Israeli conflict.

Dr. Bunche reiterated that the lack of full access to the franchise made a mockery of the guarantees in the Constitution. Bunche prepared a voluminous statistical study to document the need to extend the full measure of the law to African Americans in order to implement the ideals of the Constitution.

The future of the American Negro is a problem of the national society. It is to be solved only through opportunity for development and through assimilation into the political and economic life of the nation. The Negro has for centuries contributed his labor, his intelligence, his blood, and even his life to the development of the country. He asks nothing from American society except that it consider him as a full-fledged citizen, vested with all of the rights and privileges granted to other citizens; that the charter of liberties of the Constitution apply to the black as to all other men. The Negro citizen has long since learned that "special" treatment for him implies differentiation on a racial basis and inevitably connotes inferior status. In a world in which democracy is gravely besieged and its very foundations shaken, the United States must consider seriously the implications of its own failure to extend the democratic process in full to some thirteen million of its citizens whose present status tends to make a mockery of the Constitution. The thinking Negro appreciates fully the difficulties inherent in the American social system. He recognizes that deep-seated social attitudes are not quickly changed. Yet it can be readily understood that, in a world in which dogmas of racial superiority and racial persecution assume an increasingly dominant role, the Negro views with great alarm the stubborn persistence of racial bigotry in America.

The Negro asks only his constitutional right when he demands that the laws of the United States be designed so as to extend their benefits to black as well as to white citizens, and that political parties, governmental agencies, and officials pledge themselves to extend the full measure of law and constitution to all men, regardless of race, color, or creed. Never since the Civil War has the Constitution assumed such vital importance in the ordering of the country. The future of the Negro rests with the future of democracy, and Negroes in great numbers now know that every blow struck in behalf of democracy is a blow for the black man's future. . . .

If democracy is to survive the severe trials and buffetings to which it is being subjected in the modern world, it will do so only because it can demonstrate that it is a practical, living philosophy under which all people can live the good life most abundantly. It must prove itself in practice, or be discredited as a theory. Democratic nations such as our own have an obligation to all mankind to prove that democracy, as a form of government, as a practical means of human relationships, is a working and workable concept. This America can do only by abandoning the shallow, vulgar pretense of limited democracy—under which some are free and privileged and others are permanently fettered. The Negro, and especially the Negro in the South, already has had too vivid an experience with embryonic fascism in the very shadow of democracy. Within our own gates are found intense racial hatreds, racial ghettoes, and racial differentials that saturate the political, economic, and social life of the nation. . . .

The Negro should press with all vigor his fight before the courts for the full recognition of his constitutional rights. Court decisions, favorable or unfavorable, serve to dramatize the plight of the race more effectively than any other recourse; their propaganda and educative value is great.

Certainly appeal to the courts is a useful tactic for an oppressed minority group, and it is fortified by the fact that the Negro cause is honest and just. But the problems of the Negro cannot be solved at the bar. The courts cannot uproot deep-seated social prejudices; they can never bring on a social revolution.

The so-called Negro problem in America is only incidentally a racial one. Many of its roots go deeper than race and are themselves embedded in the fundamental problems of economic conflict and distress which afflict the entire society. The primary interests of the Negro are inextricably tied up with the interests of the masses in the dominant population. Therefore, court decisions such as those upholding the Wagner Act, social security legislation, and minimum wage and hour enactments will in the long run do much to better the condition of the Negro. Every advance made toward lessening the conflict between labor and capital, between laborer and laborer, between white and black workers—in fact, any legislation designed to increase the security of the workingman's present and future—is of the most fundamental significance for the Negro and for all other minority groups in the United States. The courts can never save the Negro from an America torn asunder by industrial conflict and its inevitable by-products, racial intolerance and bigotry. . . .

In the final analysis, however, the political burdens borne by the American Negro cannot be legislated away. The roots of Negro disabilities reach deeply into the economic and political structure of the nation. Negro political ailments are merely symptomatic of more fundamental disorders in the economic system. These disorders cannot be cured by dabbing at the symptoms. The nation's economic house needs to be put in order. In the first place, it is useless to think in terms of full Negro citizenship so long as white and black citizens must engage in daily violent struggle for the wherewithal of life. This is the process that feeds fuel to the fires of race prejudice and perpetuates those mores which stand guard against Negro entrance to the polls. The economy must afford a far larger measure of security for all before the Negro can hope for much greater political advancement. This it can do only as a result of some far-reaching changes in the direction of a socialized economy—at least insofar as the production of the necessities of life is concerned. In the second place, unless the Negro is permitted to share in the fuller fruits of a more liberal and humane economy, political privilege will become sheer mockery. The black vote will never be influential enough to initiate in and of itself any radical changes in the economy. The ballot without bread would be a tragic jest for the Negro.

uestions for Review and Reflection

1. What does Bunche say is the only real solution to the race problem? How might this assimilation occur? How has "special treatment" established an inferior status for black Americans?
2. What makes a "mockery of the Constitution," according to Bunche?
3. According to Bunche, how are the futures of democracy and of black Americans linked? What is the obligation of all democratic governments?
4. Why do you think that Bunche recommends the courts as the proper arena for the drive for civil rights in America? Do you agree? What might other courses of action be?

5

The Policies of Presidents: Liberty Broadened

Among the three branches of the federal government, Congress had dominated during the nineteenth century. National public policy was initiated from the capitol building. The twentieth century saw a shift of power to the White House, beginning with Theodore Roosevelt, who was billed as the "first modern president." A bold activist, Roosevelt completed the Panama Canal, gained major concessions for striking miners, strengthened controls over big business, and deployed U.S. troops as an international police force, especially in Latin America.

Running for president in 1912 against Roosevelt and his New Nationalism, Democrat Woodrow Wilson offered an alternative he called "The New Freedom." Like other presidents discussed in this chapter, Wilson took seriously his charge as a candidate to serve as leader of his political party and to represent the philosophy of that party during his campaign for office.

Wilson won the presidency, and his New Freedom was submitted for legislative enactment. It called for a breakup of the concentrated power that had been amassed in the previous century by big business. Such power had been used to establish monopolies in key industries and to diminish the power of the small farmer, business owner, and working man. Wilson's party supported the "little guy" and urged the use of government power to the extent necessary to restore competition and a free marketplace. Wilson's bold leadership and strong sense of the presidency went a long way toward achieving the Democratic Party's initiatives.

Article II of Section 3 of the Constitution grants the president the power to recommend legislation to the Congress. President Wilson used his powers of persuasion in 1918 to lobby for the Nineteenth Amendment, which granted the franchise to women. Earlier, he had opposed the idea of women's voting, but their contributions during World War I, both at home and at the front, changed his mind. His support for the amendment and his leadership helped to change the votes of key congressmen, so that women's long-sought right to vote was finally achieved.

Article II of Section 3 states that the president shall report to the Congress "from time to time" on the state of the Union. Strong presidents use such an opportunity to submit legislative recommendations and bold initiatives in response to the issues facing the country. They outline a plan that expresses their vision for the future.

President Franklin D. Roosevelt used his 1944 State of the Union message to declare a dramatic new set of rights which, he said, were as inalienable as those found in the original Bill of Rights and necessary to ensure economic liberty.

In determining the state of the Union, presidents can order studies that examine the current status of issues. President Harry Truman ordered such an accounting from the Commission on Civil Rights. Their report, entitled *To Secure These Rights*, urged federal action to end discrimination in education, employment, and housing. When Truman took those recommendations to Congress, it failed to act.

Always reminded by a sign on his desk that read, "The Buck Stops Here," Truman issued Executive Order 9981, which desegregated the armed forces. Presidents have authority to issue such orders that assist the executive branch in carrying out its duties.

Article II of Section 2 grants the president the power to make appointments to executive offices and to the federal bench. Appointments to the Supreme Court are particularly significant, since those seats are for life.

President Dwight D. Eisenhower appointed Earl Warren as Chief Justice of the Supreme Court. Eisenhower believed that Warren was a moderate, much like himself. To his surprise, Chief Justice Warren turned out to be a judicial activist and a liberal. The first opinion he wrote was a unanimous decision he helped to shape in the 1954 *Brown v. Board of Education* case. The Court heard arguments involving the segregation of African American school children. "Separate but equal" educational facilities had been the policy in the South since the *Plessy v. Ferguson* decision in 1896. Warren's Court ruled that such a policy violated the Fourteenth Amendment's guarantee of "equal protection," and that it had to end "with all deliberate speed." Much to the chagrin of President Eisenhower, Chief Justice Warren's court was noted for liberal decisions like this one.

Article II of Section 2 also names the president as the commander in chief of the Army and Navy and of the militia of the several states.

President Eisenhower exercised his power as commander in chief to restore order after a crisis erupted in Arkansas. Central High School in Little Rock had enrolled nine black school children in compliance with a federal court order to end segregation in schools. Arkansas Governor Faubus defied the court order, and white southerners formed an immense mob outside the school to protest integration. President Eisenhower unilaterally placed the National Guard under the authority of the president and also ordered 1,000 paratroopers deployed to the scene. They remained at Central High for the entire school year, quelling the first major challenge of federal integration laws.

These presidential actions illustrate how the authority of the executive branch expanded during the twentieth century, spurred in part by two world wars and the Great Depression, events that called for bold leadership. The scope of presidential power broadened, and strong presidents expanded the concepts of liberty and equality.

Reading 1

Woodrow Wilson, 1913

"The New Freedom"

As the son of a minister, President Woodrow Wilson (1856–1924) was raised with a strong code of ethics. He became a professor of history and political science, wrote a book called *Congressional Government*, and served as president of Princeton University. Before winning the U.S. presidency, he was elected governor of New Jersey, where he became widely known as a progressive leader.

His administration introduced a series of reforms in banking, tariff, and business policy. He also submitted some new ideas about liberty and the role of government. "We used to say that the ideal of government was for every man to be left alone. . . . But we are coming now to realize that life is so complicated . . . the law has to step in and create new conditions under which we may live."

Wilson's New Freedom meant citizens' freedom to pursue their own economic interests, aided by government intervention when necessary to level the playing field and make opportunities available for all.

We have come upon a very different age from any that preceded us. We have come upon an age when we do not do business in the way in which we used to do business,—when we do not carry on any of the operations of manufacture, sale, transportation, or communication as men used to carry them on. There is a sense in which in our day the individual has been submerged. In most parts of our country men work, not for themselves, not as partners in the old way in which they used to work, but generally as employees,—in a higher or lower grade,—of great corporations. There was a time when corporations played a very minor part in our business affairs, but now they play the chief part, and most men are the servants of corporations. . . .

There is something very new and very big and very complex about these new relations of capital and labor. A new economic society has sprung up and we must effect a new set of adjustments. We must not pit power against weakness. The employer is generally, in our day, as I have said, not an individual, but a powerful group; and yet the workingman when dealing with his employer is still, under our existing law, an individual. . . .

Our modern corporations employ thousands, and in some instances hundreds of thousands, of men. The only persons whom you see or deal with are local superintendents or local representatives of a vast organization, which is not like anything that the workingmen of the time in which our laws were framed knew anything about. A little group of workingmen, seeing their employer every day, dealing with him in a personal way, is one thing, and the modern body of labor engaged as employees of the huge enterprises that spread all over the country, dealing with men of whom they can form no personal conception, is another thing. A very different thing. You never saw a corporation, any more than you ever saw a government. Many a workingman to-day never saw the body of men who are conducting the industry in which he is employed. And they never saw him. What they know about him is written in ledgers and books and letters, in the correspondence of the office, in the reports of the superintendents. He is a long way off from them. . . .

American industry is not free, as once it was free; American enterprise is not free; the man with only a little capital is finding it harder to get into the field, more and more impossible to compete with the big fellow. Why? Because the laws of this country do not prevent the strong from crushing the weak. That is the reason, and because the strong have crushed the weak the strong dominate the industry and economic life of this country. No man can deny that the lines of endeavor have more and more narrowed and stiffened; no man who knows anything about the development of industry in this country can have failed to observe that the larger kinds of credit are more and more difficult to obtain, unless you obtain them upon the terms of uniting your efforts with those who already control the industries of the country; and nobody can fail to observe that any man who tries to set himself up in competition with any process of manufacture which has been taken under the control of large combinations of capital will presently find himself either squeezed out or obliged to sell and allow himself to be absorbed. . . .

The originative part of America, the part of America that makes new enterprises, the part into which the ambitious and gifted workingman makes his way up, the class that saves, that plans, that organizes, that presently spreads its enterprises until they have a national scope and character,—that middle class is being more and more squeezed out by the processes which we have been taught to call processes of prosperity. Its members are sharing prosperity, no doubt; but what alarms me is that they are not originating prosperity. No country can afford to have its prosperity originated by a small controlling class. The treasury of America does not lie in the brains of the small body of men now in control of the great enterprises that have been concentrated under the direction of a very small number of persons. The treasury of America lies in those ambitions, those energies, that cannot be restricted to a special favored class. It depends upon the inventions of unknown men, upon the originations of unknown men, upon the ambitions of unknown men. Every country is renewed out of the ranks of the unknown, not out of the ranks of those already famous and powerful and in control.

There has come over the land that un-American set of conditions which enables a small number of men who control the government to get favors from the government; by those favors to exclude their fellows from equal business opportunity; by those favors to extend a network of control that will presently dominate every industry in the country, and so make men forget the ancient time when America lay in every hamlet. . . .

We used to think in the old-fashioned days when life was very simple that all that government had to do was to put on a policeman's uniform, and say, 'Now don't anybody hurt anybody else.' We used to say that the ideal of government was for every man to be left alone and not interfered with, except when he interfered with somebody else; and that the best government was the government that did as little governing as possible. That was the idea that obtained in Jefferson's time. But we are coming now to realize that life is so complicated that we are not dealing with the old conditions, and that the law has to step in and create new conditions under which we may live, the conditions which will make it tolerable for us to live. . . . Whenever bodies of men employ bodies of men, it ceases to be a private relationship. . . .

There are two theories of government that have been contending with each other ever since government began. One of them is the theory which in America is associated with the name of a very great man, Alexander Hamilton. A great man, but, in my judgment, not a great American. He did not think in terms of American life. Hamilton believed that the only people who could understand government, and therefore the only people who were qualified to conduct it, were the men who had the biggest financial stake in the commercial and industrial enterprises of the country.

That theory, though few have now the hardihood to profess it openly, has been the working theory upon which our government has lately been conducted. It is astonishing how persistent it is. It is amazing how quickly the political party which had Lincoln for its first leader,—Lincoln, who not only denied, but in his own person so completely disproved the aristocratic theory,—it is amazing how quickly that party, founded on faith in the people, forgot the precepts of Lincoln and fell under the delusion that the 'masses' needed the guardianship of 'men of affairs.'

For indeed, if you stop to think about it, nothing could be a greater departure from original Americanism, from faith in the ability of a confident, resourceful, and independent people, than the discouraging doctrine that somebody has got to provide prosperity for the rest of us. . . .

You know that one of the interesting things that Mr. Jefferson said in those early days of simplicity which marked the beginnings of our government was that the best government consisted in as little governing as possible. And there is still a sense in which that is true. It is still intolerable for the government to interfere with our individual activities except where it [is] necessary to interfere with them in order to free them. But I feel confident that if Jefferson were living in our day he would see what we see: that the individual is caught in a great confused nexus of all sorts of complicated circumstances, and that to let him alone is to leave him helpless as against the obstacles with which he has to contend, and that, therefore, law in our day must come to the assistance of the individual. It must come to his assistance to see that he gets fair play; that is all, but that is much. Without the watchful interference, the resolute interference, of the government, there can be no fair play between individuals and such powerful institutions as the trusts. Freedom to-day is something more than being let alone. The program of a government of freedom must in these days be positive, not negative merely. . . .

I do not believe that America is securely great because she has great men in her now. America is great in proportion as she can make sure of having great men in the next generation. She is rich in her unborn children; rich, that is to say, if those unborn children see the sun in a day of opportunity, see the sun when they are free to exercise their energies as they will. If they open their eyes in a land where there is no special privilege, then we shall come into a new era of American greatness and American liberty; but if they open their eyes in a country where they must be employees or nothing, if they open their eyes in a land of merely regulated monopoly, where all the conditions of industry are determined by small groups of men, then they will see an America such as the founders of this Republic would have wept to think of. . . .

Since their day the meaning of liberty has deepened. But it has not ceased to be a fundamental demand of the human spirit, a fundamental necessity for the life of the soul. And the day is at hand when it shall be realized on this consecrated soil,—a New Freedom,—a Liberty widened and deepened to match the broadened life of man in modern America.

Questions for Review and Reflection

1. Describe the new economic society that has emerged in the age of corporations. How have these economic concentrations affected the nature of American government?
2. Why does Wilson claim that American industry is no longer free, as it had once been? Who is responsible?
3. According to Wilson, what factors are responsible for the difficulties of the small-business owner? What narrows his or her scope of operation? What prescription does Wilson suggest?
4. Wilson speaks of "un-American" conditions that allow a small minority of the people to capture control of the government. What are these conditions? From where do you think they come?

Reading 2

United States Congress, 1920

Nineteenth Amendment

In 1869 Wyoming became the first state to give women the vote, and women increasingly concentrated their efforts on winning the vote state by state. When, by 1910, they had achieved victory in many Western states, they focused again at the national level. President Woodrow Wilson initially opposed women's suffrage in an effort to placate Southern Democrats, who especially feared the voting power of black women. But vigorous protests, voting demonstrations, and Republican support for the women's cause wore down Wilson's resistance. Over the objections of southerners who wanted the franchise limited to white citizens, the Nineteenth Amendment of 1920 guaranteed that the right to vote could no longer be denied to citizens based on their gender. Popular participation in the American democracy was greatly expanded with the passage of this amendment.

Amendment XIX

Section 1. The right of citizens of the United States to vote shall not be denied or abridged by the United States or by any state on account of sex.

Section 2. Congress shall have power to enforce this article by appropriate legislation.

Questions for Review and Reflection

1. Read the Fourteenth Amendment on pages 63–64 in order to determine why the Nineteenth Amendment was necessary.
2. Were women citizens of the United States prior to the passage of the Nineteenth Amendment?

Reading 3

Franklin D. Roosevelt, 1944

Economic Bill of Rights

President Franklin D. Roosevelt (1882-1945) was the longest-serving president in U.S. history. First elected in 1932, he presided over the nation through the Depression, when millions of people lost their jobs, their life's savings, and their faith in democracy. Thousands of families were left homeless and without a future.

President Roosevelt came to office in 1933 with the promise of a "New Deal." Convening an emergency session of Congress, he introduced a series of legislative acts to provide "relief, recovery, and reform" from the misery that existed in America. Chief among his efforts were job creation, the hydroelectric power program called the Tennessee Valley Authority, the Federal Deposit Insurance Corporation, and federal welfare programs. The federal government thus became much more involved in the affairs of all Americans, and assumed some responsibility for their well-being.

Roosevelt's "Second Bill of Rights," under which "a new basis of security and prosperity can be established for all," signaled a departure from the traditional basic liberty, which

was the freedom to be left alone. FDR defined a more positive
liberty in which government had a responsibility to guarantee
each citizen's independence through economic security.

This Republic had its beginning, and grew to its present strength, under the
protection of certain inalienable political rights—among them the right of free
speech, free press, free worship, trial by jury, freedom from unreasonable
searches and seizures. They were our rights to life and liberty.

As our Nation has grown in size and stature, however—as our industrial
economy expanded—these political rights proved inadequate to assure us
equality in the pursuit of happiness.

We have come to a clear realization of the fact that true individual
freedom cannot exist without economic security and independence. "Neces-
sitous men are not freemen." People who are hungry and out of a job are
the stuff of which dictatorships are made.

In our day these economic truths have become accepted as self-evident.
We have accepted, so to speak, a second Bill of Rights under which a new
basis of security and prosperity can be established for all—regardless of station,
race, or creed.

Among these are—

The right to a useful and remunerative job in the industries, or shops
or farms or mines of the Nation;

The right to earn enough to provide adequate food and clothing and
recreation;

The right of every farmer to raise and sell his products at a return which
will give him and his family a decent living;

The right of every businessman, large and small, to trade in an atmos-
phere of freedom from unfair competition and domination by monopolies at
home or abroad;

The right of every family to a decent home;

The right to adequate medical care and the opportunity to achieve and
enjoy good health;

The right to adequate protection from the economic fears of old age,
sickness, accident, and unemployment;

The right to a good education.

All of these rights spell security. And after this war is won we must be
prepared to move forward, in the implementation of these rights, to new goals
of human happiness and well-being.

Questions for Review and Reflection

1. Why do you suppose Franklin Roosevelt chose to call this concept an "economic bill of rights"? What moral authority was he drawing upon with this image?
2. Roosevelt delineates certain important political rights. What had happened to threaten these traditional American rights? How did Roosevelt intend to protect these rights immediately and in the future?
3. What link did Roosevelt see between individual freedom and economic security?
4. What spelled "security" for Roosevelt?
5. Roosevelt outlined certain "economic truths" in the *Economic Bill of Rights* that appeared to cover a wide segment of American society. Can you think of any part of society that he omitted?

Reading 4

Harry Truman, 1948

Executive Order 9981

While entertaining the troops at a USO show during World War II, singer Lena Horne noticed that black troops were seated at the back of the house. She walked through the audience, faced the African American soldiers with her back to the white audience, and completed her performance. Her statement of opposition represented a growing antipathy among some Americans, black and white, toward racially discriminatory practices.

In World War II, Americans had defeated Nazi Germany and its racist ideology. The sacrifices and contributions of African American soldiers to that victory were undeniable.

But when an end to segregation in the United States armed services was proposed after the war, the opposition claimed that integration would harm morale and the cohesiveness of units. In fact, these same arguments are used today against open inclusion of gay men and women in the military.

Nevertheless, President Harry S. Truman (1884-1972), a strong and decisive leader, used the power of his office to end the policy of racial segregation and establish "equality of treatment and opportunity for all persons in the armed services without regard to race, color, religion or national origin."

Executive Order 9981

Establishing the President's Committee on Equality of Treatment and Opportunity in the Armed Services

WHEREAS it is essential that there be maintained in the armed services of the United States the highest standards of democracy, with equality of treatment and opportunity for all those who serve in our country's defense:

NOW, THEREFORE, by virtue of the authority vested in me as President of the United States, by the Constitution and the statutes of the United States, and as Commander in Chief of the armed services, it is hereby ordered as follows:

1. It is hereby declared to be the policy of the President that there shall be equality of treatment and opportunity for all persons in the armed services without regard to race, color, religion or national origin. This policy shall be put into effect as rapidly as possible, having due regard to the time required to effectuate any necessary changes without impairing efficiency or morale.

2. There shall be created in the National Military Establishment an advisory committee to be known as the President's Committee on Equality of Treatment and Opportunity in the Armed Services, which shall be composed of seven members to be designated by the President.

3. The Committee is authorized on behalf of the President to examine into the rules, procedures and practices of the armed services in order to determine in what respect such rules, procedures and practices may be altered or improved with a view to carrying out the policy of this order. The Committee shall confer and advise with the Secretary of Defense, the Secretary of the Army, the Secretary of the Navy, and the Secretary of the Air Force, and shall make such recommendations to the President and to said Secretaries as in the judgment of the Committee will effectuate the policy hereof.

4. All executive departments and agencies of the Federal Government are authorized and directed to cooperate with the Committee in its work, and to furnish the Committee such information or the services of such persons as the Committee may require in the performance of its duties.

Questions for Review and Reflection

1. Why do you suppose President Truman chose the executive order method of integrating the armed forces instead of congressional leg-

islation? What does his choice reveal about the nature of racism in American society?

2. What was the source of President Truman's authority to unilaterally integrate the armed forces of the United States of America?

3. How did he feel integration of the armed forces would facilitate the highest standards of democracy in the United States? How did Truman's move make the army stronger?

4. What was the President's Committee on Equality of Treatment and Opportunity in the Armed Services? What was the authority of this committee? What was its scope of action?

5. How might the issues surrounding America's involvement in World War II have influenced President Truman's decision to integrate the military? Do you see a similarity between the granting of women's suffrage after World War I and the adoption of desegregation following World War II? Why?

Reading 5

U.S. Supreme Court, 1954

Brown v. Board of Education, 347 U.S. 483

In the *Plessy v. Ferguson* case, the Supreme Court of the United States in 1896 upheld a Louisiana state law requiring that facilities for blacks and whites be separate in public accommodations such as railroad cars and schools. The Court reasoned that as long as the facilities were equal, a state could keep racial groups apart. This "separate but equal" doctrine legalized segregation in the South for decades afterward.

But in 1954, plaintiffs in the *Brown v. Board of Education* case contended that they were deprived of equal protection of the laws. Lawyers for eight-year-old Linda Brown argued that it was unconstitutional for Topeka, Kansas, to bus Linda five miles to a black school rather than let her attend her neighborhood school. Nor was distance the only issue. As parents were very much aware, schools for African American students were not only separate but under-equipped and vastly inferior. The Warren Court agreed, reversed *Plessy,* and ordered the integration of schools with all deliberate speed. This case secured the equal right to obtain an education and the equal protections guaranteed in the Fourteenth Amendment. Soon to follow would be a similar demand for equal access to all public facilities, spurred by Montgomery, Alabama, seamstress Rosa Parks, who bravely refused to give up her seat on the bus to a white passenger. In November 1956, the Supreme Court ordered an end to the Montgomery bus segregation.

Brown v. Board of Education

The plaintiffs contend that segregated public schools are not "equal" and cannot be made equal, and that hence they are deprived of the equal protection of the laws. . . .

Today, education is perhaps the most important function of state and local governments. Compulsory school attendance laws and the great expenditures for education both demonstrate our recognition of the importance of education to our democratic society. It is required in the performance of our most basic public responsibilities, even service in the armed forces. It is the very foundation of good citizenship. Today it is a principal instrument in awakening the child to cultural values, in preparing him for later professional training, and in helping him to adjust normally to his environment. In these days, it is doubtful that any child may reasonably be expected to succeed in life if he is denied the opportunity of an education. Such an opportunity, where the state has undertaken to provide it, is a right which must be made available to all on equal terms.

We come then to the question presented. Does segregation of children in public schools solely on the basis of race, even though the physical facilities and other "tangible" factors may be equal, deprive the children of the minority group equal educational opportunities? We believe that it does.

In *Sweatt v. Painter,* in finding that a segregated law school for Negroes could not provide them equal educational opportunities, this Court relied in large part on "those qualities which are incapable of objective measurement but which make for greatness in a law school." In *McLaurin v. Oklahoma State Regents,* the Court, in requiring that a Negro admitted to a white graduate school be treated like all other students, again resorted to intangible considerations: "his ability to study, to engage in discussions and exchange views with other students, and in, general, to learn his profession." Such considerations apply with added force to children in grade and high schools. To separate them from others of similar age and qualifications solely because of their race generates a feeling of inferiority as to their status in the community that may affect their hearts and minds in a way unlikely ever to be undone. . . .

We conclude that in the field of public education the doctrine of "separate but equal" has no place. Separate educational facilities are inherently unequal.

$\boxed{Q}$uestions for Review and Reflection

1. Describe the importance of education as defined by the Supreme Court.
2. What are the "intangible considerations" spelled out by the Court?
3. How does racial separation affect a child, according to this decision?

Reading **6**

Dwight D. Eisenhower, September 24, 1957

Address to the Nation

Brown v. Board of Education, the landmark Supreme Court decision of 1954 that declared an end to the "separate but equal" doctrine, brought strong reaction from southerners. Governor Orville Faubus of Arkansas refused to act with all deliberate speed to integrate the public schools of his state. When the Little Rock, Arkansas, school board decided to enroll nine black children in Little Rock High School, the governor ordered the National Guard to prevent the action from taking place. He later withdrew his order, but mobs of people had already begun to come into the state to protest integration.

President Dwight Eisenhower (1890–1969) reportedly disapproved of Chief Justice Earl Warren's liberal Court stance, and regretted appointing him. But Eisenhower upheld his oath to ensure "that the laws be faithfully executed." He called up 1,000 paratroopers and nationalized the Arkansas National Guardsmen to protect and enforce the rights of Little Rock schoolchildren and the principle of equal rights for all.

My *Fellow Citizens.* . . . I must speak to you about the serious situation that has arisen in Little Rock. . . . In that city, under the leadership of demagogic extremists, disorderly mobs have deliberately prevented the carrying out of proper orders from a federal court. Local authorities have not eliminated that violent opposition and, under the law, I yesterday issued a proclamation calling upon the mob to disperse.

This morning the mob again gathered in front of the Central High School of Little Rock, obviously for the purpose of again preventing the carrying out of the Court's order relating to the admission of Negro children to that school.

Whenever normal agencies prove inadequate to the task and it becomes necessary for the executive branch of the federal government to use its powers and authority to uphold federal courts, the President's responsibility is inescapable.

In accordance with that responsibility, I have today issued an Executive Order directing the use of troops under federal authority to aid in the execution of federal law at Little Rock, Arkansas. This became necessary when my Proclamation of yesterday was not observed, and the obstruction of justice still continues.

It is important that the reasons for my action be understood by all our citizens.

As you know, the Supreme Court of the United States has decided that separate public educational facilities for the races are inherently unequal and therefore compulsory school segregation laws are unconstitutional. . . .

During the past several years, many communities in our southern states have instituted public school plans for gradual progress in the enrollment and attendance of school children of all races in order to bring themselves into compliance with the law of the land.

They thus demonstrated to the world that we are a nation in which laws, not men, are supreme.

I regret to say that this truth—the cornerstone of our liberties—was not observed in this instance. . . .

Here is the sequence of events in the development of the Little Rock school case.

In May of 1955, the Little Rock School Board approved a moderate plan for the gradual desegregation of the public schools in that city. It provided that a start toward integration would be made at the present term in the high school, and that the plan would be in full operation by 1963. . . . Now this Little Rock plan was challenged in the courts by some who believed that the period of time as proposed in the plan was too long.

The United States Court at Little Rock, which has supervisory responsibility under the law for the plan of desegregation in the public schools, dismissed the challenge, thus approving a gradual rather than an abrupt change from the existing system. The court found that the school board had acted in good faith in planning for a public school system free from racial discrimination.

Since that time, the court has on three separate occasions issued orders directing that the plan be carried out. All persons were instructed to refrain from interfering with the efforts of the school board to comply with the law.

Proper and sensible observance of the law then demanded the respectful obedience which the nation has a right to expect from all its people. This, unfortunately, has not been the case at Little Rock. Certain misguided persons, many of them imported into Little Rock by agitators, have insisted upon defying the law and have sought to bring it into disrepute. The orders of the court have thus been frustrated.

The very basis of our individual rights and freedoms rests upon the certainty that the President and the Executive Branch of Government will support and insure the carrying out of the decisions of the federal courts, even, when necessary, with all the means at the President's command. . . .

Mob rule cannot be allowed to override the decisions of our courts.

Now, let me make it very clear that federal troops are not being used to relieve local and state authorities of their primary duty to preserve the peace and order of the community. . . .

The proper use of the powers of the Executive Branch to enforce the orders of a federal court is limited to extraordinary and compelling circumstances. Manifestly, such an extreme situation has been created in Little Rock. This challenge must be met and with such measures as will preserve to the people as a whole their lawfully protected rights in a climate permitting their free and fair exercise. . . .

And so, with deep confidence, I call upon the citizens of the State of Arkansas to assist in bringing to an immediate end all interference with the law and its processes. If resistance to the federal court orders ceases at once, the further presence of federal troops will be unnecessary and the City of Little Rock will return to its normal habits of peace and order and a blot upon the fair name and high honor of our nation in the world will be removed.

Thus will be restored the image of America and of all its parts as one nation, indivisible, with liberty and justice for all.

Questions for Review and Reflection

1. By what authority did Eisenhower issue his order?
2. What reasons did he give for the action?
3. What limits exist to the authority of the federal government?

6

An Era of Activism: Pursuing the American Dream

The 1960s were characterized both by disillusionment with traditional power structures in America and by optimism that unsatisfactory and unfair conditions could be changed. A collection of forces came together to make it a turbulent decade full of historic moments.

The 1950s had inspired a national civil rights movement through the action of Rosa Parks, a 43-year-old department store worker who went to jail rather than give up her seat to a white person on a Montgomery, Alabama, bus. Her brave stand energized a citywide bus boycott until segregation on the city's transportation system ended.

The Reverend Martin Luther King Jr. emerged from the success of that boycott as leader of an organized program of passive resistance to segregation laws across the South, using the tools of nonviolent protest and peaceful demonstration. In August 1963, he led over 250,000 people in a march on Washington, D.C., where he spoke of his dream one day to see America as a truly equal society.

The National Organization for Women (NOW), an interest group that worked for equal pay, reproductive rights, and an end to sex discrimination, was created in 1966 by Betty Friedan, a major figure in the women's movement. She spoke on behalf of political, social, and economic equality for all American women. The organization began to recruit female candidates for public office and revitalized the effort to ratify the Equal Rights Amendment.

The United Farm Workers organization, begun in 1962 in California, was headed by Cesar Chavez and dedicated to the improvement of working

126

conditions and wages for the migrant workers who had long been exploited by the giant farming cooperatives.

Latino political parties were launched throughout the Southwest. They worked locally and nationally for bicultural/bilingual education and bilingual balloting.

Native Americans also drew energy from the civil rights activism of the 1960s and embarked on their own form of pressure. Between 1969 and 1973, members of the activist American Indian Movement and other groups engaged in three lengthy occupations to dramatize their goals: at "The Rock," Alcatraz Island in California; at the Bureau of Indian Affairs in Washington, D.C.; and at an Indian reservation at Wounded Knee, South Dakota. They hoped to establish a Native American cultural center at Alcatraz; called the Bureau of Indian Affairs the "Trail of Broken Treaties"; and took 11 hostages in a 71-day siege at Wounded Knee. Their primary goal was self-determination and control of the resources of their own lands.

Americans, having lived through the Great Depression and World War II, seemed more attuned to the voices of the excluded than they had been in earlier decades. Perhaps their receptivity was partly because television cameras had captured the police dogs and fire hoses used against peaceful, black protesters in Birmingham, Alabama; the migrant workers' fight against agribusiness; and the grim conditions on Indian reservations. Such stories galvanized support to eradicate social injustice.

The spirit of the '60s was also fueled by a large population of young people, born shortly after World War II as families were reunited. These youthful optimists heard the challenge in President John F. Kennedy's 1960 inaugural address: "Ask not what your country can do for you, but what *you* can do for your country!" They were inspired to action. Whites joined blacks in "freedom rides" and protests. Men joined women in membership of NOW. Consumers joined farm workers in their boycott of table grapes.

When Kennedy was assassinated in November 1963 during a motorcade in Dallas, Texas, Vice President Lyndon Johnson assumed the presidency and continued the programs introduced by the Kennedy administration, with many additions of his own. Americans supported Johnson's use of federal intervention to wage his "War on Poverty" and to create the "Great Society." Congress passed the Head Start program for disadvantaged preschoolers, a Job Corps for training and remedial education, a domestic Peace Corps, a plan for urban renewal, and significant aid programs for elementary and secondary public schools.

Against this backdrop of optimism, fighting in Vietnam was a persistent thorn in the side of all American presidents during the turbulent '60s. America had become involved in the affairs of Vietnam while enforcing its cold war policy to contain communism. The entanglement began slowly but built up over time to a major commitment of over 500,000 troops. The cost in terms of money, equipment, men, and morale was staggering; it resulted in the termination of Johnson's administration. The year 1968 illustrated much of what had gone wrong. Antiwar feeling ran high because of public disillusionment with the war's purpose versus its cost. There was much campus unrest across the country among students who questioned the country's moral underpinnings and society's commitment to democratic principles. Over the prior several years, race riots had broken out in the Watts section of Los Angeles, Chicago, Detroit, and Cleveland. Muhammad Ali, heavyweight boxing champion of the world, spoke out against the "white man's war" in Vietnam and refused to be inducted. Some African American groups broke away from King's message of nonviolence. Malcolm X espoused black nationalism and violence, if necessary, against "Whitey." Violence struck another blow when Martin Luther King Jr. was assassinated. Shortly afterward, John Kennedy's brother, Robert, U.S. senator from New York, was shot and killed while campaigning for the presidential nomination.

Richard Nixon ran for and won the presidency in 1968, campaigning on behalf of the "forgotten American," described by Nixon as the hardworking, taxpaying citizen who was part of the "silent majority." He attacked dissenters who spoke against the war, against the country, and against the traditional values of American society. With his election, the burst of enthusiasm and support for economic and social equality sputtered into disillusionment toward the end of the decade. People grew weary of rebellion and unruliness; they became tired of the expense of the Kennedy-Johnson programs. The country underwent a progressive reduction in support for Great Society programs and a return to moderation in government intervention. Desegregation efforts slowed, enforcement of civil rights laws was reduced, and fewer funds were available for welfare assistance.

However, the decade had served to coalesce and organize the groups that had been so long excluded from the system. The sense of their power in numbers and the justice of their cause was not lost, and their fight for recognition became a permanent fixture in American politics.

Reading 1

Martin Luther King Jr., 1963

Letter from a Birmingham Jail

Acknowledged leader of the civil rights movement in the 1950s and 1960s and head of the Southern Christian Leadership Conference, the Reverend Martin Luther King Jr. (1929-1968) used a protest march to spotlight the injustice and brutality of the city of Birmingham, Alabama. He was arrested for acting as an "outside agitator" and breaking the law.

An advocate of passive resistance, Dr. King earned the Nobel Peace Prize in 1964. "Nonviolent direct action seeks to create such a crisis and foster such a tension that a community which has constantly refused to negotiate is forced to confront the issue."

King hoped that such action would awaken Americans to "those great wells of democracy which were dug deep by the founding fathers in their formulation of the Constitution and the Declaration of Independence" and which would lead the country toward the practice of democratic principles.

I think I should indicate why I am here in Birmingham, since you have been influenced by the view which argues against "outsiders coming in." I have the honor of serving as president of the Southern Christian Leadership Conference, an organization operating in every southern state, with headquarters in Atlanta, Georgia. We have some eighty-five affiliated organizations across the South, and one of them is the Alabama Christian Movement for Human Rights. Frequently we share staff, educational and financial resources with our affiliates. Several months ago the affiliate here in Birmingham asked us to be on call to engage in a nonviolent direct-action program if such were deemed necessary. We readily consented, and when the hour came we lived up to our promise. So I, along with several members of my staff, am here because I was invited here. I am here because I have organizational ties here. . . .

You deplore the demonstrations taking place in Birmingham. But your statement, I am sorry to say, fails to express a similar concern for the conditions that brought about the demonstrations. I am sure that none of you would want to rest content with the superficial kind of social analysis that deals merely with effects and does not grapple with underlying causes. It is unfortunate that demonstrations are taking place in Birmingham, but it is even more unfortunate that the city's white power structure left the Negro community with no alternative.

In any nonviolent campaign there are four basic steps: collection of the facts to determine whether injustices exist; negotiation; self-purification; and direct action. We have gone through all these steps in Birmingham. There can be no gainsaying the fact that racial injustice engulfs this community. Birmingham is probably the most thoroughly segregated city in the United States. Its ugly record of brutality is widely known. Negroes have experienced grossly unjust treatment in the courts. There have been more unsolved bombings of

Negro homes and churches in Birmingham than in any other city in the nation. These are the hard, brutal facts of the case. On the basis of these conditions, Negro leaders sought to negotiate with the city fathers. But the latter consistently refused to engage in good-faith negotiation. . . .

As in so many past experiences, our hopes had been blasted, and the shadow of deep disappointment settled upon us. We had no alternative except to prepare for direct action, whereby we would present our very bodies as a means of laying our case before the conscience of the local and the national community. Mindful of the difficulties involved, we decided to undertake a process of self-purification. We began a series of workshops on nonviolence, and we repeatedly asked ourselves: "Are you able to accept blows without retaliating?" "Are you able to endure the ordeal of jail?" We decided to schedule our direct-action program for the Easter season, realizing that except for Christmas, this is the main shopping period of the year. Knowing that a strong economic-withdrawal program would be the by-product of direct action, we felt that this would be the best time to bring pressure to bear on the merchants for the needed change.

You may well ask: "Why direct action? Why sit-ins, marches and so forth? Isn't negotiation a better path?" You are quite right in calling for negotiation. Indeed, this is the very purpose of direct action. Nonviolent direct action seeks to create such a crisis and foster such a tension that a community which has constantly refused to negotiate is forced to confront the issue. It seeks so to dramatize the issue that it can no longer be ignored. My citing the creation of tension as part of the work of the nonviolent resister may sound rather shocking. But I must confess that I am not afraid of the word "tension." I have earnestly opposed violent tension, but there is a type of constructive, nonviolent tension which is necessary for growth. Just as Socrates felt that it was necessary to create a tension in the mind so that individuals could rise from the bondage of myths and half-truths to the unfettered realm of creative analysis and objective appraisal, so must we see the need for nonviolent gadflies to create the kind of tension in society that will help men rise from the dark depths of prejudice and racism to the majestic heights of understanding and brotherhood.

The purpose of our direct-action program is to create a situation so crisis-packed that it will inevitably open the door to negotiation. I therefore concur with you in your call for negotiation. Too long has our beloved Southland been bogged down in a tragic effort to live in monologue rather than dialogue. . . .

We know through painful experience that freedom is never voluntarily given by the oppressor; it must be demanded by the oppressed. Frankly, I have yet to engage in a direct-action campaign that was "well timed" in the view of those who have not suffered unduly from the disease of segregation. For years now I have heard the word "Wait!" It rings in the ear of every Negro with piercing familiarity. This "Wait" has almost always meant "Never." We must come to see, with one of our distinguished jurists, that "justice too long delayed is justice denied." . . .

You express a great deal of anxiety over our willingness to break laws. This is certainly a legitimate concern. Since we so diligently urge people to obey the Supreme Court's decision of 1954 outlawing segregation in the public schools, at first glance it may seem rather paradoxical for us consciously to break laws. One may well ask: "How can you advocate breaking some laws and obeying others?" The answer lies in the fact that there are two types of laws: just and unjust. I would be the first to advocate obeying just laws. One has not only a legal but a moral responsibility to obey just laws. Conversely, one has a moral responsibility to disobey unjust laws. I would agree with St. Augustine that "an unjust law is no law at all."

Now, what is the difference between the two? How does one determine whether a law is just or unjust? A just law is a man-made code that squares with the moral law or the law of God. An unjust law is a code that is out of harmony with the moral law. To put it in the terms of St. Thomas Aquinas: An unjust law is a human law that is not rooted in eternal law and natural law. Any law that uplifts human personality is just. Any law that degrades human personality is unjust. All segregation statutes are unjust because segregation distorts the soul and damages the personality. It gives the segregator a false sense of superiority and the segregated a false sense of inferiority. Segregation, to use the terminology of the Jewish philosopher Martin Buber, substitutes an "I-it" relationship for an "I-thou" relationship and ends up relegating persons to the status of things. Hence segregation is not only politically, economically and sociologically unsound, it is morally wrong and sinful. Paul Tillich has said that sin is separation. Is not segregation an existential expression of man's tragic separation, his awful estrangement, his terrible sinfulness? Thus it is that I can urge men to obey the 1954 decision of the Supreme Court, for it is morally right; and I can urge them to disobey segregation ordinances, for they are morally wrong. . . .

I hope you are able to see the distinction I am trying to point out. In no sense do I advocate evading or defying the law, as would the rabid segregationist. That would lead to anarchy. One who breaks an unjust law must do so openly, lovingly, and with a willingness to accept the penalty. I submit that an individual who breaks a law that conscience tells him is unjust, and who willingly accepts the penalty of imprisonment in order to arouse the conscience of the community over its injustice, is in reality expressing the highest respect for law.

Of course, there is nothing new about this kind of civil disobedience. It was evidenced sublimely in the refusal of Shadrach, Meshach and Abednego to obey the laws of Nebuchadnezzar, on the ground that a higher moral law was at stake. It was practiced superbly by the early Christians who were willing to face hungry lions and the excruciating pain of chopping blocks rather than submit to certain unjust laws of the Roman Empire. To a degree, academic freedom is a reality today because Socrates practiced civil disobedience. In our own nation, the Boston Tea Party represented a massive act of civil disobedience. . . .

Before closing I feel impelled to mention one other point in your statement that has troubled me profoundly. You warmly commended the Birmingham police force for keeping "order" and "preventing violence." I doubt that you would have so warmly commended the police force if you had seen its dogs sinking their teeth into unarmed, nonviolent Negroes. I doubt that you would so quickly commend the policemen if you were to observe their ugly and inhumane treatment of Negroes here in the city jail; if you were to watch them push and curse old Negro women and young Negro girls; if you were to see them slap and kick old Negro men and young boys; if you were to observe them, as they did on two occasions, refuse to give us food because we wanted to sing our grace together. I cannot join you in your praise of the Birmingham police department.

It is true that the police have exercised a degree of discipline in handling the demonstrators. In this sense they have conducted themselves rather "nonviolently" in public. But for what purpose? To preserve the evil system of segregation. Over the past few years I have consistently preached that nonviolence demands that the means we use must be as pure as the ends we seek. I have tried to make clear that it is wrong to use immoral means to attain moral ends. But now I must affirm that it is just as wrong, or perhaps even more so, to use moral means to preserve immoral ends. Perhaps Mr. Connor and his policemen have been rather nonviolent in public, as was Chief Pritchett in Albany, Georgia, but they have used the moral means of nonviolence to maintain the immoral end of racial injustice. As T. S. Eliot has said: "The last temptation is the greatest treason: To do the right deed for the wrong reason."

I wish you had commended the Negro sit-inners and demonstrators of Birmingham for their sublime courage, their willingness to suffer and their amazing discipline in the midst of great provocation. One day the South will recognize its real heroes. They will be the James Merediths, with the noble sense of purpose that enables them to face jeering and hostile mobs, and with the agonizing loneliness that characterizes the life of the pioneer. They will be old, oppressed, battered Negro women, symbolized in a seventy-two-year-old woman in Montgomery, Alabama, who rose up with a sense of dignity and with her people decided not to ride segregated buses, and who responded with ungrammatical profundity to one who inquired about her weariness: "My feets is tired, but my soul is at rest." They will be the young high school and college students, the young ministers of the gospel and a host of their elders, courageously and nonviolently sitting in at lunch counters and willingly going to jail for conscience' sake. One day the South will know that when these disinherited children of God sat down at lunch counters, they were in reality standing up for what is best in the American dream and for the most sacred values in our Judaeo-Christian heritage, thereby bringing our nation back to those great wells of democracy which were dug deep by the founding fathers in their formulation of the Constitution and the Declaration of Independence.

Q uestions for Review and Reflection

1. According to King, why was he in Birmingham? What were the conditions that brought about the demonstration in the city?
2. King states that they had no alternative but to engage in "direct action." What was the nature of this direct action? Why was it necessary? How did the workshops on nonviolence prepare the protesters for Birmingham? Were they successful?
3. What had history taught King regarding the acquisition of freedom from the oppressors? How did this lesson impact the civil rights movement?
4. What distinction does King draw between laws that should be obeyed and those that should not? Do you agree or disagree? What might lead you to civil disobedience?
5. How did King employ T. S. Eliot's statement, "The last temptation is the greatest treason: To do the right deed for the wrong reason"? Is this an effective argument?

Reading 2

Betty Friedan, 1963

The Feminine Mystique

Women were accepted into nontraditional fields of work during World War II to replace men lost to the war effort. Women built planes, serviced ships, manufactured weaponry. But when the war was over, they were urged to return to their homes to make room for servicemen coming back. Postwar publicity attempted to glorify the homemaker and her role as wife and mother. Girls were encouraged to marry, have children, and be satisfied with family life. Women who remained at work continued to face legal inequities such as disparate wages and unequal access to job opportunities.

Born in 1921, Betty Friedan was a middle-class housewife who had completed a college degree in psychology, married, and begun to raise a family. She conducted a study from her home in the early '60s by sampling her former fellow college students about the contentment they felt with staying at home. She discovered a "problem that had no name" among the dissatisfied suburban housewives who wanted more out of life.

In 1966 Friedan formed the National Organization for Women, an interest group that advocated absolute political, social, and economic equality. Friedan put forth "a new life plan" for women, which would entitle them to the same rights as men "to compete then, not as a woman, but as a human being."

T he problem lay buried, unspoken, for many years in the minds of American women. It was a strange stirring, a sense of dissatisfaction, a yearning that women suffered in the middle of the 20th century in the United States. Each suburban wife struggled with it alone. As she made the beds, shopped for groceries, matched slipcover material, ate peanut butter sandwiches with her children, chauffeured cub scouts and brownies, lay beside her husband at night, she was afraid to ask even of herself the silent question—is this all?

... The problem that has no name—which is simply the fact that American women are kept from growing to their full human capacities—is taking a far greater toll on the physical and mental health of our country than any known disease.

... These problems cannot be solved by medicine, or even by psychotherapy. We need a drastic reshaping of the cultural image of femininity that will permit women to reach maturity, identity, completeness of self, without conflict with sexual fulfillment. A massive attempt must be made by educators and parents—and ministers, magazine editors, manipulators, guidance counselors—to stop the early-marriage movement, stop girls from growing up wanting to be "just a housewife," stop it by insisting, with the same attention from childhood that parents and educators give to boys, that girls develop the resources of self, goals that will permit them to find their own identity.

... It is perhaps beside the point to remark that bowling alleys and supermarkets have nursery facilities, while schools and colleges and scientific laboratories and government offices do not. But it is very much to the point to say that if an able American woman does not use her human energy and ability in some meaningful pursuit ... she will fritter away her energy in neurotic symptoms, or unproductive exercise, or destructive "love."

It also is time to stop giving lip service to the idea that there are no battles left to be fought for women in America, that women's rights have already been won. It is ridiculous to tell girls to keep quiet when they enter a new field, or an old one, so that men will not notice they are there. In almost every professional field, in business and in the arts and sciences, women are still treated as second-class citizens. It would be a great service to tell girls who plan to work in society to expect this subtle, uncomfortable discrimination—tell them not to be quiet, and hope it will go away, but fight it. A girl should not expect special privileges because of her sex, but neither should she "adjust" to prejudice and discrimination.

She must learn to compete then, not as a woman, but as a human being. Not until a great many women move out of the fringes into the mainstream, will society itself provide the arrangements for their new life plan.

[Q]uestions for Review and Reflection

1. What is this problem that Friedan claims lay buried, unspoken, for many years? In other words, what is the problem with no name? What is the solution?
2. How might Friedan's suggestion about a "drastic reshaping of the culture" take place? Do you think she is being practical?
3. What does she say is the danger of early marriage for young American women? Do you agree or disagree?
4. What point do you think Friedan was trying to make when she pointed out that bowling alleys and supermarkets have nursery facilities, while schools, colleges, and government buildings do not? How might this point advance her goals?
5. What evidence might Friedan employ to prove her assertion that women in America are still second-class citizens? Do you agree or disagree?

Reading 3

Martin Luther King Jr., 1963

"I Have a Dream" Speech

African Americans endured the segregationist policies of the South for decades. Blacks sat in the back of public buses, for example, unless there were unused seats, but had to defer to any white rider. One day in December 1955, Rosa Parks, a black woman, refused to give up her seat to a white person and was arrested. A young minister organized a year-long bus boycott to protest such customs and began the modern civil rights movement.

Dr. Martin Luther King Jr., (1929–1968) was that minister and eventual leader of the Southern Christian Leadership Conference. His was a nonviolent approach. Passive resistance, he said, would eventually bring about the justice so long denied. His oratory rallied not just African Americans but the whole nation, as they watched on television the hatred and brutality that he and the protesters faced day after day. The success of the bus boycott led to a full-scale effort across the South for equal rights through the integration of schools, lunchrooms, and other public facilities.

In August 1963, King led an impressive march on Washington, D.C., where his power and eloquence were spotlighted in this now-famous speech, in which he spoke on behalf of equal rights for all Americans.

I say to you today, my friends, that in spite of the difficulties and frustrations of the moment I still have a dream. It is a dream deeply rooted in the American dream.

I have a dream that one day this nation will rise up and live out the true meaning of its creed: "We hold these truths to be self-evident; that all men are created equal."

I have a dream that one day on the red hills of Georgia the sons of former slaves and the sons of former slaveowners will be able to sit down together at the table of brotherhood.

I have a dream that one day even the state of Mississippi, a desert state sweltering with the heat of injustice and oppression, will be transformed into an oasis of freedom and justice.

I have a dream that my four little children will one day live in a nation where they will not be judged by the color of their skin but by the content of their character.

I have a dream today.

I have a dream that one day the state of Alabama, whose governor's lips are presently dripping with the words of interposition and nullification, will be transformed into a situation where little black boys and black girls will be able to join hands with little white boys and white girls and walk together as sisters and brothers.

I have a dream today.

I have a dream that one day every valley shall be exalted, every hill and mountain shall be made low, the rough places will be made plain, and the crooked places will be made straight, and the glory of the Lord shall be revealed, and all flesh shall see it together.

This is our hope. This is the faith with which I return to the South. With this faith we will be able to hew out of the mountain of despair a stone of hope. With this faith we will be able to transform the jangling discords of our nation into a beautiful symphony of brotherhood.

With this faith we will be able to work together, to pray together, to struggle together, to go to jail together, to stand up for freedom together, knowing that we will be free one day.

This will be the day when all of God's children will be able to sing with new meaning, "My country 'tis of thee, sweet land of liberty, of thee I sing. Land where my fathers died, land of the Pilgrims' pride, from every mountainside, let freedom ring."

And if America is to be a great nation, this must become true. So let freedom ring from the prodigious hilltops of New Hampshire. Let freedom ring from the mighty mountains of New York. Let freedom ring from the heightening Alleghenies of Pennsylvania!

Let freedom ring from the snowcapped Rockies of Colorado! Let freedom ring from the curvaceous peaks of California! But not only that; let freedom ring from Stone Mountain of Georgia! Let freedom ring from Lookout Mountain of Tennessee!

Let freedom ring from every hill and molehill of Mississippi. From every mountainside, let freedom ring.

When we let freedom ring, when we let it ring from every village and every hamlet, from every state and every city, we will be able to speed up that day when all of God's children, black men and white men, Jews and gentiles, Protestants and Catholics, will be able to join hands and sing in the words of the old Negro spiritual, "Free at last! Free at last! Thank God Almighty, we are free at last!"

Questions for Review and Reflection

1. In what way does King draw upon the same natural rights philosophy that the framers of the Constitution did? What are the similarities? What are the differences?
2. Why do you suppose King's emotional appeal struck such a harmonious chord with so many Americans?
3. How do you think King's appeal was received by those who did not agree with his goals?
4. How does King make an appeal to the religious traditions in American history? How effective was this appeal to Christian ideals?

5. In what ways does King both draw upon and challenge traditional American ideals?

Reading 4

Malcolm X, 1964

Speech to New York Meeting

So familiar is Malcolm X's name, especially among African Americans, that the shorthand "X" on a cap is enough to evoke it. Born Malcolm Little as one of 11 children, he was a high school dropout and convicted burglar who joined the Nation of Islam and became a follower of Elijah Mohammed while serving a 10-year prison sentence. He adopted the X, he said, because he became an "ex-smoker, ex-drinker, ex-Christian and ex-slave."

Once out of prison, Malcolm X (1925–1965) became a spokesperson for the Black Muslims to large audiences, both black and white. He was provocative, charismatic, and his words brought him a following. His militant rhetoric advocated black nationalism as the way to achieve full economic and political rights, "by any means necessary," which frightened many white Americans.

Malcolm X eventually broke with Elijah Mohammed and in 1964 went on a pilgrimage to Mecca. There he met white Muslims who were free of prejudice; this experience caused him to reconsider his absolutist position on separatism. Upon returning to America, he formed the Organization of African Unity. He was assassinated following a public speech in 1965, allegedly by jealous partisans of Elijah Mohammed.

Following his trip to Mecca, Malcolm's words continued to have a threatening quality, but his proposals were more conciliatory. "The full use of the ballot in every one of the fifty states," which was essential and fundamental, was the only alternative to a revolution of interracial violence. Those limited choices only underscored the frustration felt by Malcolm X and other black leaders with a system that denied the representation they had been promised since Reconstruction days. He delivered the speech excerpted here to the Militant Labor Forum, a socialist group.

Any kind of racial explosion that takes place in this country today, in 1964, is not a racial explosion that can be confined to the shores of America. It is a racial explosion that can ignite the racial powder keg that exists all over the planet that we call Earth. I think that nobody would disagree that the dark masses of Africa and Asia and Latin America are already seething with bitterness, animosity, hostility, unrest, and impatience with the racial intolerance that they themselves have experienced at the hands of the white West.

And just as they have the ingredients of hostility toward the West in general, here we also have 22 million African-Americans, black, brown, red, and yellow people, in this country who are also seething with bitterness and impatience and hostility and animosity at the racial intolerance not only of the white West but of white America in particular.

And by the hundreds of thousands today we find our own people have become impatient, turning away from your white nationalism, which you call democracy, toward the militant, uncompromising policy of black nationalism. I point out right here that as soon as we announced we were going to start a black nationalist party in this country, we received mail from coast to coast, especially from young people at the college level, the university level, who expressed complete sympathy and support and a desire to take an active part in any kind of political action based on black nationalism, designed to correct or eliminate immediately evils that our people have suffered here for 400 years. . . .

1964 will be America's hottest year, her hottest year yet, a year of much racial violence and much racial bloodshed. But it won't be blood that's going to flow only on one side. The new generation of black people that have grown up in this country during recent years are already forming the opinion, and it's a just opinion, that if there is to be bleeding, it should be reciprocal— bleeding on both sides.

It should also be understood that the racial sparks that are ignited here in America today could easily turn into a flaming fire abroad, which means it could engulf all the people of this earth into a giant race war. You cannot confine it to one little neighhorhood, or one little community, or one little country. What happens to a black man in America today happens to the black man in Africa. What happens to a black man in America and Africa happens to the black man in Asia and to the man down in Latin America. What happens to one of us today happens to all of us. And when this is realized, I think that the whites—who are intelligent even if they aren't moral or aren't just or aren't impressed by legalities—those who are intelligent will realize that when they touch this one, they are touching all of them, and this in itself will have a tendency to be a checking factor. . . .

We have to keep in mind at all times that we are not fighting for integration, nor are we fighting for separation. We are fighting for recognition as human beings. We are fighting for the right to live as free humans in this society. In fact, we are actually fighting for rights that are even greater than civil rights and that is human rights. . . .

So in this country you find two different types of Afro-Americans—the type who looks upon himself as a minority and you as the majority, because his scope is limited to the American scene; and then you have the type who looks upon himself as part of the majority and you as part of a microscopic minority. And this one uses a different approach in trying to struggle for his rights. He doesn't beg. He doesn't thank you for what you give him, because you are only giving him what he should have had a hundred years ago. He doesn't think you are doing him any favors.

He doesn't see any progress that he has made since the Civil War. He sees not one iota of progress because, number one, if the Civil War had freed him, he wouldn't need civil-rights legislation today. If the Emancipation Proclamation, issued by that great shining liberal called Lincoln, had freed him, he wouldn't be singing "We Shall Overcome" today. If the amendments to the Constitution had solved his problem, his problem wouldn't still be here today. And if the Supreme Court desegregation decision of 1954 was genuinely and sincerely designed to solve his problem, his problem wouldn't be with us today. . . .

There is no system more corrupt than a system that represents itself as the example of freedom, the example of democracy, and can go all over this earth telling other people how to straighten out their house, when you have citizens of this country who have to use bullets if they want to cast a ballot.

The greatest weapon the colonial powers have used in the past against our people has always been divide and conquer. America is a colonial power. She has colonized 22 million Afro-Americans by depriving us of first-class citizenship, by depriving us of civil rights, actually by depriving us of human rights. She has not only deprived us of the right to be a citizen, she has deprived us of the right to be human beings, the right to he recognized and respected as men and women. In this country the black can be fifty years old and he is still a "boy."

I grew up with white people. I was integrated before they even invented the word and I have never met white people yet—if you are around them long enough—who won't refer to you as a "boy" or a "gal," no matter how old you are or what school you came out of, no matter what your intellectual or professional level is. In this society we remain "boys."

So America's strategy is the same strategy as that which was used in the past by the colonial powers: divide and conquer. She plays one Negro leader against the other. She plays one Negro organization against the other. She makes us think we have different objectives, different goals. As soon as one Negro says something, she runs to this Negro and asks him, "What do you think about what he said?" Why, anybody can see through that today—except some of the Negro leaders.

All of our people have the same goals, the same objective. That objective is freedom, justice, equality. All of us want recognition and respect as human beings. We don't want to be integrationists. Nor do we want to be separationists. We want to be human beings. Integration is only a method that is used by some groups to obtain freedom, justice, equality and respect as human beings. Separation is only a method that is used by other groups to obtain freedom, justice, equality or human dignity.

Our people have made the mistake of confusing the methods with the objectives. As long as we agree on objectives, we should never fall out with each other just because we believe in different methods or tactics or strategy to reach a common objective.

Why is America in a position to bring about a bloodless revolution? Because the Negro in this country holds the balance of power, and if the Negro in this country were given what the Constitution says he is supposed to have, the added power of the Negro in this country would sweep all of the racists and the segregationists out of office. It would change the entire political structure of the country. It would wipe out the Southern segregationism that now controls America's foreign policy, as well as America's domestic policy.

And the only way without bloodshed that this can be brought about is that the black man has to be given full use of the ballot in every one of the fifty states. But if the black man doesn't get the ballot, then you are going to be faced with another man who forgets the ballot and starts using the bullet.

Revolutions are fought to get control of land, to remove the absentee landlord and gain control of the land and the institutions that flow from that land. The black man has been in a very low condition because he has had no control whatsoever over any land. He has been a beggar economically, a beggar politically, a beggar socially, a beggar even when it comes to trying to get some education. The past type of mentality, that was developed in this colonial system among our people, today is being overcome. And as the young ones come up, they know what they want. And as they listen to your beautiful preaching about democracy and all those other flowery words, they know what they're supposed to have.

So you have a people today who not only know what they want, but also know what they are supposed to have. And they themselves are creating another generation that is coming up that not only will know what it wants and know what it should have, but also will be ready and willing to do whatever is necessary to see that what they should have materializes immediately. Thank you.

Questions for Review and Reflection

1. How do you think the public at large responded to Malcolm's suggestion that there will be "bleeding on both sides"?
2. In what way does Malcolm see the race problem in global terms?

3. What parallels does Malcolm see between the strategy of the colonial powers and Americans regarding race?
4. Describe the two different kinds of Afro-Americans in this country that Malcolm X sees. How would Malcolm X describe himself?
5. How might Malcolm X's contemporaries see his attitudes as fostering a rebellion?

Reading 5

National Organization for Women, 1966

Organizing Statement

Seeking a "full partnership with men," the National Organization for Women was founded in order to eliminate all sexual discrimination. The 300 members were mostly professional women who were well educated and politically savvy. They became one of the largest civil rights groups for women in the U.S., with a membership of over 250,000.

NOW sought reforms in employment and educational opportunities, salaries, abortion rights, day care access, and an end to the discriminatory practices that existed in economic, political, and social life—essentially the same agenda that the organization currently follows.

The organizing statement asserted that these were issues for men and women and that "the power of American law and the protection guaranteed by the U.S. Constitution . . . must be effectively applied and enforced." NOW founders called on the authority of the federal government to assist in such an achievement.

We, men and women who hereby constitute ourselves as the National Organization for Women, believe that the time has come for a new movement toward true equality for all women in America, and toward a fully equal partnership of the sexes, as part of the worldwide revolution of human rights now taking place within and beyond our national borders.

The purpose of NOW is to take action to bring women into full participation in the mainstream of American society now, exercising all the privileges and responsibilities thereof in truly equal partnership with men.

We believe the time has come to move beyond the abstract argument, discussion and symposia over the status and special nature of women which have raged in America in recent years; the time has come to confront, with concrete action, the conditions that now prevent women from enjoying the equality of opportunity and freedom of choice which is their right, as individual Americans, and as human beings.

NOW is dedicated to the proposition that women, first and foremost, are human beings, who, like all other people in our society, must have the chance to develop their fullest human potential. We believe that women can achieve such equality only by accepting to the full the challenges and responsibilities they share with all other people in our society, as part of the decision-making mainstream of American political, economic, and social life.

We organize to initiate or support action, nationally, or in any part of this nation, by individuals or organizations, to break through the silken curtain of prejudice and discrimination against women in government, industry, the professions, the churches, the political parties, the judiciary, the labor unions, in education, science, medicine, law, religion, and every other field of importance in American society. . . .

WE BELIEVE that the power of American law, and the protection guaranteed by the U.S. Constitution to the civil rights of all individuals, must be effectively applied and enforced to isolate and remove patterns of sex discrimination, to ensure equality of opportunity in employment and education, and equality of civil and political rights and responsibilities on behalf of women, as well as for Negroes and other deprived groups.

We realize that women's problems are linked to many broader questions of social justice; their solution will require concerted action by many groups. Therefore, convinced that human rights for all are indivisible, we expect to give active support to the common cause of equal rights for all those who suffer discrimination and deprivation, and we call upon other organizations committed to such goals to support our efforts toward equality for women.

WE DO NOT ACCEPT the token appointment of a few women to high-level positions in government and industry as a substitute for a serious continuing effort to recruit and advance women according to their individual abilities. To this end, we urge American government and industry to mobilize the same resources of ingenuity and command with which they have solved problems of far greater difficulty than those now impeding the progress of women.

WE BELIEVE that this nation has a capacity at least as great as other nations, to innovate new social institutions which will enable women to enjoy true equality of opportunity and responsibility in society, without conflict with their responsibilities as mothers and homemakers. In such innovations, America does not lead the Western world, but lags by decades behind many European countries. We do not accept the traditional assumption that a woman has to choose between marriage and motherhood, on the one hand, and serious participation in industry or the professions on the other. . . .

WE BELIEVE that it is as essential for every girl to be educated to her full potential of human ability as it is for every boy—with the knowledge that such education is the key to effective participation in today's economy and that, for a girl as for a boy, education can only be serious where there is expectation that it will be used in society. . . .

WE REJECT the current assumptions that a man must carry the sole burden of supporting himself, his wife, and family, and that a woman is automatically entitled to lifelong support by a man upon her marriage, or that marriage, home, and family are primarily woman's world and responsibility— hers to dominate—his to support. We believe that a true partnership between the sexes demands a different concept of marriage, an equitable sharing of the responsibilities of home and children and of the economic burdens of their support. We believe that proper recognition should be given to the economic and social value of homemaking and child care. To these ends, we will seek to open a re-examination of laws and mores governing marriage and divorce, for we believe that the current state of "half-equality" between the sexes discriminates against both men and women, and is the cause of much unnecessary hostility between the sexes.

WE BELIEVE that women must now exercise their political rights and responsibilities as American citizens. They must refuse to be segregated on the basis of sex into separate-and-not-equal ladies' auxiliaries in the political parties, and they must demand representation according to their numbers in the regularly constituted party committees—at local, state, and national levels—and in the informal power structure, participating fully in the selection of candidates and political decision-making, and running for office themselves. . . .

WE BELIEVE that women will do most to create a new image of women by *acting* now, and by speaking out in behalf of their own equality, freedom, and human dignity—not in pleas for special privilege, nor in enmity toward men, who are also victims of the current, half-equality between the sexes—but in an active, self-respecting partnership with men. By so doing, women will develop confidence in their own ability to determine actively, in partnership with men, the conditions of their life, their choices, their future, and their society.

Questions for Review and Reflection

1. What is the essential goal of the National Organization for Women? What is the purpose of NOW?

2. According to the authors, what are the conditions that bar women from achieving true equality? What kind of "concrete action" do you think will be necessary to change this?
3. How are women's problems linked to the larger problems in society? What are these larger problems?
4. What dangers do the authors see in token appointments of a few women to high governmental and industry positions? Do you agree or disagree?
5. What current assumptions do the authors reject? How are these assumptions about the role of women societal, rather than biological?

Reading 6

American Indian Task Force, 1969

Statement to U.S. House of Representatives

Treaty negotiations with Indian tribes ended in 1871. The Dawes Act of 1887 attempted to adapt Indians to American society through individual land ownership. This policy of assimilation included the education of Native American children in American public schools, where they were forced to give up much of their tribal cultures as well as their languages. The 1934 Reorganization Act returned some authority to Indians, promoting self-government, economic development, and a revival of tribalism. These were lofty goals, but funds were never available to implement the law's provisions.

Native American tribes continued to hope for sovereignty, and a movement was organized in the 1960s that laid a set of demands before Congress to bring about more independence. Representatives of 42 tribes came together to form the activist American Indian Task Force, which was dissatisfied not only with Congress as a whole, but also with the National Council on Indian Opportunity, their official representation in Washington (see Reading 9). They felt the council, which was headed by the vice president and other Cabinet officials, contained too few Native American participants who had too little voice in council decisions. The task force said, "We come to seek a new arrangement with the Congress." Task force members complained that their way of life, "an American way of life," needed to be understood and respected. Courts had ruled that Congress had primary authority with regard to Indian affairs, according to Article 1, Section 8, Clause 3 of the Constitution. The task force's statement was therefore directed to the legislature, requesting federal lawmakers to use their authority to redress the tribes' grievances.

W e, the first Americans, come to the Congress of the United States that you give us the chance to try to solve what you call the Indian problem. You have had 200 years and you have not succeeded by your standards. It is clear that you have not succeeded in ours.

On Monday, we asked the vice president of the United States to set into motion a process which would insure that our people could secure redress of grievances and could shape the government programs that affect and control their lives.

We know that a request to the executive branch—even if heeded—is not sufficient. We know that there are three branches—the executive, the legislative, and the judiciary.

We come here today to ask you to do three things:

1. To serve as watchdog on the executive branch.
2. To facilitate—and certainly, not to bar—our access to the judicial branch; and
3. To use your legislative powers to make it possible for Indians to shape their own lives and control their own destinies.

We have asked the vice president of the United States for Indian boards of inquiries which would hold hearings throughout the areas where Indians live, for area conferences, for red ribbon grand juries, for circuit riders to take complaints, and for a national board of inquiry to meet and make national recommendations received on the grass roots level.

And we ask you to help us see that the process we proposed to the vice president somehow becomes a reality. We hope that he will be willing to do it on his own. But we ask you, as the representatives of the people of the United States, to serve as our representatives too—to help us see that assurances do not become empty promises. And, if necessary, to enact legislation which will create such a process where Indians can really shape government policy and control their own lives and destinies if that is not done by the executive branch.

We come to you with a sense of impending betrayal, at a moment when we wish to seek redress of grievances, to ask you to broaden our access to the courts to protect the rights guaranteed us by your treaties and statutes. And we find, with a sense of horror and impending doom, that instead, the Congress of the United States is on the verge of passing an amendment to the Economic Opportunity Act which would effectively diminish the slight access to the courts we have gained in recent years through the advent of the OEO [Office of Economic Opportunity] Legal Service Program. And it is an even greater irony that we find this to be the case when the governor's veto in at least one state has already killed a legal service program for Indians. What right do the governors have to interfere with what goes on on the reservation? What right do state governors have to interfere with the solemn promises made to us by the federal government in statutes and treaties which can only be enforced by resort to the courts? What right do you, or any generation of Americans, have to rip up the solemn promises of the past— promises made to us both by the Constitution and by the President of a nation which still holds and enjoys the land received in exchange for those treaties. There are none among you who would suggest that rights—and above all the right to petition one's government—can have any meaning at all without lawyers and without access to the forum where the people traditionally petition their government.

We come to you today to ask that you set your own house in order. We say that until the congressional committees which control nearly all Indian legislation cease to be hostile to the interests of the Indian, then we have been deprived of one of the three branches of what we have been repeatedly told is our government as well as yours. . . .

Today, we come to seek a new arrangement with the Congress. We have come to seek a change in the committees that deal in Indian Affairs. We ask that the committees of Congress not be dominated by interests which are hostile to our own survival. We ask that these committees act as a watchdog on federal programs which are passed especially for our benefit but which do not in fact benefit us because of the way the BIA runs them. And we ask that these committees insure that we get our fair share of general legislation passed to help all citizens—highway legislation, health legislation, education legislation, economic development legislation. We do not get our fair share of these programs now. And we do not have any means to seek redress when the very programs that are passed to help us in fact are used as means to enslave and oppress us.

We come here today to remind you that you are not just the representatives of local districts or of states. You are members of the Congress of the United States. You have national obligations. We know you are highly conscious of your national obligations when you deliberate on such problems as the war in Vietnam. We know that you have even taken those obligations seriously enough to go to Vietnam in order to personally inform yourself on how the executive carries out the commitments of the United States.

We ask that you do no less at home—for the United States has made older and more sacred national commitments to the people who have occupied these shores for 25,000 years. The United States has made national commitments in the form of treaties, legislation, and the Constitution itself, to our peoples. We ask you to come to our homes—in the cities and on the reservations. We ask that you seek with equal vigilance to determine whether national commitments have been kept to us. Guided tours by bureaucrats will only serve to hamper you in your search for truth.

You, the Congress of the United States, are being asked to come to see how we really live and to try to understand the values, the culture, and the way of life we are fighting to preserve—an American way of life. A way of life which we believe is built upon respect for differences, a tolerance of diversity.

We cannot come to Washington. We are not rich. And we cannot afford the high price of democracy.

In essence, we ask the restoration of what you claimed at the founding of your nation—the inalienable right to pursue happiness. We cannot fail worse than the experts and the bureaucrats. We do not lack for knowledge— and we are not ashamed to hire experts and technicians. But our people do not lack for leaders, for sensitivity, for talent and ability. We ask for the right to pursue our dream—and we ask for you to respect that dream. That is the American way. We claim our birthright.

Questions for Review and Reflection

1. Why did the authors petition the legislative branch of the United States government in addition to the executive? What three things do the authors ask of the government?
2. How might legislation allow the Indians to shape government policy in order to gain some control over their own lives?
3. What do the authors mean when they say that they are making this petition with a sense of impending betrayal? What might account for this feeling? Is it justified?
4. What was the authors' greatest fear if the Economic Opportunity Act should pass Congress? What new arrangement with Congress are the authors seeking?
5. The authors ask members of Congress to come to their homes and see for themselves the plight of the Indians. What do the authors hope this will accomplish? Are their hopes well-founded?

Reading 7

Reies Tijerina, 1969

Letter from a Santa Fe Jail

In many ways Chicanos' experiences with treaty violations and a gold rush were similar to those of Native Americans. Reies Tijerina was a student of land grants and a Chicano activist of the 1960s who traveled the migrant labor camps as a preacher. He believed that Chicanos had been cheated out of their lands following the Treaty of Guadalupe-Hidalgo, which settled the Mexican-American War. Mexico ceded huge territories, and America promised to protect the titles of property holders. Instead, the U.S. government stood by as land speculators spread across the new territories, swindling and defrauding people who did not understand their rights.

Tijerina's message appealed to a number of Mexican Americans who found themselves impoverished and politically powerless. Tijerina and his followers held public demonstrations and called for treaty obligations to be met. One such protest landed him in jail, where he wrote, "I am in jail for defending and fighting for the rights of my people." His group called for the U.S. government to uphold the supremacy of the Treaty of Guadelupe-Hidalgo by returning property to the heirs of the original landholders.

From my cell block in this jail I am writing these reflections. I write them to my people, the Indo-Hispanos, to my friends among the Anglos, to the agents of the federal government, the state of New Mexico, the Southwest, and the entire Indo-Hispano world—"Latin America."

I write to you as one of the clearest victims of the madness and racism in the hearts of our present-day politicians and rulers.

At this time, August 17, I have been in jail for 65 days—since June 11, 1969, when my appeal bond from another case was revoked by a federal judge. I am here today because I resisted an assassination attempt led by an agent of the federal government—an agent of all those who do not want anybody to speak out for the poor, all those who do not want Reies Lopez Tijerina to stand in their way as they continue to rob the poor people, all those many rich people from outside the state with their summer homes and

ranches here whose pursuit of happiness depends on thievery, all those who
have robbed the people of their land and culture for 120 years. . . .

What is my real crime? As I and the poor people see it, especially the
Indo-Hispanos, my only crime is UPHOLDING OUR RIGHTS AS PROTECTED
BY THE TREATY OF GUADALUPE-HIDALGO which ended the so-called
Mexican-American War of 1846–48. My only crime is demanding the respect
and protection of our property, which has been confiscated illegally by the
federal government. Ever since the treaty was signed in 1848, our people have
been asking every elected president of the United States for a redress of
grievances. Like the Black people, we too have been criminally ignored. Our
right to the Spanish land grant pueblos is the real reason why I am in prison
at this moment. . . .

This truth is denied by the conspirators against the poor and by the press
which they control. There are also the Silent Contributors. The Jewish people
accused the Pope of Rome for keeping silent while Hitler and his machine
persecuted the Jews in Germany and other countries. I support the Jews in
their right to accuse those who contributed to Hitler's acts by their SILENCE.
By the same token, I denounce those in New Mexico who have never opened
their mouths at any time to defend or support the thousands who have been
killed, robbed, raped of their culture. I don't know of any church or Establishment organization or group of elite intellectuals that has stood up for the
Treaty of Guadalupe-Hidalgo. We condemn the silence of these groups and
individuals and I am sure that, like the Jewish people, the poor of New Mexico
are keeping a record of the Silence which contributes to the criminal con-
spiracy against the Indo-Hispano in New Mexico. . . .

This government must show its good faith to the Indo-Hispano in respect
to the Treaty of Guadalupe-Hidalgo and the land question by forming a
presidential committee to investigate and hold open hearings on the land
question in the northern part of New Mexico. We challenge our own
government to bring forth and put all the facts on the conference table. We
have the evidence to prove our claims to property as well as to the cultural
rights of which we have been deprived. WE ARE RIGHT—and therefore ready
and willing to discuss our problems and rights under the Treaty with the Anglo
federal government in New Mexico or Washington, D.C., directly or through
agents.

This government must also reform the whole educational structure in
the Southwest before it is too late. It should begin in the northern part of New
Mexico, where 80% of the population are Indo-Hispanos, as a pilot center.
If it works here, then a plan can be developed based on that experience in
the rest of the state and wherever the Indo-Hispano population requires it.

Because I know WE ARE RIGHT, I have no regrets as I sit in my jail
cell. I feel very, very proud and happy to be in jail for the reason that I am.
. . . I am sure that not one of my prison days is lost. Not one day has been
in vain. While others are free, building their personal empires, I am in jail

for defending and fighting for the rights of my people. Only my Indo-Hispano people have influenced me to be what I am. I am what I am, for my brothers.

Questions for Review and Reflection

1. What was Tijerina's "real crime"?
2. What solidarity with the Jewish people does Tijerina articulate in this letter? What similarities does he draw between the Catholic Church's attitude toward the Holocaust and American attitudes toward Mexican Americans? Do you agree?
3. According to Tijerina, how can the federal government redress the Indo-Hispanos' grievances with the American people?

Reading 8

Delano Grape Workers, 1969

Delano Grape Workers' Proclamation

Political, social and economic equality did not exist for the migrant workers of the Southwest any more than it did for the Latino workers in the major cities.

Big-business farming needed cheap migrant labor but offered subsistence wages, substandard living conditions, and a dangerous work environment. Decades of poor wages and working conditions had persisted with little public notice or concern until the 1960s, when the Black Revolution caught the imagination of the Hispanic community. The Chicanos' struggle for equality captured headlines due to a lengthy strike in Delano, California, which eventually led to national boycotts, first of table grapes and later of lettuce.

Educated by the civil rights movement and led by the grape pickers, the field workers of California banded together to proclaim their liberation from their exploitation. They wrote a set of aims which expressed their ambitions for social justice and equal protection of the laws.

We, the striking grape workers of California, join on this International Boycott Day with the consumers across the continent in planning the steps that lie ahead on the road to our liberation. As we plan, we recall the footsteps that brought us to this day and the events of this day. The historic road of our pilgrimage to Sacramento later branched out, spreading like the unpruned vines in struck fields, until it led us to willing exile in cities across this land. There, far from the earth we tilled for generations, we have cultivated the strange soil of public understanding, sowing the seed of our truth and our cause in the minds and hearts of men.

We have been farm workers for hundreds of years and pioneers for seven. Mexicans, Filipinos, Africans and others, our ancestors were among those who founded this land and tamed its natural wilderness. But we are still pilgrims on this land, and we are pioneers who blaze a trail out of the wilderness of hunger and deprivation that we have suffered even as our ancestors did. We are conscious today of the significance of our present quest. If this road we chart leads to the rights and reforms we demand, if it leads to just wages, humane working conditions, protection from the misuse of pesticides, and to the fundamental right of collective bargaining, if it changes the social order that relegates us to the bottom reaches of society, then in our wake will follow thousands of American farm workers. Our example will make them free. But if our road does not bring us to victory and social change, it will not be because our direction is mistaken or our resolve too weak, but only because our bodies are mortal and our journey hard. For we are in the midst of a great social movement, and we will not stop struggling 'til we die, or win!

We have been farm workers for hundreds of years and strikers for four. It was four years ago that we threw down our plowshares and pruning hooks. These Biblical symbols of peace and tranquility to us represent too many lifetimes of unprotesting submission to a degrading social system that allows us no dignity, no comfort, no peace. We mean to have our peace, and to win it without violence, for it is violence we would overcome—the subtle spiritual and mental violence of oppression, the violence subhuman toil does to the human body. So we went and stood tall outside the vineyards where we had stooped for years. But the tailors of national labor legislation had left us naked. Thus exposed, our picket lines were crippled by injunctions and harassed by growers; our strike was broken by imported scabs; our overtures to our employers were ignored. Yet we knew the day must come when they would talk to us, *as equals.*

We have been farm workers for hundreds of years and boycotters for two. We did not choose the grape boycott, but we had chosen to leave our peonage, poverty and despair behind. Though our first bid for freedom, the strike, was weakened, we would not turn back. The boycott was the only way forward the growers left to us. We called upon our fellow men and were answered by consumers who said—as all men of conscience must—that they would no longer allow their tables to be subsidized by our sweat and our sorrow: They shunned the grapes, fruit of our affliction.

We marched alone at the beginning, but today we count men of all creeds, nationalities, and occupations in our number. Between us and the justice we seek now stand the large and powerful grocers who, in continuing to buy table grapes, betray the boycott their own customers have built. These stores treat their patrons' demands to remove the grapes the same way the growers treat our demands for union recognition—by ignoring them. The consumers who rally behind our cause are responding as we do to such treatment—with a boycott! They pledge to withhold their patronage from stores that handle grapes during the boycott, just as we withhold our labor from the growers until our dispute is resolved.

Grapes must remain an unenjoyed luxury for all as long as the barest human needs and basic human rights are still luxuries for farm workers. The grapes grow sweet and heavy on the vines, but they will have to wait while we reach out first for our freedom. The time is ripe for our liberation.

Questions for Review and Reflection

1. According to the authors, what were the circumstances and conditions that necessitated the boycott? What were the goals of this movement?
2. What reverse biblical symbolism do the authors draw upon when they say that they have thrown down their "plowshares and pruning hooks?" Is this an effective appeal?
3. According to the authors, how would violence detract from the movement's goals? How does this square with the "plowshares" analogy?
4. What do the authors mean by claiming that the "tailors of national labor legislation had left us naked"? To whom do you think that they were referring? Do you agree?

Reading 9

National Council on Indian Opportunity, January 26, 1970

Statement of Indian Members

In response to growing demands from Native Americans for the right to participate in the making of Indian public policy, the federal government established a council in 1968, chaired by the vice president of the United States and made up of Indian representatives and cabinet secretaries. This agency provided the means for Indians and federal officials to communicate directly on decisions affecting Indians' living conditions.

Native Americans utilized this means to submit a very specific agenda that called for programs and funding to provide greater opportunities and civil rights in education, health, welfare, and economic development. Many of their recommendations were directly incorporated into the Nixon administration's policy toward Native Americans, implemented between 1970 and Nixon's resignation in 1974.

Despite this group's progress in framing recommendations, other Native Americans mistrusted the council's ability to represent them adequately. The American Indian Task Force, whose opinions are excerpted in Reading 6, was among the factions who felt the council lacked real influence and served only as a rubber stamp for the executive branch's initiatives.

Statement of the Indian Members

- In 1970, when men have landed on the moon, many American Indians still do not have adequate roads to the nearest market.
- In 1970, when almost every American baby can look forward to a life expectancy of 70 years, the Indian infant mortality rate is three times higher than the national average after the first month of life.
- In 1970, when personal income in America is at an unprecedented level, unemployment among American Indians runs as high as 60%.

These are reasons why the National Council on Indian Opportunity—the first agency of the Federal Government where Indian leaders sit as equals with members of the President's Cabinet in overseeing Federal Indian programs and in recommending Federal Indian policy—is of the most vital importance to Indians all across the Nation. Because the essential requirement of any Indian policy must be active and prior Indian consultation and input before major decisions are taken which affect Indian lives, Indian membership on the Council is not only of symbolic importance, but is insurance that such consultation will be sought.

We wonder if the Vice President and the Cabinet Officers fully appreciate the fact of their physical presence here today—the meaning that it has for Indian people? We realize that every group in America would like to have you arrayed before them, commanding your attention.

For the Indian people across the nation to know that at this moment the Vice President and Cabinet Officers are sitting in a working session with Indian leaders is to alleviate some of the cynicism and despair rife among them.

Thus, the Council and the visibility of its Federal members is of great symbolic importance to the Indian people. However, symbolism is not enough. We must be able to report that we have come away from this meeting with commitments on the part of the Federal members that Indian people and their problems will be considered even out of proportion to their numbers or political impact. Otherwise the distrust, the suspicion on the part of the Indians, which has dogged the Federal Government and has defeated most of its attempts to help the Indian people, will continue.

The National Council has a concern with the well-being of all Indians everywhere—whether they live on the reservations or off; in cities or rural areas; on Federal Indian Reservations or on those established by particular states.

Indian Tribes on Federal reservations have had a very long relationship with the Federal Government. However, in the last decade and a half, longstanding latent suspicion and fear brought about by broken promises, humiliation, and defeat have sharpened into an almost psychological dread of the termination of Federal responsibility. This fear permeates every negotiation, every meeting, every encounter with Indian tribes. Whether this fear can be overcome is debatable, but Federal agencies—especially those represented on this Council—must understand it and be aware of its strangling implications.

Co-existent with this attitude, criticism of the Bureau of Indian Affairs by the Indian people has begun to rise. The criticism has two aspects, the latter of which seems to contradict the opposition to termination.

First, a growing awareness among Indians of how far they have been left behind in achieving the American dream and rising expectations have led to the realization that Bureau services have been grossly inadequate.

Second, a quest for self-determination and control over their own destiny has led to criticism of the paternalistic attitude with which these services have been given in the past. The Indian people are aware that this approach has led to a sense of over-dependency on the Bureau and want to overcome this without losing their special relationship with the Bureau.

In short, the Indian people want more services, more self-determination and relief from the hovering spectre of termination.

The Indian problem has been studied and re-studied, stated and re-stated. There is little need for more study. In 1970, the Indians are entitled to some action, some programs, and some results. To that end we are setting forth a series of specific goals. These goals can and must be met. Such positive federal action will create Indian confidence in the sincerity and capability of the Federal Government. . . .

Education

It is an appalling fact that between 50 and 60% of all Indian children drop out of school. In some areas the figure is as high as 75%. This stands in sharp contrast to the national average of 23%. The suicide rate among all young Indians is over three times the national average. Estimates place it at five to seven times the national average for boarding school students.

A full generation of Indian adults have been severely damaged by an unresponsive and destructive educational system. At a time when economic survival in society requires increasing comprehension of both general knowledge and technical skills, Indians are lost at the lowest level of achievement of any group within our society. We must not lose this generation of Indian children as well. There is a desperate need for both a massive infusion of funds and complete restructuring of basic educational concepts. . . .

Health

It is a recognized fact that despite considerable improvement the health status of the American Indian is far below that of the general population of the United States. Indian infant mortality after the first month of life is three times the national average. This means, in plain language, that children are dying needlessly. The average life span of Indians is 44 years, one-third short of the national average of 64 years; in Alaska it is only 36 years. In light of the dire need for all health facilities and health needs, it is criminal to impose a personnel and budget freeze on Indian health programs. Even without a freeze, Indian hospitals are woefully understaffed and undersupplied, even to the extent of lacking basic equipment and medicine. We deplore the budget decisions that have caused this state of inadequacy.

There are a number of specific actions that can be taken now to improve Indian health services:

1. An Indian health aide program has been established. A review should be undertaken of its recruitment, training and assignment policies.
2. The Division of Indian Health and the regular U.S. Public Health Service should establish communication for ascertaining their respective areas of responsibility. There is no excuse for the plight of a sick individual, who also happens to be Indian, to be denied access to health facilities due to jurisdictional conflicts.
3. The establishment of Indian advisory boards at hospitals should be continued and expanded. However, to be meaningful, these boards must be given actual authority in the administrative areas of patient care.
4. The establishment of a program to bring Indian health services into communities rather than simply at the central office location, e.g., traveling clinics.

5. Lastly, the Council goes on record in support of a national health insurance system.

Welfare

President Nixon's proposal for a Family Assistance Program is a major step toward restoring dignity to the individuals involved. We support the concept of this program and urge its enactment and adequate funding. We also request Indian input into its planning and delivery, for without a mutual exchange this new, innovative program will not satisfy the unique needs of the Indian people.

We specifically recommend today the following:

1. That an immediate investigation be undertaken of the system whereby many welfare recipients are exploited by trading post and grocery store owners. These trading posts and grocery stores are the mailing address for large numbers of Indian welfare recipients in the surrounding areas. By isolated location, overcharging and credit, and the custom of dependency, the traders and store owners have complete control over the disbursement of the welfare checks;
2. That training programs in the culture and value systems of the Indian populations be required for social workers serving Indian people;
3. That Indian tribes be given the option of contracting with the Federal government for the administration of their own welfare programs.

Economic Development

Indian people in general have been deprived of the opportunity of obtaining business acumen and have not participated in the benefits of the American free enterprise system. This fact has led to the present economic plight of the first Americans and has been an embarrassment to principles upon which this country was founded. But in recent years, because of a cooperative effort involving government agencies and of the private groups, industrial development on Indian reservations is starting to become a reality. This development is greatly desired by most tribes to improve the economics of the communities and to provide jobs for the individuals of those communities.

However, where large industries have located in Indian communities, the inadequacies of the reservation to accommodate the sudden concentration of employee populations have created serious problems. In most of these new industrial communities there are inadequate schools, too few houses, insufficient hospital and medical capability and generally inadequate community facilities for the population. While Indians desire and deserve job opportunities near their homes, most of the industries thus far attracted to reservations have chiefly employed women. This leaves the male head of the family still unemployed and disrupts the family. Attention of those federal agencies concerned with industrial development should be directed to this problem and they should maximize employment for Indian men.

[Q]uestions for Review and Reflection

1. What is the purpose of the National Council on Indian Affairs?
2. What are some of the agenda items of Native Americans?
3. What would be the role of government vis-à-vis Native Americans if all of these demands were met?
4. What has caused industrial development on tribal lands? What has been the impact of industrial development?

Reading 10

Armando Rodriguez, 1970

Testimony to Congress

Armando Rodriguez was Director of Spanish-Speaking Affairs for the U.S. Department of Health, Education and Welfare in 1970. His testimony to Congress reported on the second-largest minority group in the United States, which had become 8 percent of the population.

While some Hispanics, particularly in California, were moving toward the middle class, many remained impoverished, with high dropout rates from school.

Some states in the Southwest had segregated Spanish-speaking students in separate schools, while many schools in other states prohibited the use of Spanish. The suppression of language and culture was reminiscent of the Indian assimilation schools that were part of the Dawes Act.

Director Rodriguez made a case for "La Raza," Mexican Americans who are proud of their culture and want to protect its integrity while being assimilated into American life. He argued that equal opportunity was denied to Latino students when their culture was suppressed and that such a policy held them back rather than advanced them. Rodriguez asked for an equal status for all cultures in America, "where cultural heritage and language assets are prime instruments in the acceptance of human diversity as a major national goal."

We are fast becoming America's most promising human catalyst for the creation of a democratic society where cultural heritage and language assets are prime instruments in the acceptance of human diversity as a major national goal. I refute that television report in April of last year that identified La Raza as "The Invisible Minority." If the producers could sense what I feel and see in my travels, La Raza would be identified as the "dynamic and responsible minority." The old image that the Puerto Rican or the Mexican American is neither Puerto Rican, Mexican nor American: he is suspended between two cultures, neither of which claims him, is rapidly disappearing. Tomorrow's Puerto Rican and Mexican American—those forceful, creative, bold youngsters under 25 will be the American citizens who successfully retain and cherish their cultural heritage and simultaneously participate fully in the larger cultural environment of our society. And I suggest that the frontier of this movement will be found in the urban areas of our cities throughout this country. Who is the Puerto Rican or the Mexican American? He is that unique individual who has suffered from cultural isolation, language rejection, economic and educational inequalities, but who has now begun to take those instruments of oppression and turn them into instruments of change. Bilingual and bicultural education in our public schools will be a reality very shortly. The national moral and legal commitment of our federal government for educational programs that reflect the culture and language of the students will be a common part of curriculums throughout the country. And to a great extent this sweeping movement must be credited to the patience and perseverance of our youth—cultural qualities that for so many years was termed "passivity." . . .

"Who am I?" asks a young Mexican American high school student. "I am a product of myself. I am a product of you and my ancestors. We came to California long before the Pilgrims landed at Plymouth Rock. We settled California, the Southwestern part of the United States including the states of Arizona, New Mexico, Colorado and Texas. We built the missions, we cultivated the ranches. We were at the Alamo in Texas, both inside and outside. You know we owned California—that is, until gold was found here. Who am I? I'm a human being. I have the same hopes that you do, the same fears, the same drives, same desires, same concerns, same abilities; and I want the same chance that you have to be an individual. Who am I? In reality I am who you want me to be."

Questions for Review and Reflection

1. In what ways are Latinos suspended between two cultures, according to the author?
2. What is the author's attitude about assimilation into the larger culture? What are the consequences of assimilation?
3. What do the author's concluding remarks reveal about his values and goals?

Reading 11

Mary Frances Berry, 1971

Black Resistance/White Law

The civil rights movement of the 1950s and 1960s led to momentous changes in the laws of the nation. The 1964 Civil Rights Act brought about integration of public facilities and equal employment protections. The 1965 Voting Rights Act promised federal protection during voter registration and elections. The 1968 Civil Rights Act cemented the guarantees against discrimination and extended fuller opportunities for all minorities in America. But Martin Luther King Jr. was assassinated in 1968, and the momentum was lost. America fell quiet when the Kerner report, commissioned by the federal government, found that the nation was "moving toward two societies, one black, one white, separate and unequal."

The election of Richard Nixon in 1968 and the retirement of Earl Warren in 1969 signaled that perhaps the civil rights efforts had come to an end.

Author and scholar Mary Frances Berry served as an assistant secretary for education and on the U.S. Commission for Civil Rights during this period. She warned in her book that "if real black revolution comes, it will result from this failure of the larger society . . . to use the Constitution to effect needed social, economic and political reform." She charged that white America used the Constitution to suppress rather than support black achievement.

White oppression and black resistance has been a persistent part of the American scene since the colonial period. The response of the government in its effort to suppress racial disorder has reflected the tension between the lofty ideals expressed in the documents on which constitutional government is based and the tendency of the white majority to desire summary disposition of those they regard as unpopular, unlovely, hateful, or powerless. The predilection of the white majority to suppress efforts by black people to acquire real freedom and equality in America (as black *people,* not as single individuals who may achieve some recognition of the rights), even when white repression means resorting to illegal violence and brutality, has added to that tension. Black people have not been, of course, the only oppressed group in American society—the labor movement, Mexican-Americans, Indians, Mormons, and white radicals have experienced suppression. The black experience is unique because black people have been oppressed from the day they first set foot on English-American soil. The American government and people have persistently defended the repression of blacks in the name of law and order, without admitting that the Constitution was designed and has been interpreted to maintain the racial status quo. Racism, the promotion of white nationalism, is the primary reason why black people have served as the mudsills of American society. The need to respect constitutional government has been so twisted and perverted in the name of this objective that it is no wonder that its victims see beyond the fiction and regard law and order as a mere instrument for their repression.

The reflex action of the national government to black requests for federal action to aid in the improvement of their economic and social condition has always been token measures or assertions that no problem exists. If these tactics failed and black people persisted too vigorously, then force and suppression were used. If the slave experience is any indicator, a serious dislocation of American society might be necessary before the institutional response is changed. Also, if the failure of the economic promises of Reconstruction is relevant, satisfactory improvement in the conditions and status of blacks so as to remove the factors that give rise to riots and rebellion will be a long time in coming.

From 1789 through 1970, governmental action in response to the problem of black-white violence and black rebellion has been slow and uneven until some great cataclysm threatening white people has occurred. While white America and the government generally vacillated on the issue, black advances have been met with repression. And repression has proceeded in the guise of constitutionalism, despite the fact that the Constitution is much more flexible than those who hide behind its provisions will admit. Further, no concerted effort has been made to fully utilize its person-oriented and general welfare provisions to remove the economic and social causes of black rebellion.

Additionally, the government has demonstrated a lack of imagination in eradicating the racial prejudice which undergirds the constitutional suppression of black people. If blacks are to be a part of American society, the removal of racism should have the highest priority. Although racism may not be erased by legislation, educational techniques, even-handed justice, and black self-determination as positive government programs might prove effective. Since Americans are apparently enamored of the profit motive, perhaps a government policy for paying grants or giving tax credits to people and programs designed to end racial antagonism might be useful. Even if these ideas seem utopian, one superficial indicator of prejudice—continued racial violence—is amenable to solution. The enforcement of laws designed to make contact between whites and blacks less abrasive and a willingness on the part of the government to respond as quickly when blacks are the victims as when the persons or property of white people are at stake would be a good beginning.

This study also supports the view that the government allocates military power, as everything else, to defend those who are its friends and to injure those who are its enemies. Unfortunately, blacks in general and militants in particular have always been regarded as enemies. So long as the government possesses a virtual monopoly of military power, is unencumbered by widespread internal disorder, such as that which occurred during the Civil War, and remains able to cope with its enemies at home and abroad, white Americans apparently see no need to deal seriously with the factors which cause black rebellion. If real black revolution comes, it will result from this failure of the larger society to come quickly to an acceptable determination of the status of black people and to use the Constitution to effect needed social, economic, and political reform.

Questions for Review and Reflection

1. According to Berry, what has been a consistent pattern since colonial days?
2. What recent events have added to the racial tension?
3. In addition to blacks, what other oppressed groups are there in American society?
4. What does Berry see as unique in the black experience among the oppressed groups?
5. How does Berry define "racism"?
6. In what ways are the laws instruments for repression, in Berry's opinion? Do you agree? Why?
7. How did the government respond to black petitions for federal action on their behalf?

8. Berry argues that repression has "proceeded in the guise of constitutionalism." To what is Berry referring? Do you agree? Why?
9. According to Berry, what is necessary for blacks to become part of American society? What methods will accomplish this?
10. What will be the result if Americans do not come to an adequate determination of "the status of black people"? What is this adequate determination?

Reading 12

Cesar Chavez, 1973

An Interview

Born in 1927, Cesar Chavez grew up in migrant labor camps and knew first-hand the indignities and hardships of Mexican American second-class citizenship. He attended more than 30 elementary schools as a child. Early on, he served in voter registration drives to earn power for Chicanos, but he became even more active in the issues surrounding workers' rights. In the early 1960s, he founded the United Farm Workers (UFW) organization known as La Causa. Chavez sought economic power through decent wages, labor contracts, and worker education about their rights. He used boycotts as an effective tool to force growers to the bargaining table. He believed that political equality would result from economic strength. "I think that we can develop economic power and put it in the hands of the people . . . and then begin to change the system." Cesar Chavez left behind a membership of about 100,000 in the UFW. His death in 1993 brought renewed interest and support to his cause. An effort to boycott grapes in protest of the use of pesticides is now moving across the state of California.

Once we have reached our goal and have farm workers protected by contracts, we must continue to keep our members involved. The only way is to continue struggling. It's just like plateaus. We get a Union, then we want to struggle for something else. The moment we sit down and rest on our laurels, we're in trouble.

Once we get contracts and good wages, we know the tendency will be for the majority to lose interest, unless the Union is threatened or a contract is being renegotiated. The tendency will be for just a few to remain active and involved, while everybody else just holds out until something very big happens. That's true of other unions that we've seen; that's true of other institutions; that's true of our country.

To avoid that, to keep people's attention and continuing interest, we've got to expand and get them involved in other things. The Union must touch them daily.

Our best education, the most lasting, has been out on the picket line. But when the initial membership gets old and dies off, the new people coming in won't have had the same experience of building a Union. So we must get them involved in other necessary struggles.

Poor people are going to be poor for a long time to come, even though we have contracts, and economic action is an exciting thing for them. If they see an alternative, they will follow it. And we've probably got now the best organization of any poor people in all the country. That's why we can go any place in California where there are farm workers and get a whole group of people together and in action. We are hitting at the real core problems.

After we've got contracts, we have to build more clinics and co-ops, and we've got to resolve the whole question of mechanization. That can become a great issue, not fighting the machines, but working out a program ahead of time so the workers benefit.

Then there's the whole question of political action, so much political work to be done taking care of all the grievances that people have, such as the discrimination their kids face in school, and the whole problem of the police. I don't see why we can't exchange those cops who treat us the way they do for good, decent human beings like farm workers. Or why there couldn't be any farm worker judges.

We have to participate in the governing of towns and school boards. We have to make our influence felt everywhere and anywhere. It's a long struggle that we're just beginning, but it can be done because the people want it.

To get it done, there's a lot of construction work needed with our members. Many are not citizens, and others are not registered to vote. We must work toward the day when the majority of them are citizens with a vote.

But political power alone is not enough. Although I've been at it for some twenty years, all the time and the money and effort haven't brought about any significant change whatsoever. Effective political power is never going to come, particularly to minority groups, unless they have economic power. And however poor they are, even the poor people can organize economic power.

Political power by itself, as we've tried to fathom it and to fashion it, is like having a car that doesn't have any motor in it. It's like striking a match that goes out. Economic power is like having a generator to keep that bulb burning all the time. So we have to develop economic power to assure a continuation of political power.

I'm not advocating black capitalism or brown capitalism. At the worst it gets a black to exploit other blacks, or a brown to exploit others. At the best, it only helps the lives of a few. What I'm suggesting is a cooperative movement.

Power can come from credit in a capitalistic society, and credit in a society like ours means people. As soon as you're born, you're worth so much—not in money, but in the privilege to get in debt. And I think that's a powerful weapon. If you have a lot of people, then you have a lot of credit. The idea is to organize that power and transfer it into something real.

I don't have the answers yet. I'm at the point where I was in 1955 about organizing a farm workers' union. Then I was just talking about ideas and what could be done. A lot of people thought I was crazy. But this is how I learn, by talking and expounding and getting arguments back. That's why we're starting a three-year program to study all of these things. I still know very little about economic theory, but I'm going to learn because the whole fight, if you're poor, and if you're a minority group, is economic power.

As a continuation of our struggle, I think that we can develop economic power and put it into the hands of the people so they can have more control of their own lives, and then begin to change the system. We want radical change. Nothing short of radical change is going to have any impact on our lives or our problems. We want sufficient power to control our own destinies. This is our struggle. It's a lifetime job. The work for social change and against social injustice is never ended.

I know we're not going to see the change, but if we can get an idea and put legs under it, that's all we want. Let it go. Let it start, like the Union.

I guess I have an ideology, but it probably cannot be described in terms of any political or economic system.

Once I was giving a talk in Monterey about the Christian doctrine. When I got through, one man came back and said, "It's very radical, very socialistic."

I didn't say anything, but I was convinced it was very Christian. That's my interpretation. I didn't think it was so much political or economic.

Actually, I can't see where the poor have fared that well under any political or economic system. But I think some power has to come to them so they can manage their lives. I don't care what system it is, it's not going to work if they don't have the power.

That's why if we make democracy work, I'm convinced that's by far the best system. And it will work if people want it to. But to make it work for the poor, we have to work at it full time. And we have to be willing to just give up everything and risk it all.

In the last twenty years, the farm workers' outlook has radically changed, just like day and night. Twenty years ago, to get one person to talk to me about the Union was an effort. They were afraid. Now, we've overcome that.

And the idea of serving without pay—they had never heard about that. Right now we need a good education program, a meaningful education, not just about the Union, but about the whole idea of the Cause, the whole idea of sacrificing for other people.

Fighting for social justice, it seems to me, is one of the profoundest ways in which man can say yes to man's dignity, and that really means sacrifice. There is no way on this earth in which you can say yes to man's dignity and know that you're going to be spared some sacrifice. . . .

I've learned two very big things that I knew and had forgotten. The same methods that we used to build a Union, very effective in the beginning, still apply today and much more so. We thought because we had contracts that there were other things we could do. But I'm convinced we can't. We've got to do exactly what we did back in 1962, 1963, 1964. We must go back to the origins of the Union and do service-center work. The contracts are no substitute for the basic help we provide workers in all aspects of their lives. In some cases we thought that this work didn't deal with what we consider to be trade union business. But they deal very directly with human problems.

The second thing I know from experience is that whenever a critical situation hits us, the best source of power, the best source of hope, is straight from the people. It's happened to me so often.

There's a Mexican dicho [saying] that says there's always a good reason why bad news comes. And I think that in our case probably this will save the Union.

Questions for Review and Reflection

1. What does Chavez say happens when the union gets contracts and good wages?
2. What generalization does Chavez make concerning all unions?
3. What role does Chavez see for political action in the union's struggle?
4. Why does Chavez stress economic power over political power? What limitations does he see in exclusive political power?
5. Chavez suggests a "cooperative movement." What does he mean? How would it work?
6. Why do you suppose Chavez believes that his "ideology" cannot be described in terms of any political or economic system?
7. What political system does Chavez believe is the best?
8. According to Chavez, what does fighting for social justice do for the individual?
9. What is the best source of power and the best source for hope in the struggle?

7

All Persons Shall Be Entitled: Extending the Ideal of Equality

T he American system of government offers a variety of access points for people to influence public policy. In this chapter of government responses to the voices raised in the 1960s, we will see public policy emanating from a wide range of sources.

Power is divided between the national government and state governments. The Constitution defines federal authority, and the Tenth Amendment reserves to the states all power that is neither delegated solely to the national government nor denied to the states. One advantage of such a system is that states can act as laboratories to experiment with new ideas while maintaining their local approach to matters of public policy. For example, California chose to protect the rights of farm workers to organize unions and to bargain collectively (see Reading 11).

States can exercise their power as long as their laws comply with the supreme law of the land, the Constitution of the United States. For example, Idaho state law was struck down in *Reed v. Reed* (Reading 8) because it permitted only a father to be executor of a child's estate, violating the equal protection clause of the Fourteenth Amendment. Congressional law also supersedes state law. When the Voting Rights Act of 1965 was passed, it annulled state laws that denied or abridged the right to vote on account of race or color.

Power is allocated at the national level among three branches of government. The executive branch administers law; the legislative branch enacts law; the judicial branch interprets law. Consequently, people have multiple access points to influence government at the national level.

Congress is granted power over such matters as interstate commerce and defense and is able to do whatever is "necessary and proper" to carry out those delegated powers. Congress exercised its power over interstate commerce when it found it necessary and proper to pass the Civil Rights Act of 1964 (Reading 2).

Bicameralism divides the legislative branch even further; the Senate and the House of Representatives make up the U.S. Congress. They act independently of one another, with separate terms of office and rules; yet they must agree on a bill before it becomes law. The Senate's rule allowing unlimited debate enabled the opposition to conduct a filibuster during the debate over civil rights in 1964. History was made when, for the first time during a civil rights debate, "talking the bill to death" was halted by a cloture vote (forcing an end to debate), and the landmark act was passed.

Once a bill becomes law, it is the separate responsibility of the executive branch to carry it out. Various departments and agencies are created to administer the law. The Equal Employment Opportunity Commission came into being in order to enforce civil rights legislation. Presidential leadership is often required for effective administration of the law. In a public address at Howard University, President Lyndon Johnson exercised his own brand of leadership as he outlined what he insisted was necessary to accomplish equal rights and opportunities for all Americans (see Reading 4).

The Supreme Court acts independently as it interprets the laws of the country. Justices are nominated by the president and confirmed by the Senate to serve on the court for life "during good behavior." Judges must distinguish between policy questions for the executive and legislative branches and constitutional questions for the court. Such was the case in *Roe v. Wade* (Reading 9). The state of Texas asserted that abortion was a matter best left to the state legislature. The Supreme Court disagreed. It recognized instead a right to privacy "broad enough to encompass a woman's decision" about whether or not to terminate a pregnancy. Since that decision, the beliefs and values of judicial nominees have become an issue. Critics on both sides accuse presidents and members of Congress of requiring that judicial candidates pass a "litmus test" on the issue of abortion.

The president recommends and the Congress enacts. This was the case when President Richard Nixon recommended and Congress enacted an Indian self-determination policy in the 1970s. Once Congress has enacted law, the president can issue orders to assist in its enforcement. President Johnson issued Executive Order 11246 following passage of the 1964 Civil Rights Act. His order went even further than the law by requiring federal agencies to take "affirmative steps" to end discrimination by recruiting, hiring, training, and promoting without regard to "race, creed, color, or national origin."

All levels of power were active during the 1960s, producing a stream of action in response to calls for justice by the excluded. The results were rapid and encompassing.

Reading 1

United States Supreme Court, 1964

Reynolds v. Sims, 377 U.S. 533

Registered voters and taxpayers of Alabama brought suit against their state over district apportionment. At issue was the unequal representation that existed between geographic areas due to differences in population density. Some representatives to the upper house of the Alabama state legislature had constituencies of 15,000, while others had over ten times that number. Despite Alabama's argument that United States senators represent unequal numbers of people, the Supreme Court found that counties are unlike states. The Court concluded that "the right of suffrage can be denied by a debasement of suffrage or dilution of the weight of a citizen's vote just as effectively as by wholly prohibiting the free exercise of the franchise." When the Court ordered reapportionment based on population, the one-person, one-vote rule was affirmed, based on the equal protection clause of the Fourteenth Amendment. This key decision helped future groups to challenge other forms of discriminatory election structures.

Legislators represent people, not trees or acres. Legislators are elected by voters, not farms or cities or economic interests. As long as ours is a representative form of government, and our legislatures are those instruments of government elected directly by and directly representative of the people, the right to elect legislators in a free and unimpaired fashion is a bedrock of our political system. It could hardly be gainsaid that a constitutional claim had been asserted by an allegation that certain otherwise qualified voters had been entirely prohibited from voting for members of their state legislature. And, if a State should provide that the votes of citizens in one part of the State should be given two times, or five times, or 10 times the weight of votes of citizens in another part of the State, it could hardly be contended that the right to vote of those residing in the disfavored areas had not been effectively diluted. It would appear extraordinary to suggest that a State could be constitutionally permitted to enact a law providing that certain of the State's voters could vote two, five, or 10 times for their legislative representatives, while voters living elsewhere could vote only once. And it is inconceivable that a state law to the effect that, in counting votes for legislators, the votes of citizens in one part of the State would be multiplied by two, five, or 10, while the votes of persons in another area would be counted only at face value, could be constitutionally sustainable. . . .

Overweighting and overvaluation of the votes of those living here has the certain effect of dilution and undervaluation of the votes of those living there. The resulting discrimination against those individual voters living in disfavored areas is easily demonstrable mathematically. Their right to vote is simply not the same right to vote as that of those living in a favored part of the State. Two, five, or 10 of them must vote before the effect of their voting is equivalent to that of their favored neighbor. Weighting the votes of citizens differently, by any method or means, merely because of where they happen to reside, hardly seems justifiable. One must be ever aware that the Constitution forbids "sophisticated as well as simple-minded modes of discrimination." . . . As we stated in Wesberry v Sanders, supra:

"We do not believe that the Framers of the Constitution intended to permit the same vote-diluting discrimination to be accomplished through the device of districts containing widely varied numbers of inhabitants." . . .

State legislatures are, historically, the fountainhead of representative government in this country. A number of them have their roots in colonial times, and substantially antedate the creation of our nation and our federal government. In fact, the first formal stirrings of American political independence are to be found, in large part, in the views and actions of several of the colonial legislative bodies. . . .

But representative government is in essence self-government through the medium of elected representatives of the people, and each and every citizen has an inalienable right to full and effective participation in the political processes of his State's legislative bodies. Most citizens can achieve this participation only as qualified voters through the election of legislators to represent them. Full and effective participation by all citizens in state government requires, therefore, that each citizen have an equally effective voice in the election of members of his state legislature. Modern and viable state government needs, and the Constitution demands, no less. . . .

To conclude differently, and to sanction minority control of state legislative bodies, would appear to deny majority rights that might otherwise be thought to result. Since legislatures are responsible for enacting laws by which all citizens are to be governed, they should be bodies which are collectively responsive to the popular will. And the concept of equal protection has been traditionally viewed as requiring the uniform treatment of persons standing in the same relation to the governmental action questioned or challenged. With respect to the allocation of legislative representation, all voters, as citizens of a State, stand in the same relation regardless of where they live. . . .

$\boxed{Q}$ uestions for Review and Reflection

1. In the case at issue here, how is a vote multiplied in force as a result of geographic location?
2. What is the "fountainhead" of republican government?
3. Can you see that this concept of "one-person, one-vote" could be applied to factors other than geography?
4. Could a vote be diluted by where it is placed within a district?

Reading 2

United States Congress, 1964

The Civil Rights Act

The 1964 Civil Rights Act was a landmark piece of legislation that resulted from the civil rights movement of the 1950s and 1960s. Congress enacted the law by exercising its authority to regulate the nation's commerce. The new law prohibited discrimination on the basis of race, color, religion, or national origin in places of public accommodation and employment, and it established the Equal Employment Opportunity Commission to investigate complaints. Other acts followed, such as the Age Discrimination in Employment Act of 1967, the Fair Housing Act of 1968, and Title IX of the Education Act of 1972 that banned gender discrimination in education programs. With these decisions, lawmakers brought the full force of the federal government to bear on the issue of equal protection before the law. The Civil Rights Act had been proposed during John F. Kennedy's administration, but it was enacted after his death. It was the first of many steps to achieve what Kennedy's successor, Lyndon Johnson, called the Great Society.

Subchapter II—Public Accommodations

§ 2000a. Prohibition against discrimination or segregation in places of public accommodation

Equal Access

(a) All persons shall be entitled to the full and equal enjoyment of the goods, services, facilities, privileges, advantages, and accommodations of any place of public accommodation, as defined in this section, without discrimination or segregation on the ground of race, color, religion, or national origin.

Establishments affecting interstate commerce or supported in their activities by State action as places of public accommodation; lodgings; facilities principally engaged in selling food for consumption on the premises; gasoline stations; places of exhibition or entertainment; other covered establishments

(b) Each of the following establishments which serves the public is a place of public accommodation within the meaning of this subchapter if its operations affect commerce, or if discrimination or segregation by it is supported by State action:

(1) any inn, hotel, motel, or other establishment which provides lodging to transient guests, other than an establishment located within a building which contains not more than five rooms for rent or hire and which is actually occupied by the proprietor of such establishment as his residence;

(2) any restaurant, cafeteria, lunchroom, lunch counter, soda fountain, or other facility principally engaged in selling food for consumption on the premises, including, but not limited to, any such facility located on the premises of any retail establishment; or any gasoline station;

(3) any motion picture house, theater, concert hall, sports arena, stadium or other place of exhibition or entertainment; and

(4) any establishment (A)(i) which is physically located within the premises of any establishment otherwise covered by this subsection, or (ii) within the premises of which is physically located any such covered establishment, and (B) which holds itself out as serving patrons of such covered establishment. . . .

Historical Note

Short Title of 1972 Amendment.   Pub.L. 92–261, § 1, Mar. 24, 1972, 86 Stat. 103, provided: "That this Act [which enacted sections 2000e–16 and 2000e–17 of this title, amended sections 5108 and 5314 to 5316 of Title 5, Government Organization and Employees, and sections 2000e to 2000e–6, 2000e–8, 2000e–9, 2000e–13, and 2000e–14 of this title, and enacted provisions set out as a note under section 2000e–5 of this title] may be cited as the 'Equal Employment Opportunity Act of 1972'."

Short Title. Section 1 of Pub.L. 88–352 provided: "That this Act [which enacted subchapters II to IX of this chapter, amended sections 2204 and 2205 of former Title 5, Executive Departments and Government Officers and Employees, section 1447(d) of Title 28, Judiciary and Judicial Procedure, and sections 1971 and 1975a to 1975d of this title, and enacted provisions set out as a note under section 2000e of this title] may be cited as the 'Civil Rights Act of 1964'."

Legislative History. For legislative history and purpose of Pub.L. 88–352, see 1964 U.S. Code Cong. and Adm. News, p. 2355.

§ 2000e–2. Unlawful employment practices

Employer Practices

(a) It shall be an unlawful employment practice for an employer—

(1) to fail or refuse to hire or to discharge any individual, or otherwise to discriminate against any individual with respect to his compensation, terms, conditions, or privileges of employment, because of such individual's race, color, religion, sex, or national origin; or

(2) to limit, segregate, or classify his employees or applicants for employment in any way which would deprive or tend to deprive any individual of employment opportunities or otherwise adversely affect his status as an employee, because of such individual's race, color, religion, sex, or national origin.

Employment Agency Practices

(b) It shall be an unlawful employment practice for an employment agency to fail or refuse to refer for employment, or otherwise to discriminate against, any individual because of his race, color, religion, sex, or national origin, or to classify or refer for employment any individual on the basis of his race, color, religion, sex, or national origin.

Labor Organization Practices

(c) It shall be an unlawful employment practice for a labor organization—

(1) to exclude or to expel from its membership, or otherwise to discriminate against, any individual because of his race, color, religion, sex, or national origin;

(2) to limit, segregate, or classify its membership or applicants for membership, or to classify or fail or refuse to refer for employment any individual, in any way which would deprive or tend to deprive any individual of employment opportunities, or would limit such employment opportunities or otherwise adversely affect his status as an employee or as an applicant for employment, because of such individual's race, color, religion, sex, or national origin; or

(3) to cause or attempt to cause an employer to discriminate against an individual in violation of this section.

Training Programs

(d) It shall be an unlawful employment practice for any employer, labor organization, or joint labor-management committee controlling apprenticeship or other training or retraining, including on-the-job training programs to discriminate against any individual because of his race, color, religion, sex, or national origin in admission to, or employment in, any program established to provide apprenticeship or other training.

$\boxed{Q}$ uestions for Review and Reflection

After reading this section of the *U.S. Code Annotated:*
1. Distinguish between 2000a and 2000e-2 in terms of who is protected and from what.
2. Identify what is defined as a "public accommodation."
3. What kinds of exceptions are noted and why?

Reading 3

Hubert Humphrey, 1965

Civil Rights Commission Report

The Civil Rights Act was an omnibus law that spawned many more decisions supporting, strengthening, and enhancing the initial legislation. The Civil Rights Act of 1968 prohibited dis crimination in the sale or rental of housing. The 1972 Equal Employment Opportunity Act broadened opportunities for the disadvantaged. The 1972 Education Amendment prohibited sex discrimination in school programs and activities.

Long an advocate on behalf of minorities, Vice President Hubert Humphrey (1911-1978) was assigned by Lyndon Johnson to assist in the implementation of the civil rights legislation. This report reflects the number of agencies and commissions involved and the scope of the commitment to exercise federal authority to enforce constitutional principles.

A. Department of Justice.

The Department, through civil law suits and criminal prosecutions, acts to protect certain rights guaranteed by Federal law. Prior to 1964, its major statutory responsibilities involved protection of voting rights, enforcement of the Civil Rights Acts of 1957 and 1960 and prior civil rights statutes, representation of other Federal agencies in law suits, and assistance in enforcement of court orders. In addition, the Attorney General serves as chief legal advisor to the President on civil rights as well as other matters.

The 1964 Civil Rights Act added the following responsibilities: initiation of suits to require desegregation of governmentally owned or operated facilities and public schools, upon complaint of individuals who themselves are unable to sue, initiation of suits to end discrimination in public accommodations or in employment, where such discrimination is part of a pattern or practice; intervention in private law suits involving discrimination in places of public accommodation and in employment, or in suits alleging denial of equal protection of the laws.

B. U.S. Commission on Civil Rights.

Established by the Civil Rights Act of 1957, the Commission investigates denials of the right to vote, studies legal developments, and appraises Federal policies relating to the equal protection of the laws in such areas as education, housing, employment, the administration of justice, use of public facilities, and transportation. It makes recommendations to the President and Congress and serves as a national clearing house for civil rights information.

C. Community Relations Service.

The Service was established by the Civil Rights Act of 1964 as a unit of the Department of Commerce to assist communities in resolving disputes arising from discriminatory practices which impair rights guaranteed by Federal law or which affect interstate commerce. It conciliates complaints referred by Federal courts in law suits to desegregate public accommodations and seeks, through conferences, publications, and technical assistance, to aid communities in developing plans to improve racial relations and understanding.

D. Equal Employment Opportunity Commission.

Established by the Civil Rights Act of 1964, the Commission will investigate charges of discrimination and through conciliation seek to resolve disputes involving discrimination by employers, unions and employment agencies covered by Title VII of the 1964 Act. It will carry out technical studies, make assistance available to persons subject to the Act, and may refer matters for action by the Department of Justice.

E. President's Committee on Equal Employment Opportunity.

This Committee, established by Executive Order 10925, enforces the requirements of the Order and of Executive Order 11114 that there be equal job opportunities in Federal employment, in work performed under government contract, and in all Federally-assisted construction projects. It supervises the compliance activities of each Federal contracting agency subject to the Orders.

F. Housing and Home Finance Agency.

The Agency is responsible for securing compliance with Executive Order 11063 and other Federal laws which require nondiscrimination in the sale and rental of Federal and Federally-assisted housing, including public housing, urban renewal, college housing, FHA-insured homes, and community facilities. It also has responsibility for insuring non-discrimination in employment under Executive Order 11114 in Federal and Federally-assisted housing construction projects.

G. President's Committee on Equal Opportunity in Housing.

Established by Executive Order 11063, the Committee coordinates the activities of departments and agencies in preventing discrimination in housing and also conducts educational programs designed to foster acceptance of the Federal policy of equal opportunity in housing.

H. Department of Health, Education, and Welfare.

Several constituent units of the Department have civil rights responsibilities.

The Office of Education is charged by the 1964 Civil Rights Act to conduct a survey on the availability of equal educational opportunity and to provide technical and financial assistance to school boards in carrying out plans for the desegregation of public schools and for assisting in resolution of problems incident to desegregation. The Office is also responsible for assuring non-discrimination in Federal aid-to-education programs including aid to colleges and universities, elementary and secondary schools, and libraries.

The Public Health and the Welfare Administrations are responsible under Title VI of the 1964 Civil Rights Act for assuring non-discrimination in Federally-assisted health and welfare programs, including aid to hospitals, State and county welfare departments, health clinics, and community mental health centers.

I. Department of Defense.

The Department implements programs requiring equal opportunity in the recruitment, training, and promotion of military personnel in the Armed Forces, the Reserves, and the National Guard. The Department also carries out, through base-community relations committees, programs designed to secure equal treatment for military personnel and their families in such off-base facilities as public schools, housing, and public accommodations. Because of its volume of expenditures, the Department has substantial responsibility for implementing Executive Order 10925 requiring non-discrimination in employment by Government contractors, and is responsible for assuring that grants and loans made by the Department to colleges, universities, and other institutions are administered without discrimination. The President's Committee on Equal Opportunity in the Armed Forces has submitted reports on efforts to eliminate discrimination against members of the uniformed services and their dependents.

J. Office of Economic Opportunity.

Established in 1964 to administer anti-poverty programs under the Economic Opportunity Act, the Office is directly responsible for operating the Job Corps, the Community Action Program, and the VISTA volunteers program. It also supervises a number of delegated programs, including the Neighborhood Youth Corps, college work-study, adult literacy, rural loans, small business loans, and work-experience programs.

Activities of the Office are significant in the civil rights field not only because they will be administered on a completely non-segregated basis, but also because they seek to involve the disadvantaged in the planning and administration of the anti-poverty programs. With more than half of all Negro, Spanish-speaking and Puerto Rican families afflicted with poverty, this emphasis is likely to produce significant benefits in bringing these groups more into local community life.

K. Other Agencies with Civil Rights Responsibilities.

Education.   In addition to the Department of Health, Education and Welfare, the Department of Defense, and the Housing and Home Finance Agency, several other agencies and are responsible for assuring non-discrimination in college and university programs for which they provide Federal financial assistance. These include the Atomic Energy Commission, the National Science Foundation, the National Aeronautics and Space Administration, and the Departments of Agriculture and Interior.

Employment.   In addition to the President's Committee on Equal Employment Opportunity and the Equal Employment Opportunity Commission, other agencies having civil rights responsibilities in employment include:

— the Department of Labor, which is responsible for securing non-discrimination in Federally-financed recruitment, training, referral, employment service and apprenticeship programs;

— the National Labor Relations Board, which has held certain racially discriminatory practices to be unfair labor practices;

— the Department of Commerce which offers technical assistance to business through its Task Force on Equal Employment Opportunities and which has major responsibilities under Executive Order 11114 and Title VI of the 1964 Civil Rights Act through the Bureau of Public Roads, the Area Redevelopment Administration, and other programs;

— the U.S. Civil Service Commission, which carries out certain responsibilities for the President's Committee on Equal Employment Opportunity to eliminate discrimination within the Federal service;

— the General Services Administration which, through its letting of contracts for government buildings and facilities, is involved in implementation of Executive Order 11114 barring discrimination in employment by government contractors.

Federal Financial Assistance. Of course, all Federal agencies are responsible under Title VI of the 1964 Act for assuring nondiscrimination in Federally-financed programs administered by them. Some have already been mentioned. Others include:

— the Department of Agriculture, which helps finance State Extension Services, and other agricultural programs;

— the General Services Administration, which is responsible for the disposal of surplus government property;

— the Federal Aviation Agency, which assists in the construction and maintenance of airport terminal facilities;

In addition, the Small Business Administration operates a program of special services aimed at expanding business opportunities among minority groups.

$\boxed{Q}$ uestions for Review and Reflection

1. In this report, distinguish between existing agencies and new bureaucratic agencies created to enforce the law.
2. What specific responsibilities are outlined for the new agencies created?
3. What does all this additional federal protection say about the federal government's role in civil rights?

Reading 4

Lyndon B. Johnson, 1965

Howard University Speech

Lyndon B. Johnson (1908-1973) took over the presidency of the United States following the assassination of President John F. Kennedy in 1963. Johnson was elected into office in 1964, and during his tenure he put forward the Great Society, a government program to combat poverty and assume a much greater role in assisting all citizens to achieve the American dream.

In Johnson's view, government's obligation began with ensuring political and legal equality for all, but it did not end there. "We seek not just legal equity but human ability, not just equality as a right and a theory but equality as a fact and equality as a result." Jobs, homes, and social welfare programs were part of the equation. Using the Civil Rights Act as a foundation, Johnson built a series of laws and programs to fulfill this broad interpretation of government's role.

In far too many ways American Negroes have been another nation; deprived of freedom, crippled by hatred, the doors of opportunity closed to hope.

In our time change has come to this nation. The American Negro, acting with impressive restraint, has peacefully protested and marched, entered the courtrooms and the seats of government, demanding a justice that has long been denied. The voice of the Negro was the call to action. But it is a tribute to America that, once aroused, the courts and the Congress, the President and most of the people, have been the allies of progress.

The voting rights bill will be the latest, and among the most important, in a long series of victories. But this victory—as Winston Churchill said of another triumph for freedom—"is not the end. It is not even the beginning of the end. But it is, perhaps, the end of the beginning."

That beginning is freedom; and the barriers to that freedom are tumbling down. Freedom is the right to share, share fully and equally, in American society—to vote, to hold a job, to enter a public place, to go to school. It is the right to be treated in every part of our national life as a person equal in dignity and promise to all others.

But freedom is not enough. You do not wipe away the scars of centuries by saying: Now you are free to go where you want, and do as you desire, and choose the leaders you please.

You do not take a person who for years has been hobbled by chains and liberate him, bring him up to the starting line of a race and then say, "you are free to compete with all the others," and still justly believe that you have been completely fair.

Thus it is not enough just to open the gates of opportunity. All our citizens must have the ability to walk through those gates.

This is the next and the more profound stage of the battle for civil rights. We seek not just freedom but opportunity. We seek not just legal equity but human ability, not just equality as a right and a theory but equality as a fact and equality as a result. . . .

Of course Negro Americans as well as white Americans have shared in our rising national abundance. But the harsh fact of the matter is that in the battle for true equality too many—far too many—are losing ground every day.

We are not completely sure why this is. We know the causes are complex and subtle. But we do know the two broad basic reasons. And we do know that we have to act.

First, Negroes are trapped—as many whites are trapped—in inherited, gateless poverty. They lack training and skills. They are shut in, in slums, without decent medical care. Private and public poverty combine to cripple their capacities.

We are trying to attack these evils through our poverty program, through our education program, through our medical care and our other health programs, and a dozen more of the Great Society programs that are aimed at the root causes of this poverty.

We will increase, and we will accelerate, and we will broaden this attack in years to come until this most enduring of foes finally yields to our unyielding will.

But there is a second cause—much more difficult to explain, more deeply grounded, more desperate in its force. It is the devastating heritage of long years of slavery; and a century of oppression, hatred, and injustice.

For Negro poverty is not white poverty. Many of its causes and many of its cures are the same. But there are differences—deep, corrosive, obstinate differences—radiating painful roots into the community, and into the family, and the nature of the individual.

These differences are not racial differences. They are solely and simply the consequence of ancient brutality, past injustice, and present prejudice. They are anguishing to observe. For the Negro they are a constant reminder of oppression. For the white they are a constant reminder of guilt. But they must be faced and they must be dealt with and they must be overcome, if we are ever to reach the time when the only difference between Negroes and whites is the color of their skin.

Nor can we find a complete answer in the experience of other American minorities. They made a valiant and a largely successful effort to emerge from poverty and prejudice.

The Negro, like these others, will have to rely mostly upon his own efforts. But he just cannot do it alone. For they did not have the heritage of centuries to overcome, and they did not have a cultural tradition which had been twisted and battered by endless years of hatred and hopelessness, nor were they excluded—these others—because of race or color—a feeling whose dark intensity is matched by no other prejudice in our society.

Nor can these differences be understood as isolated infirmities. They are a seamless web. They cause each other. They result from each other. They reinforce each other.

Much of the Negro community is buried under a blanket of history and circumstance. It is not a lasting solution to lift just one corner of that blanket. We must stand on all sides and we must raise the entire cover if we are to liberate our fellow citizens. . . .

There is no single easy answer to all of these problems.

Jobs are part of the answer. They bring the income which permits a man to provide for his family.

Decent homes in decent surroundings and a chance to learn—an equal chance to learn—are part of the answer.

Welfare and social programs better designed to hold families together are part of the answer.

Care for the sick is part of the answer.

An understanding heart by all Americans is another big part of the answer.

And to all of these fronts—and a dozen more—I will dedicate the expanding efforts of the Johnson Administration.

Questions for Review and Reflection

1. To whom does President Johnson attribute the advancement in black Americans' civil rights? Who deserves the credit?
2. Why does Johnson employ Winston Churchill's statement that this victory is "not the end, not the beginning, but the end of the beginning"? What does Johnson mean by the statement "freedom is not enough"? Do you agree?
3. Although poor blacks and poor whites both bear the devastation of poverty, what special burden does Johnson see causing even more hardship on America's black population? How might wealthy blacks respond to this aspect of the black experience?
4. How does the special burden experienced by American blacks inhibit them from fully taking part in American society? Can this ever be overcome?
5. According to Johnson, what extra burden does the disintegration of the Negro family structure place upon the black family? How would his administration's programs help in this area?

Reading **5**

United States Congress, 1965

The Voting Rights Act

Despite its intent, the Fifteenth Amendment did not result in full voting rights for African Americans. For nearly a century, effective barriers continued to stand between these citizens and the polling booths. A "grandfather clause" exempted white voters from tests and taxes by enfranchising those whose grandfathers had had the vote. Literacy tests and poll taxes were placed on every "newer" citizen. From Reconstruction forward, the South was remarkably successful in shutting down the black vote. The exemptions of grandfather clauses were found unconstitutional in 1915, but literacy tests, character tests, property requirements, and polling taxes continued.

In 1965, Congress passed the Voting Rights Act to provide a series of remedies to Southern roadblocks. Federal agents were sent into districts where less than 50 percent of the population was registered to vote. At long last, literacy and other qualifying tests were outlawed; poll taxes had been eliminated with the passage of the Twenty-fourth Amendment in 1964. Any procedures that had the effect of denying the right to vote based on color or race were interdicted. The Voting Rights Act of 1965 had a dramatic impact on the number of American voters. It was a major step in making political equality a reality, and it was the second building block in Johnson's Great Society.

1971. Sec. Voting rights.

(a) Race, color, or previous condition not to affect right to vote; uniform standards for voting qualification; errors or omissions from papers; literacy tests; agreements between Attorney General and State or local authorities; definitions.

    (b) Intimidation, threats, or coercion.

    (c) Prevention relief; injunction; rebuttable literacy presumption; liability of United States for costs; State as party defendant.

    (d) jurisdiction; exhaustion of other remedies.

    (e) Order qualifying person to vote; application; hearing; voting referees; transmittal of report and order; certification of qualification; definitions.

(f) Contempt; assignment of counsel; witnesses.

(g) Three-judge district court: hearing, determination, expedition of action, review by Supreme Court; single-judge district court: hearing, determination, expedition of action.

1972. Interference with freedom of elections.

Subchapter I-A—Enforcement of Voting Rights

1973. Denial or abridgement of right to vote on account of race or color through voting qualifications or prerequisites.

1973a. Proceeding to enforce right to vote.

(a) Authorization by court for appointment of federal examiners.

(b) Suspension of use of tests and devices which deny or abridge right to vote.

(c) Retention of jurisdiction to prevent commencement of new devices to deny or abridge right to vote.

1973b. Suspension of use of tests or devices in determining eligibility to vote.

(a) Action by State or political subdivision for declaratory judgment of no denial or abridgement; three-judge district court; appeal to Supreme Court; retention of jurisdiction by three-judge court.

(b) Required factual determinations necessary to allow suspension of compliance with tests and devices; publication in Federal Register.

(c) Definition of test or device.

(d) Required frequency, continuation and probable recurrence of incidents of denial or abridgement to constitute forbidden use of tests or devices.

(e) Completion of requisite grade level of education in American-flag schools in which predominant classroom language was other than English.

(f) Congressional findings of voting discrimination against language minorities; prohibition of English-only elections; other remedial measures.

1973c. Alteration of voting qualifications and procedures; action by State or political subdivision for declaratory judgment of no denial or abridgement of voting rights; three-judge district court; appeal to Supreme Court.

1973d. Federal voting examiners; appointment.

1973e. Examination of applicants for registration.

(a) Form of application; requisite allegation of non-registration.

(b) Placement of eligible voters on official lists; transmittal of lists.

(c) Certificate of eligibility.

(d) Removal of names from list by examiners.

1973f. Observers at elections; assignment; duties; reports.

1973g. Challenges to eligibility listings.

(a) Filing of challenge; supplementary affidavits; service upon person challenged; hearing; review.

(b) Rules and regulations by Director of Office of Personnel Management.

(c) Subpoena power of Director of Office of Personnel Management; contempt.

1973h. Poll taxes.

(a) Congressional finding and declaration of policy against enforced payment of poll taxes as device to impair voting rights.

(b) Authority of Attorney General to institute actions for relief against enforcement of poll tax requirement.

(c) Jurisdiction of three-judge district courts; appeal to Supreme Court.

1973i. Prohibited acts.

(a) Failure or refusal to permit casting or tabulation of vote.

(b) Intimidation, threats, or coercion.

Questions for Review and Reflection

According to the Voting Rights Act in the *United States Code Annotated:*

1. What practices are not allowed when carrying out the vote?
2. Can education be a prerequisite for voting?
3. Can certificates of eligibility be required?
4. Does it appear that intimidation had been used as a tactic to deny the right to vote?

Reading 6

Lyndon B. Johnson, 1965

Executive Order 11246

"It is the policy of the Government of the United States to provide equal opportunity in Federal employment for all qualified persons, to prohibit discrimination in employment because of race, creed, color or national origin."

With these words, President Lyndon Johnson (1908–1973), author of the Great Society, began a program of affirmative action in which government contractors were required to take steps not only to employ people but also to recruit, train, and promote them without engaging in any discriminatory practices.

Government was no longer neutral in its handling of the principle of equality. A ban on discrimination had not achieved the desired results of integration in the workplace, so government undertook the new responsibility of affirming equality of opportunity through action.

In addition to the Civil Rights and Voting Rights Acts, other parts of Johnson's ambitious social program were the Office of Economic Opportunity, Project Head Start, the Job Corps, and Medicaid and Medicare.

Equal Employment Opportunity

Under and by virtue of the authority vested in me as President of the United States by the Constitution and statutes of the United States, it is ordered as follows:

Part I—Nondiscrimination in Government Employment

Section 101. It is the policy of the Government of the United States to provide equal opportunity in Federal employment for all qualified persons, to prohibit discrimination in employment because of race, creed, color, or national origin, and to promote the full realization of equal employment opportunity through a positive, continuing program in each executive department or agency. The policy of equal opportunity applies to every aspect of Federal employment policy and practice.

Sec. 102. The head of each executive department and agency shall establish and maintain a positive program of equal employment opportunity for all civilian employees and applicants for employment within his jurisdiction in accordance with the policy set forth in Section 101.

Sec. 103. The Civil Service Commission shall supervise and provide leadership and guidance in the conduct of equal employment opportunity programs for civilian employees and of applications for employment within the executive departments and agencies and shall review agency program accomplishments periodically. In order to facilitate the achievement of a model program for equal employment opportunity in the Federal service, the Commission may consult from time to time with such individuals, groups, or organizations as may be of assistance in improving the Federal program and realizing the objectives of this Part.

Sec. 104. The Civil Service Commission shall provide for the prompt, fair, and impartial consideration of all complaints of discrimination in Federal employment on the basis of race, creed, color, or national origin. Procedures for the consideration of complaints shall include at least one impartial review within the executive department or agency and shall provide for appeal to the Civil Service Commission.

Sec. 105. The Civil Service Commission shall issue such regulations, orders, and instructions as it deems necessary and appropriate to carry out its responsibilities under this Part, and the head of each executive department and agency shall comply with the regulations, orders, and instructions issued by the Commission under this Part.

Part II—Nondiscrimination in Employment by Government Contractors and Subcontractors

Subpart A—Duties of the Secretary of Labor Sec. 201. The Secretary of Labor shall be responsible for the administration of Parts II and III of this Order and shall adopt such rules and regulations and issue such orders as he deems necessary and appropriate to achieve the purposes thereof.

Subpart B—Contractors' Agreements Sec. 202. Except in contracts exempted in accordance with Section 204 of this Order, all Government contracting agencies shall include in every Government contract hereafter entered into the following provisions:

"During the performance of this contract, the contractor agrees as follows:

"(1) The Contractor will not discriminate against any employee or applicant for employment because of race, creed, color, or national origin. The contractor will take affirmative action to ensure that applicants are employed, and that employees are treated during employment, without regard to their race, creed, color, or national origin. Such action shall include, but not be limited to the following: employment, upgrading, demotion, or transfer; recruitment or recruitment advertising; layoff or termination; rates of pay or other forms of compensation; and selection for training, including apprenticeship. The contractor agrees to post in conspicuous places, available to employees and applicants for employment, notices to be provided by the contracting officer setting forth the provisions for this nondiscrimination clause.

   "(2) the Contractor will, in all solicitations or advertisements for employees placed by or on behalf of the contractor, state that all qualified applicants will receive consideration for employment without regard to race, creed, color, or national origin."

Questions for Review and Reflection

1. Compare and contrast this executive order with the executive order issued by President Truman to integrate the military (Chapter 5, Reading 4). What was the goal of each order?
2. What was the scope of this executive order? Were there any areas of the federal bureaucracy that were not covered by this order?
3. What role does the Civil Service Commission have in the implementation of President Johnson's executive order? Can you think of another appropriate agency to oversee the policies established by this order?
4. By what authority did President Johnson seek to require private contractors to abide by the terms and conditions of this executive order? What groups might be exempted by this executive order?
5. Are there any differences between the requirements placed by this executive order on federal agencies and those for private contractors?

Reading 7

Richard Nixon, 1970

Message to Congress

Native Americans had spent the 1960s asking for more self-determination. President Richard Nixon (1913–1994) responded to that call in his 1970 recommendations to Congress regarding Indian-American relations. His comments reflected a sensitivity to the issues and concerns so long communicated by the many Indian organizations. His message abandoned government's historic policy of trying to assimilate the tribes, replacing it with one that sought a new sovereignty for Native Americans.

The Nixon administration worked with Indian groups to formulate a series of bills, which were then submitted to the Congress. The resulting legislation helped to bring about a new self-governing authority for the Native American tribes in the United States. "It is a new and balanced relationship between the U.S. Government and the first Americans that is at the heart of our approach to Indian problems." A framework was established for respectful coexistence, rather than the subjugation Native Americans had suffered for so long.

To the Congress of the United States:

The first Americans—the Indians—are the most deprived and most isolated minority group in our nation. On virtually every scale of measurement—employment, income, education, health—the condition of the Indian people ranks at the bottom.

This condition is the heritage of centuries of injustice. From the time of their first contact with European settlers, the American Indians have been oppressed and brutalized, deprived of their ancestral lands and denied the opportunity to control their own destiny. Even the Federal programs which are intended to meet their needs have frequently proven to be ineffective and demeaning.

But the story of the Indian in America is something more than the record of the white man's frequent aggression, broken agreements, intermittent remorse and prolonged failure. It is a record also of endurance, of survival, of adaptation and creativity in the face of overwhelming obstacles. It is a record of enormous contributions to this country—to its art and culture, to its strength and spirit, to its sense of history and its sense of purpose.

It is long past time that the Indian policies of the Federal government began to recognize and build upon the capacities and insights of the Indian people. Both as a matter of justice and as a matter of enlightened social policy, we must begin to act on the basis of what the Indians themselves have long been telling us. The time has come to break decisively with the past and to create the conditions for a new era in which the Indian future is determined by Indian acts and Indian decisions.

Self-Determination Without Termination

The first and most basic question that must be answered with respect to Indian policy concerns the historic and legal relationship between the Federal government and Indian communities. In the past, this relationship has oscillated between two equally harsh and unacceptable extremes.

On the one hand, it has—at various times during previous Administrations—been the stated policy objective of both the Executive and Legislative branches of the Federal government eventually to terminate the trusteeship relationship between the Federal government and the Indian people. As recently as August of 1953, in House Concurrent Resolution 108, the Congress declared that termination was the long-range goal of its Indian policies. This would mean that Indian tribes would eventually lose any special standing they had under Federal law; the tax exempt status of their lands would be discontinued; Federal responsibility for their economic and social well-being would be repudiated; and the tribes themselves would be effectively dismantled. Tribal property would be divided among individual members who would then be assimilated into the society at large.

This policy of forced termination is wrong, in my judgment, for a number of reasons. First, the premises on which it rests are wrong. Termination implies that the Federal government has taken on a trusteeship responsibility for Indian communities as an act of generosity toward a disadvantaged people and that it can therefore discontinue this responsibility on a unilateral basis whenever it sees fit. But the unique status of Indian tribes does not rest on any premise such as this. The special relationship between Indians and the Federal government is the result instead of solemn obligations which have been entered into by the United States Government. Down through the years, through written treaties and through formal and informal agreements, our government has made specific commitments to the Indian people. For their part, the Indians have often surrendered claims to vast tracts of land and have accepted life on government reservations. In exchange, the government has agreed to provide community services such as health, education and public safety, services which would presumably allow Indian communities to enjoy a standard of living comparable to that of other Americans.

This goal, of course, has never been achieved. But the special relationship between the Indian tribes and the Federal government which arises from these agreements continues to carry immense moral and legal force. To terminate this relationship would be no more appropriate than to terminate the citizenship rights of any other American.

The second reason for rejecting forced termination is that the practical results have been clearly harmful in the few instances in which termination actually has been tried. The removal of Federal trusteeship responsibility has produced considerable disorientation among the affected Indians and has left them unable to relate to a myriad of Federal, State and local assistance efforts. Their economic and social condition has often been worse after termination than it was before.

The third argument I would make against forced termination concerns the effect it has had upon the overwhelming majority of tribes which still enjoy a special relationship with the Federal government. The very threat that this relationship may someday be ended has created a great deal of apprehension among Indian groups and this apprehension, in turn, has had a blighting effect on tribal progress. Any step that might result in greater social, economic or political autonomy is regarded with suspicion by many Indians who fear that it will only bring them closer to the day when the Federal government will disavow its responsibility and cut them adrift. . . .

I believe that both of these policy extremes are wrong. Federal termination errs in one direction, Federal paternalism errs in the other. Only by clearly rejecting both of these extremes can we achieve a policy which truly serves the best interests of the Indian people. Self-determination among the Indian people can and must be encouraged without the threat of eventual termination. In my view, in fact, that is the only way that self-determination can effectively be fostered.

This, then, must be the goal of any new national policy toward the Indian people: to strengthen the Indian's sense of autonomy without threatening his sense of community. We must assure the Indian that he can assume control of his own life without being separated involuntarily from the tribal group. And we must make it clear that Indians can become independent of Federal control without being cut off from Federal concern and Federal support. My specific recommendations to the Congress are designed to carry out this policy.

Rejecting Termination

Because termination is morally and legally unacceptable, because it produces bad practical results, and because the mere threat of termination tends to discourage greater self-sufficiency among Indian groups, I am asking the Congress to pass a new Concurrent Resolution which would expressly renounce, repudiate and repeal the termination policy as expressed in House Concurrent Resolution 108 of the 83rd Congress. This resolution would explicitly affirm the integrity and right to continued existence of all Indian tribes and Alaska native governments, recognizing that cultural pluralism is a source of national strength. . . .

For years we have talked about encouraging Indians to exercise greater self-determination, but our progress has never been commensurate with our promises. Part of the reason for this situation has been the threat of termination. But another reason is the fact that when a decision is made as to whether a Federal program will be turned over to Indian administration, it is the Federal authorities and not the Indian people who finally make that decision.

This situation should be reversed. In my judgment, it should be up to the Indian tribe to determine whether it is willing and able to assume administrative responsibility for a service program which is presently administered by a Federal agency. To this end, I am proposing legislation which would empower a tribe or a group of tribes or any other Indian community to take over the control or operation of Federally-funded and administered programs in the Department of the Interior and the Department of Health, Education and Welfare whenever the tribal council or comparable community governing group voted to do so. . . .

Consistent with our policy that the Indian community should have the right to take over the control and operation of federally funded programs, we believe every Indian community wishing to do so should be able to control its own Indian schools. This control would be exercised by school boards selected by Indians and functioning much like other school boards throughout the nation. To assure that this goal is achieved, I am asking the Vice President, acting in his role as Chairman of the National Council on Indian Opportunity, to establish a Special Education Subcommittee of that Council. The members of that Subcommittee should be Indian educators who are selected by the Council's Indian members. . . .

Economic deprivation is among the most serious of Indian problems. Unemployment among Indians is ten times the national average; the unemployment rate runs as high as 80 percent on some of the poorest reservations. Eighty percent of reservation Indians have an income which falls below the poverty line; the average annual income for such families is only $1,500. As I said in September of 1968, it is critically important that the Federal government support and encourage efforts which help Indians develop their own economic infrastructure. To that end, I am proposing the "Indian Financing Act of 1970."

This act would do two things:

1. It would broaden the existing Revolving Loan Fund, which loans money for Indian economic development projects. I am asking that the authorization for this fund be increased from approximately $25 million to $75 million.

2. It would provide additional incentives in the form of loan guarantees, loan insurance and interest subsidies to encourage *private* lenders to loan more money for Indian economic projects. An aggregate amount of $200 million would be authorized for loan guarantee and loan insurance purposes. . . .

The Indians of America need Federal assistance—this much has long been clear. What has not always been clear, however, is that the Federal government needs Indian energies and Indian leadership if its assistance is to be effective in improving the conditions of Indian life. It is a new and balanced relationship between the United States Government and the first Americans that is at the heart of our approach to Indian problems. And that is why we now approach these problems with new confidence that they will successfully be overcome.

Questions for Review and Reflection

1. How does Nixon describe the American Indian?
2. What is the most basic issue, according to Nixon, with regard to Indian rights?
3. What are some of the specific problems addressed by President Nixon?
4. Does Nixon's policy respond to the Indian demands made earlier?

Reading **8**

United States Supreme Court, 1971

Reed v. Reed, 404 U.S. 71

Sex discrimination was a major agenda item for the women's movement of the 1960s and 1970s. Under the Constitution, state and federal laws could differentiate people according to gender, but only on a reasonable and relevant basis. Increasingly, women took their cases to court, charging violations of their constitutional guarantee of equal protection.

In the *Reed* case, Mr. and Mrs. Reed both applied to become the administrator of their son's estate. Idaho law required the Probate Court, when hearing several claims for the position of administrator, to favor male over female applications. Mrs. Reed challenged the law on the grounds that it violated her right to equal protection.

The Court, in a unanimous decision, agreed that a law that arbitrarily based its decision solely on gender was unconstitutional. "By providing dissimilar treatment for men and women who are thus similarly situated, the challenged section violates the Equal Protection Clause." This was the first time the standard of rationality was applied to laws involving gender-based differential treatment. In subsequent cases, a Florida law exempting widows, but not widowers, from property taxes was upheld; a Utah law requiring divorced fathers to support daughters to age 18 but sons to age 21 was struck down.

Richard Lynn Reed, a minor, died intestate in Ada County, Idaho, on March 29, 1967. His adoptive parents, who had separated sometime prior to his death, are the parties to this appeal. Approximately seven months after Richard's death, his mother, appellant Sally Reed, filed a petition in the Probate Court of Ada County, seeking appointment as administratrix of her son's estate. Prior to the date set for a hearing on the mother's petition, appellee Cecil Reed, the father of the decedent, filed a competing petition seeking to have himself appointed administrator of the son's estate. The probate court held a joint hearing on the two petitions and thereafter ordered that letters of administration be issued to appellee Cecil Reed upon his taking the oath and filing the bond required by law. The court treated §§ 15–312 and 15–314 of the Idaho Code as the controlling statutes and read those sections as compelling a preference for Cecil Reed because he was a male. . . .

Sally Reed appealed from the probate court order, and her appeal was treated by the District Court of the Fourth Judicial District of Idaho as a constitutional attack on §15–314. In dealing with the attack, that court held that the challenged section violated the Equal Protection Clause of the Fourteenth Amendment and was, therefore void; the matter was ordered "returned to the Probate Court for its determination of which of the two parties" was better qualified to administer the estate.

This order was never carried out, however, for Cecil Reed took a further appeal to the Idaho Supreme Court, which reversed the District Court and reinstated the original order naming the father administrator of the estate. In reaching this result, the Idaho Supreme Court first dealt with the governing statutory law and held that under § 15–312 "a father and mother are 'equally entitled' to letters of administration," but the preference given to males by § 15–314 is "mandatory" and leaves no room for the exercise of a probate court's discretion in the appointment of administrators. Having thus definitively and authoritatively interpreted the statutory provisions involved, the Idaho Supreme Court then proceeded to examine, and reject, Sally Reed's contention that § 15–314 violates the Equal Protection Clause by giving a mandatory preference to males over females, without regard to their individual qualifications as potential estate administrators. . . .

Sally Reed thereupon appealed for review by this court. . . . Having examined the record and considered the briefs and oral arguments of the parties, we have concluded that the arbitrary preference established in favor of males by § 15–314 of the Idaho Code cannot stand in the face of the Fourteenth Amendment's command that no State deny the equal protection of the laws to any person within its jurisdiction. . . .

In applying that clause, this Court has consistently recognized that the Fourteenth Amendment does not deny to States the power to treat different classes of persons in different ways. . . . The Equal Protection clause of that amendment does, however, deny to States the power to legislate that different treatment be accorded to persons placed by a statute into different classes on the basis of criteria wholly unrelated to the objective of that statute. A classification "must be reasonable, not arbitrary, and must rest upon some ground of difference having a fair and substantial relation to the object of the legislation, so that all persons similarly circumstanced shall be treated alike." *Royster Guano Co. v. Virginia,* 253 U.S. 412, 415 (1920). The question presented by this case, then, is whether a difference in the sex of competing applicants for letters of administration bears a rational relationship to a state objective that is sought to be advanced by the operation of §§ 15–312 and 15–314. . . .

We note finally that if § 15–314 is viewed merely as a modifying appendage to § 15–312 and as aimed at the same objective, its constitutionality is not thereby saved. The objective of § 15–312 clearly is to establish degrees of entitlement of various classes of persons in accordance with their varying degrees and kinds of relationship to the intestate. Regardless of their sex, persons within any one of the enumerated classes of that section are similarly situated with respect to that objective. By providing dissimilar treatment for men and women who are thus similarly situated, the challenged section violates the Equal Protection Clause.

Questions for Review and Reflection

1. What was the probate court policy regarding assigning an administrator to a child's estate?
2. Why did the Idaho Supreme Court reverse the district court's decision?
3. What does the Fourteenth Amendment provide that is violated by the Idaho Supreme Court?
4. When can a law treat people differently?

Reading 9

United States Supreme Court, 1973

Roe v. Wade, 410 U.S. 113

In the 1870s the Comstock Laws were passed, banning distribution of all "obscene, lewd, lascivious, filthy, indecent" materials, including those that contained contraception information.

Under these federal laws, birth control clinics like the one established by Margaret Sanger in 1914 were shut down, and Sanger and other practitioners were arrested (see Chapter 4, Reading 11).

State governments extended the restrictions by outlawing abortion toward the end of the nineteenth century. Their goal was to discourage illicit sexual conduct as well as to protect prenatal life.

Nearly a century later, a Texas statute of this type was challenged in the Supreme Court. The Court, in an opinion written by Associate Justice Harry Blackmun, acknowledged a right to privacy that extended to control over one's own body, at least during the first trimester of pregnancy. In this decision, which remains controversial, women won additional rights over their reproductive systems and a measure of freedom from government control over their childbearing decisions. The Supreme Court in 1993 refused to overturn *Roe v. Wade*, but its provisions will probably continue to be hotly contested for some time.

Excerpts from *Roe v. Wade*

Mr. Justice BLACKMUN delivered the opinion of the Court. . . .

II

Jane Roe, a single woman who was residing in Dallas County, Texas, instituted this federal action in March 1970 against the District Attorney of the county. She sought a declaratory judgment that the Texas criminal abortion statutes were unconstitutional on their face, and an injunction restraining the defendant from enforcing the statutes.

Roe alleged that she was unmarried and pregnant; that she wished to terminate her pregnancy by an abortion "performed by a competent, licensed physician, under safe, clinical conditions"; that she was unable to get a "legal" abortion in Texas because her life did not appear to be threatened by the continuation of her pregnancy; and that she could not afford to travel to another jurisdiction in order to secure a legal abortion under safe conditions. She claimed that the Texas statutes were unconstitutionally vague and that they abridged her right of personal privacy, protected by the First, Fourth, Fifth, Ninth and Fourteenth Amendments. . . .

V

The principal thrust of appellant's attack on the Texas statutes is that they improperly invade a right, said to be possessed by the pregnant woman, to choose to terminate her pregnancy. Appellant would discover this right in the concept of personal "liberty" embodied in the Fourteenth Amendment's Due Process Clause. . . .

VII

Three reasons have been advanced to explain historically the enactment of criminal abortion laws in the 19th century and to justify their continued existence.

It has been argued occasionally that these laws were the product of a Victorian social concern to discourage illicit sexual conduct. Texas, however, does not advance this justification in the present case, and it appears that no court or commentator has taken the argument seriously. The appellants and *amici* contend, moreover, that this is not a proper state purpose at all and suggest that if it were, the Texas statutes are overbroad in protecting it since the law fails to distinguish between married and unwed mothers.

A second reason is concerned with abortion as a medical procedure. When most criminal abortion laws were first enacted, the procedure was a hazardous one for the woman. This was particularly true prior to the development of antisepsis. Antiseptic techniques, of course, were based on discoveries by Lister, Pasteur, and others first announced in 1867, but were not generally accepted and employed until about the turn of the century. Abortion mortality was high, even after 1900, and perhaps until as late as the development of antibiotics in the 1940's, standard modern techniques such as dilation and curettage were not nearly so safe as they are today. Thus, it has been argued that a State's real concern in enacting a criminal abortion law was to protect the pregnant woman, that is, to restrain her from submitting to a procedure that placed her life in serious jeopardy.

Modern medical techniques have altered this situation. . . .

The third reason is the State's interest—some phrase it in terms of duty—in protecting prenatal life. Some of the argument for this justification rests on the theory that a new human life is present from the moment of conception. The State's interest and general obligation to protect life then extends, it is argued, to prenatal life. Only when the life of the pregnant mother herself is at stake, balanced against the life she carries within her, should the interest of the embryo or fetus not prevail. Logically, of course, a legitimate state interest in this area need not stand or fall on acceptance of the belief that life begins at conception or at some other point prior to live birth. In assessing the State's interest, recognition may be given to the less rigid claim that as long as at least *potential* life is involved, the State may assert interests beyond the protection of the pregnant woman alone. . . .

It is with these interests, and the weight attached to them, that this case is concerned.

VIII

The constitution does not explicitly mention any right of privacy. In a line of decisions, however, going back perhaps as far as *Union Pacific R. Co. v. Botsford,* 141 U.S. 250, 251, 11 S.Ct. 1000, 1001, the Court has recognized that a right of personal privacy, or a guarantee of certain areas or zones of privacy, does exist, under the Constitution. . . .

This right of privacy, whether it be founded in the Fourteenth Amendment's concept of personal liberty and restrictions upon state action, as we feel it is, or, as the District Court determined, in the Ninth Amendment's reservation of rights of people, is broad enough to encompass a woman's decision whether or not to terminate her pregnancy. . . . The Court's decisions recognizing a right of privacy also acknowledge that some state regulation in areas protected by that right is appropriate. As noted above, a State may properly assert important interests in safeguarding health, in maintaining medical standards, and in protecting *potential* life. At some point in pregnancy, these respective interests become sufficiently compelling to sustain regulation of the factors that govern the abortion decision. The privacy right involved, therefore, cannot be said to be absolute. In fact, it is not clear to us that the claim asserted by some *amici* that one has an unlimited right to do with one's body as one pleases bears a close relationship to the right of privacy previously articulated in the Court's decision. The Court has refused to recognize an unlimited right of this kind in the past. . . .

We, therefore, conclude that the right to personal privacy includes the abortion decision, but that this right is not unqualified and must be considered against important state interests in regulation. . . .

XI

. . . To summarize and to repeat

1. A state criminal abortion statute of the current Texas type, that excepts from criminality only a *life*-saving procedure on behalf of the mother, without regard to pregnancy stage and without recognition of the other interests involved, is violative of the Due Process Clause of the Fourteenth Amendment.

(a) For the stage prior to approximately the end of the first trimester, the abortion decision and its effectuation must be left to the medical judgment of the pregnant woman's attending physician.

(b) For the stage subsequent to approximately the end of the first trimester, the State, in promoting its interest in the health of the mother, may, if it chooses, regulate the abortion procedure in ways that are reasonably related to maternal health.

(c) For the stage subsequent to viability, the State in promoting its interest in the potentiality of human life may, if it chooses, regulate, and even proscribe, abortion except where it is necessary, in appropriate medical judgment, for the preservation of the life, or health of the mother. . . .

XII

Our conclusion that Art. 1196 is unconstitutional means, of course, that the Texas abortion statutes, as a unit, must fall.

. . . In all other respects, the judgment of the District Court is affirmed. Costs are allowed to the appellee.

It is so ordered. Affirmed in part and reversed in part.

Questions for Review and Reflection

1. What were the conditions under which Jane Roe sought an abortion?
2. What were the three reasons offered for making abortion a criminal offense?
3. What new right was established as a result of this decision?
4. What are the rights of the unborn, according to this decision?

Reading 10

United States Congress, 1975

The Indian Self-Determination and Assistance Act

Spurred by President Richard Nixon's leadership and advocacy, the federal government undertook major reforms in its relationship with Native Americans. Congress concluded that "the prolonged Federal domination of Indian service programs has served to retard rather than enhance the progress of Indian people." In 1975, members enacted the legislation excerpted here to ensure "maximum Indian participation" in federal services. While it led to increased Indian sovereignty, some Native Americans criticized the law as a perpetuation of the "domestic dependent" status for Indians, on the basis that the federal government retained its "unique and continuing relationship with and responsibility toward the Indian people." The statute resulted in greater freedom from government control for the tribes, while it perpetuated the federal government's role in Native American affairs.

Pub.L. 93–638, Jan. 4, 1975.

§ 450. Congressional statement of findings

(a) The Congress, after careful review of the Federal government's historical and special legal relationship with, and resulting responsibilities to, American Indian people, finds that—

(1) the prolonged Federal domination of Indian service programs has served to retard rather than enhance the progress of Indian people and their communities by depriving Indians of the full opportunity to develop leadership skills crucial to the realization of self-government, and has denied to the Indian people an effective voice in the planning and implementation of programs for the benefit of Indians which are responsive to the true needs of Indian communities; and

(2) the Indian people will never surrender their desire to control their relationships both among themselves and with non-Indian governments, organizations, and persons.

(b) The Congress further finds that—

(1) true self-determination in any society of people is dependent upon an educational process which will insure the development of qualified people to fulfill meaningful leadership roles;

(2) the Federal responsibility for and assistance to education of Indian children has not effected the desired level of educational achievement or created the diverse opportunities and personal satisfaction which education can and should provide; and

(3) parental and community control of the educational process is of crucial importance to the Indian people.

§ 450a. Congressional declaration of policy

(a) The Congress hereby recognizes the obligation of the United States to respond to the strong expression of the Indian people for self-determination by assuring maximum Indian participation in the direction of educational as well as other Federal services to Indian communities so as to render such services more responsive to the needs and desires of those communities.

(b) The Congress declares its commitment to the maintenance of the Federal Government's unique and continuing relationship with and responsibility to the Indian people through the establishment of a meaningful Indian self-determination policy which will permit an orderly transition from Federal domination of programs for and services to Indians to effective and meaningful participation by the Indian people in the planning, conduct, and administration of those programs and services.

(c) The Congress declares that a major national goal of the United States is to provide the quantity and quality of educational services and opportunities which will permit Indian children to compete and excel in the life areas of their choice, and to achieve the measure of self-determination essential to their social and economic well-being. . . .

§ 450b. Definitions

For the purposes of this Act, the term—

(a) "Indian" means a person who is a member of an Indian tribe;

(b) "Indian tribe" means any Indian tribe, band, nation, or other organized group or community, including any Alaska Native village or regional or village corporation as defined in or established pursuant to the Alaska Native Claims Settlement Act [43 U.S.C.A. § 1601 et seq.] which is recognized as eligible for the special programs and services provided by the United States to Indians because of their status as Indians;

(c) "Tribal organization" means the recognized governing body of any Indian tribe; any legally established organization of Indians which is controlled, sanctioned, or chartered by such governing body or which is democratically elected by the adult members of the Indian community to be served by such organization and which includes the maximum participation of Indians in all phases of its activities: *Provided,* That in any case where a contract is let or grant made to an organization to perform services benefitting more than one Indian tribe, the approval of each such Indian tribe shall be a prerequisite to the letting or making of such contract or grant;

(d) "Secretary", unless otherwise designated, means the Secretary of the Interior;

(f) "State education agency" means the State board of education or other agency or officer primarily responsible for supervision by the State of public elementary and secondary schools, or, if there is no such officer or agency, an officer or agency designated by the Governor or by State law.

Questions for Review and Reflection

According to the Indian Self-Determination Act:

1. How does Congress define the relationship between the federal government and the Indians?
2. How is self-determination accomplished?
3. What does the federal government owe the Indian people?
4. What is the definition of an Indian?
5. What is the definition of a tribal organization?

Reading 11

State of California, 1975

The California Agricultural Labor Relations Act

The Chicano farm workers of California eventually won the right to organize and bargain, to have secret ballot elections, and to be free from "restraint" or "coercion." After many years of strikes and boycotts, agribusiness and fieldworkers declared a truce through the California Agricultural Labor Relations Act of 1975, which attempted to address many of the issues raised by the United Farm Workers (UFW) in earlier decades. The law also created the Agricultural Labor Relations Board, whose functions are to investigate unfair labor practices, to mediate disputes, and to supervise elections.

Implementation of the law under Governor Jerry Brown seemed to favor the interests of farm workers. However, new appointments to the board by subsequent governors have led to UFW charges that the law and its board are now pro-farmer. Although the Chicano workers' struggle is far from over, this state legislation remains a potentially useful tool. It also set a precedent for legislation elsewhere in the nation, paving the way for the 1983 federal Migrant and Seasonal Agricultural Workers Act, which mandates health and safety standards, timely payment of wages, posting of hours and wages, and much more.

§ 1140.2. State policy

It is hereby stated to be the policy of the State of California to encourage and protect the right of agricultural employees to full freedom of association, self-organization, and designation of representatives of their own choosing, to negotiate the terms and conditions of their employment, and to be free from the interference, restraint, or coercion of employers of labor, or their agents, in the designation of such representatives or in self-organization or in other concerted activities for the purpose of collective bargaining or other mutual aid or protection. For this purpose this part is adopted to provide for collective-bargaining rights for agricultural employees.

§ 1141. Creation; membership; appointment; tenure; vacancies; removal

(a) There is hereby created in state government the Agricultural Labor Relations Board, which shall consist of five members.

(b) The members of the board shall be appointed by the Governor with the advice and consent of the Senate. The term of office of the members shall be five years, and the terms shall be staggered at one-year intervals. Upon the initial appointment, one member shall be appointed for a term ending January 1, 1977, one member shall be appointed for a term ending January 1, 1978, one member shall be appointed for a term ending January 1, 1979, one member shall be appointed for a term ending January 1, 1980, and one member shall be appointed for a term ending January 1, 1981. Any individual appointed to fill a vacancy of any member shall be appointed only for the unexpired term of the member to whose term he is succeeding. The Governor shall designate one member to serve as chairperson of the board. Any member of the board may be removed by the Governor, upon notice and hearing, for neglect of duty or malfeasance in office, but for no other cause. . . .

§ 1142. Principal office; regional offices; delegation of powers; review by board

(a) The principal office of the board shall be in Sacramento, but it may meet and exercise any or all of its power at any other place in California.

(b) Besides the principal office in Sacramento, as provided in subdivision (a), the board may establish offices in such other cities as it shall deem necessary. The board may delegate to the personnel of these offices such powers as it deems appropriate to determine the unit appropriate for the purpose of collective bargaining, to investigate and provide for hearings, to determine whether a question of representation exists, to direct an election by a secret ballot pursuant to the provisions of Chapter 5 (commencing with Section 1156), and to certify the results of such election, and to investigate, conduct hearings and make determinations relating to unfair labor practices. The board may review any action taken pursuant to the authority delegated under this section upon a request for a review of such action filed with the board by an interested party. Any such review made by the board shall not, unless specifically ordered by the board, operate as a stay of any action taken. The entire record considered by the board in considering or acting upon any such request or review shall be made available to all parties prior to such consideration or action, and the board's findings and action thereon shall be published as a decision of the board.

Questions for Review and Reflection

According to the Agricultural Labor Relations Act:
1. What rights do agricultural employees enjoy?
2. What is the role of the Agricultural Labor Relations Board?
3. Who should serve on the board?
4. How should elections take place?

8

The New Politics:
Redefining Democracy

The unity that existed among groups during the era of the civil rights movement had given way to a "me decade" by the 1980s, a period when gains in civil rights and opportunities for minorities made in prior decades sustained some backlash.

Ronald Reagan's conservative agenda won public favor, and he was inaugurated as president in 1981. He had campaigned on a platform that touted the theory of "supply side economics." It replaced Keynesian theory, relied on a giant tax cut to reinvigorate investment, and required a decrease in government spending. The conservative backlash was evident in a reduction in discretionary programs, such as food stamps, welfare benefits, and subsidized programs for education and housing. This reversal of public policy was supported by a political bloc of traditionalists and neo-conservatives, coupled with the "New Right," a coalition of evangelical Christian organizations. The religious right also spoke out against the erosion of traditional family values they perceived to have occurred. They fought the Equal Rights Amendment, as well as the right to abortion, and challenged the "new feminism" as an offense against the family.

Women were divided among themselves on women's rights versus women's role in society. The backlash came from those who feared that any new legal status of equality could deprive a woman of respect for her roles as wife and mother. This faction helped defeat the Equal Rights Amendment, believing that it could force women into the military and out of such gender-separate facilities as toilets or dormitories. The ERA failed, three votes short of ratification. Women also found themselves on opposite sides of the abortion issue. The controversial *Roe v. Wade* decision in 1973 that legalized abortion created considerable backlash. Intense lobbying efforts occurred across the country to deny public funding for abortion and to restrain access to the procedure through state government regulation. Some state legislatures passed laws that required a waiting period or counseling. Other states raised issues of parental notification or spousal consent. The makeup of the Supreme Court had changed by the time some of these state laws were challenged. President Reagan had named William Rehnquist to the position of Chief Justice and had appointed Sandra Day O'Connor, Antonin Scalia, and Anthony Kennedy to the bench. While the Court continued to uphold the right to abortion, the justices also upheld state laws that restricted access, so long as the statutes did not place an "undue burden" on the mother.

Some women complained that the conservative backlash was clearly coming from a male-dominated government that failed to respond to the growing "feminization of poverty" experienced by women in the 1960s and 1970s. The divorce rate had soared during this era, with marriages having little more than a 50 percent chance for success. Women found themselves as single-parent heads of households, unable to keep their homes or provide for their children. When they looked to government for help, they received instead a reduction of social services. According to Congresswoman Bella Abzug, there was a "gender gap" between men and women over public policy. The only solution, she offered, was to get more women into the political process through voting and holding public office.

The backlash also affected affirmative action programs that had begun in the 1960s. Whites charged that hiring and admissions policies had become numbers games that required employers to hire and schools to admit a "quota" of minorities and women in order to comply with the law. This "preferential treatment," it was charged, led to "reverse discrimination" and denied equal opportunities to white men. The backlash manifested itself in a series of challenges in the courts and in Congress on the meaning of a "color blind" Constitution.

Minority communities themselves experienced backlash, becoming divided over the effectiveness of affirmative action. Some people believed that they were stigmatized by affirmative action programs—left with little self-esteem and the conviction that they could only compete and win through some form of preferential treatment. Others insisted that race-based hiring, promotion, and admissions policies were the only way to end blatant, long-standing, and pervasive discrimination.

So much backlash brought with it anger, frustration, and impatience on the part of all groups with government's inability to deal with the meaning and intent of equality in America. Some defended assimilation as the quickest path to equal opportunity. Others rejected the "melting pot," demanding cultural recognition and independence rather than absorption. Native Americans had always subscribed to such a notion and continued to fight for autonomy. Several other minority groups lobbied for a different form of autonomy; they wanted multicultural education and ethnic studies that taught their history and traditions, asserting that legitimacy for all cultures can be achieved only when each culture is recognized and respected for its unique contributions to society.

Still others saw such demands as leading to culture wars. The Reverend Jesse Jackson, a leading spokesperson from the minority community, spoke on behalf of finding the "common ground." Equality, he insisted, could be achieved only on the basis of a core set of values and principles to which all groups, regardless of race, ethnicity, or gender, could subscribe.

Immigration, both legal and illegal, rose significantly between 1960 and 1990. Diversity was fundamentally changing the face of American society, forcing a reexamination of American politics and a reappraisal of democracy. Learning to live with America's diversity had become a major issue.

Reading 1

Phyllis Schlafly, 1977

The Power of the Positive Woman

Following the publication of *The Feminine Mystique* in the 1960s, a new women's movement got under way. The National Organization for Women was founded, called for an equal rights amendment to the Constitution, and wrote a NOW bill of rights that included women's rights to maternity leave from work, social security benefits, tax deductions for child care expenses, equal job training, and other equal opportunities.

Journalist, attorney, and author Phyllis Schlafly became a spokesperson for traditional family values. Her book, the source of this reading, criticized the positions of NOW and the women's "liberation" movement.

Schlafly objected to identical treatment for men and women, rejected the "gender-free" approach to public policy, and accepted some sex-based differences. Equal opportunity should be offered to each individual rather than to groups, she proposed.

Equal opportunity included the right to employment and education without regard to sex, she maintained, but it also included the right of employers to give job preference to a wage

earner who was supporting dependents. Women's rights included the right of a woman to stay home, be wife and mother,
and protect the institution of the family.

Schlafly can be seen as speaking for women who defeated
the ERA because they did not support the level of equality it
would have afforded them.

The Five Principles

When the women's liberationists enter the political arena to promote legislation and litigation in pursuit of their goals, their specific demands are based
on five principles.

(1) They demand that a "gender-free" rule be applied to every federal
and state law, bureaucratic regulation, educational institution, and expenditure
of public funds. Based on their dogma that there is no real difference between
men and women (except in sex organs), they demand that males and females
have identical treatment always. Thus, if fathers are not expected to stay home
and care for their infant children, then neither should mothers be expected
to do so; and, therefore, it becomes the duty of the government to provide
kiddy-care centers to relieve mothers of that unfair and unequal burden.

The women's lib dogma demands that the courts treat sex as a "suspect"
classification—just as race is now treated—so that no difference of treatment
or separation between the sexes will ever be permitted, no matter how
reasonable or how much it is desired by reasonable people. . . .

The Positive Woman rejects the "gender-free" approach. She knows that
there are many differences between male and female and that we are entitled
to have our laws, regulations, schools, and courts reflect these differences and
allow for reasonable differences in treatment and separations of activities that
reasonable men and women want.

The Positive Woman also rejects the argument that sex discrimination
should be treated the same as race discrimination. There is vastly more
difference between a man and a woman than there is between a black and
a white, and it is nonsense to adopt a legal and bureaucratic attitude that
pretends that those differences do not exist. Even the United States Supreme
Court has, in recent and relevant cases, upheld "reasonable" sex-based
differences of treatment by legislatures and by the military.

(2) The women's lib legislative goals seek an irrational mandate of
"equality" at the expense of justice. The fact is that equality cannot always
be equated with justice, and may sometimes even be highly unjustified if we
had absolutely equal treatment in regard to taxes, then everyone would pay
the same income tax, or perhaps the same rate of income tax, regardless of
the size of the income.

If we had absolutely equal treatment in regard to federal spending programs, we would have to eliminate welfare, low-income housing benefits, food stamps, government scholarships, and many other programs designed to benefit low-income citizens. If we had absolutely equal treatment in regard to age, then seventeen-year-olds, or even ten-year-olds, would be permitted to vote, and we would have to eliminate Social Security unless all persons received the same benefits that only those over sixty-two receive now.

Our legislatures, our administrative departments, and our courts have always had and still retain the discretion to make reasonable differences in treatment based on age, income, or economic situation. The Positive Woman believes that it makes no sense to deprive us of the ability to make reasonable distinctions based on sex that reasonable men and women want.

(3) The women's liberation movement demands that women be given the benefit of "reverse discrimination." The Positive Woman recognizes that this is mutually exclusive with the principle of equal opportunity for all. Reverse discrimination is based on the theory that "group rights" take precedence over individual rights, and that "reverse discrimination" (variously called "preferential treatment," "remedial action," or "affirmative action") should be imposed in order to compensate some women today for alleged past discriminations against other women. The word "quotas" is usually avoided, but it amounts to the same thing.

The fallacy of reverse discrimination has been aptly exposed by Professor Sidney Hook. No one would argue, he wrote, that because many years ago blacks and women were denied the right to vote, we should now compensate by giving them an extra vote or two, or by barring white men from voting at all.

The Positive Woman supports equal opportunity for individuals of both sexes, as well as of all faiths and races. She rejects the theories of reverse discrimination and "group rights." It does no good for the woman who may have been discriminated against twenty-five years ago to know that an unqualified woman today receives preferential treatment at the expense of a qualified man. Only the vindictive radical would support such a policy of revenge.

(4) The women's liberation movement is based on the unproven theory that uniformity should replace diversity—or, in simpler language, the federalization of all remaining aspects of our life. The militant women demand that *all* educational institutions conform to federally determined rules about sex discrimination.

There is absolutely no evidence that HEW bureaucrats can do a better or fairer job of regulating our schools and colleges than local officials. Nor is there any evidence that individuals, or women, or society as a whole, would be better off under a uniform system enforced by the full power of the federal government than they would be under a free and competitive system, under local control, using diverse methods and regulations. It is hard to see why anyone would want to put more power into the hands of federal bureaucrats who cannot cope with the problems they already have.

The militant women demand that HEW regulations enforce a strict gender-free uniformity on all schools and colleges. Everything from sports to glee clubs must be coed, regardless of local customs or wishes. The militants deplore the differences from state to state in the laws governing marriage and divorce. Yet does anyone think our nation would be improved if we were made subject to a national divorce law devised by HEW?

The Positive Woman rejects the theory that Washington, D.C., is the fountainhead of all wisdom and professional skill. She supports the principle of leaving all possible control and discretion in the hands of local school and college officials and their elected boards.

(5) The women's liberation movement pushes its proposals on the premise that everything must be neutral as between morality and immorality, and as between the institution of the family and alternate lifestyles: for example, that homosexuals and lesbians should have just as much right to teach in the schools and to adopt children as anyone else; and that illegitimate babies and abortions by married or single mothers should be accepted as normal behavior for teachers—and funded by public money. . . .

The Positive Woman believes that our educational institutions have not only the right, but the obligation, to set minimum standards of moral conduct at the local level. She believes that schools and colleges have no right to use our public money to promote conduct that is offensive to the religious and moral values of parents and taxpayers. . . .

Here is a starting checklist of goals that can be restored to America if Positive Women will apply their dedicated efforts:

(1) The right of a woman to be a full-time wife and mother and to have this right recognized by laws that obligate her husband to provide the primary financial support and a home for her and their children.

(2) The responsibility of parents (not the government) for the care of preschool children.

(3) The right of parents to insist that the schools:

    a. permit voluntary prayer,

    b. teach the "fourth R," right and wrong, according to the precepts of Holy Scriptures,

    c. use textbooks that do not offend the religious and moral values of the parents,

    d. use textbooks that honor the family, monogamous marriage, woman's role as wife and mother, and man's role as provider and protector,

    e. teach such basic educational skills as reading and arithmetic before time and money are spent on frills,

    f. permit children to attend school in their own neighborhood, and

    g. separate the sexes for gym classes, athletic practice and competition, and academic and vocational classes, if so desired.

(4) The right of employers to give job preference (where qualifications are equal) to a wage earner supporting dependents.

(5) The right of a woman engaged in physical-labor employment to be protected by laws and regulations that respect the physical differences and different family obligations of men and women.

(6) The right to equal opportunity in employment and education for all persons regardless of race, creed, sex, or national origin.

(7) The right to have local governments prevent the display of printed or pictorial materials that degrade women in a pornographic, perverted, or sadistic manner.

(8) The right to defend the institution of the family by according certain rights to husbands and wives that are not given to those choosing immoral lifestyles.

(9) The right to life of all innocent persons from conception to natural death.

(10) The right of citizens to live in a community where state and local government and judges maintain law and order by a system of justice under due process and punishment that is swift and certain.

(11) The right of society to protect itself by designating different roles for men and women in the armed forces and police and fire departments, where necessary.

(12) The right of citizens to have the federal government adequately provide for the common defense against aggression by any other nation.

Questions for Review and Reflection

1. Why do you think Schlafly claims that the real goal of the women's movement is an "irrational mandate of 'equality' "?
2. Why does Schlafly argue that racial discrimination is nothing like gender discrimination? Do you agree? Why?
3. Describe Schlafly's "Positive Woman." Do you find Schlafly's arguments reasonable? Somewhat reasonable? Absurd? Why?
4. Schlafly argues that the women's liberation movement is based on the "unproven" theory that "uniformity should replace diversity." Is this an accurate assessment of the movement, in your opinion? How might Gloria Steinem respond to Schlafly?
5. On which points in Schlafly's "checklist of goals" for the Positive Woman do you think feminists would agree? On which might they disagree? Are there more areas of agreement or disagreement between these two positions?

Reading 2

Gloria Steinem, 1983

Outrageous Acts and Everyday Rebellions

Gloria Steinem is a recognized spokesperson on behalf of women's issues. She is cofounder of *Ms.* magazine and used her publication as a vehicle to promote the agenda of full economic, political, and social equality for women. She has also written several widely read books on these topics.

When the ERA Amendment failed in 1982, Steinem wrote a book, from which this reading is taken, to explain why and to offer a plan of action to defy such intransigence toward equal rights.

Steinem rejected the usual tactics of a full-scale assault. Instead, she recommended a protracted battle of small steps and individual acts rather than a grand revolution. She acknowledged that changing the status quo requires a unity of purpose among both men and women who believe in the vision of a more democratic and equal society.

How many of us have had our dreams set free but still can't budge everyday realities? How many of us went courageously back to school, for instance, only to find ourselves among the female unemployed who grow larger in number and better educated every year? Or with one full-time job outside the home and one in it? How many of us are trying to help children become free, individual people, but face a whole culture devoted to mass-producing them as roles? How many of us try to keep love and mutual support flowing between equals, only to find it damned up by some imbalance of self-confidence or power?

This seems to be where we are, after the first full decade of the second wave of feminism. Raised hopes, a hunger for change, and years of hard work are running head-on into a frustrating realization that each battle must be fought over and over again at different depths. One inevitable result of winning a majority change in consciousness is a backlash from those forces whose power depended on the old one.

Perhaps that's the first Survival Lesson we need to remember if we are to keep going: *serious opposition is a measure of success.* Women have been trained to measure our effectiveness in love and approval, not conflict or resistance. That makes it tough to be personally independent or to advocate change. But the truth is that there was no major organized backlash against us when we were still paying for women's conferences out of our own pockets and living-room benefits. That happened only after we were strong enough to get a few of our own tax dollars back. Traditional churches and fundamentalist leaders didn't organize against feminists politically until the contagion of justice caused nuns to question the authority of priests, Mormon women to chafe at the sex-race restrictions by which that well-to-do establishment is run, Jewish and Protestant women to become rabbis and ministers, and the very personification of God the Father to be questioned. . . .

It also takes a while for a critical mass of any movement as enormous as this wave of feminism to learn that the paths to change prescribed in our civics texts are just not enough. Working inside political parties, explaining problems to leaders, electing or diselecting, gaining the support of the majority—all these make sense. Occasionally they even work. But our textbooks didn't prepare us for the fact that some power considerations have nothing to do with majorities (for instance, which special interests make the biggest political contributions, who appoints committee chairs, who can quash some legislator's ethics rap, and which legislators just are not going to vote for equality because "God didn't intend women to be equal"); or that majority support can exist for years on some issue (like gun control, full employment, or getting out of Vietnam) without giving it the power to win. . . .

In fact, however, the most recognizable characteristic of feminists and feminist acts is their effort to be inclusive. The radical vision of feminism depends on its possibility of transforming the status of all women, not just a correct few. . . .

Ideas for actions, conflict resolution, and a reminder of similar hostility in the past—all these are practical reasons for Survival Lesson number three: *we need to know the history of our sisters, both for inspiration and for accumulating a full arsenal of ideas, and adopt what translates into the present.* Very few tactics are either completely new, or completely out-of-date. Even after we as individuals have exhausted our ability to make them fresh, other feminists can repeat, enlarge, and change them.

We are all organizers, and no organizer should ever end a meeting or a book or an article without ideas for practical action. After all, a movement depends on people moving. What *are* we going to do differently when we get up tomorrow?

In fact, the great strength of feminism—like that of the black movement here, the Gandhian movement in India, and all the organic struggles for self-rule and simple justice—has always been encouragement for each of us to act, without waiting and theorizing about some future takeover at the top.

It's no accident that, when some small group does accomplish a momentous top-down revolution, the change seems to benefit only those who made it. Even with the best intentions of giving "power to the people," the revolution is betrayed.

Power can be taken, but not given. The process of the taking is empowerment in itself.

So we ask ourselves: What might a spectrum of diverse, mutually supportive tactics really look like for us as individuals, for family and community groups, for men who care about equality, for children, and for political movements as a whole? Some actions will always be unique to particular situations and thus unforeseeable. Others will be suited to times of great energy in our lives, and still others will make sense for those who are burnt out and need to know that a time of contemplation and assessment is okay. But here are some that may inspire action, if only to say, "No, that's not right. But this is what I choose to do instead."

As Individuals

In the early 1970s when I was traveling and lecturing with feminist lawyer and black activist Florence Kennedy, one of her many epigrams went like this: "Unity in a movement situation is overrated. If you were the Establishment, which would you rather see coming in the door, five hundred mice or one lion?"

Mindful of her teaching, I now often end lectures with an organizer's zeal. If each person in the room promises that in the twenty-four hours beginning the very next day she or he will do at least *one outrageous thing* in the cause of simple justice, then I promise I will, too. It doesn't matter whether the act is as small as saying, "Pick it up yourself" (a major step for those of us who have been our family's servants) or as large as calling a strike. The point is that, if each of us does as promised, we can be pretty sure of two results. First, the world one day later won't be quite the same. Second, we will have such a good time that we will never again get up in the morning saying, *"Will* I do anything outrageous?" but only *"What* outrageous act will I do today?"

Here are some samples I've recorded from the outrageous acts of real life.

- Announced a permanent refusal to contribute more money to a church or synagogue until women too can become priests, ministers, and rabbis.
- Asked for a long-deserved raise, or, in the case of men and/or white folks, refused an undeserved one that is being given over the heads of others because of their race or sex.

- Written a well-reasoned critique of a sexist or racist textbook and passed it out on campus.
- Challenged some bit of woman-hating humor or imagery with the seriousness more often reserved for slurs based on religion or race.
- Shared with colleagues the knowledge of each other's salaries so that unfairnesses can be calculated. (It's interesting that employers try to keep us from telling the one fact we know.)
- Cared for a child or children so that an overworked mother could have a day that is her own. (This is especially revolutionary when done by a man.)
- Returned to a birth name or, in the case of a man, gave his children both parents' names.
- Left home for a week so that the father of your young child could learn to be a parent. (As one woman later reported calmly, "When I came home, my husband and the baby had bonded, just the way women and babies do.")
- Petitioned for a Women's Studies section in a local library or bookstore.
- Checked a corporate employer's giving programs, see if they are really inclusive by benefiting women with at least half of their dollars, and made suggestions if not.

Questions for Review and Reflection

1. According to Gloria Steinem, what is the measure of success for a "movement"?
2. What does Steinem feel caused the backlash against the women's movement?
3. What does she state is the most recognizable characteristic of feminists?
4. What is the importance of history for Steinem?
5. Share some other acts that could contribute to the women's movement.
6. How might Steinem respond to Phyllis Schlafly?

Reading 3

Thurgood Marshall, 1987

Speech on the Bicentennial of the Constitution

Justice Thurgood Marshall (1908–1993) was the first black judge ever to be appointed to the Supreme Court. Earlier in his career, Marshall had argued the landmark case of *Brown v. Board of Education* before the Supreme Court; he won the decision that stated that separate is inherently unequal, which forced the integration of public schools.

A champion of minority rights, Justice Marshall cautioned Americans to be aware of the "evolving nature of the Constitution." He reminded people in a speech during the bicentennial of the Constitution that when the framers wrote, "We the People," that "they did not have in mind the majority of America's citizens."

He challenged his audience to see the "defects" of the Constitution, which were only overcome through the persistent courage of many different groups. It was their struggle that brought about the amendments incorporating and extending many democratic principles, which have made the Constitution of the United States as relevant to our lives today as it was to those of eighteenth-century Americans.

1987 marks the 200th anniversary of the United States Constitution. A Commission has been established to coordinate the celebration. The official meetings, essay contests, and festivities have begun.

The planned commemoration will span three years, and I am told 1987 is "dedicated to the memory of the Founders and the document they drafted in Philadelphia." We are to "recall the achievements of our Founders and the knowledge and experience that inspired them, the nature of the government they established, its origins, its character, and its ends, and the rights and privileges of citizenship, as well as its attendant responsibilities."

Like many anniversary celebrations, the plan for 1987 takes particular events and holds them up as the source of all the very best that has followed.

Patriotic feelings will surely swell, prompting proud proclamations of the wisdom, foresight, and sense of justice shared by the Framers and reflected in a written document now yellowed with age. This is unfortunate—not the patriotism itself, but the tendency for the celebration to oversimplify, and overlook the many other events that have been instrumental to our achievements as a nation. The focus of this celebration invites a complacent belief that the vision of those who debated and compromised in Philadelphia yielded the "more perfect Union" it is said we now enjoy.

I cannot accept this invitation, for I do not believe that the meaning of the Constitution was forever "fixed" at the Philadelphia Convention. Nor do I find the wisdom, foresight, and sense of justice exhibited by the Framers particularly profound. To the contrary, the government they devised was defective from the start, requiring several amendments, a civil war, a momentous social transformation to attain the system of constitutional government, and its respect for the individual freedoms and human rights, we hold as fundamental today. When contemporary Americans cite "The Constitution," they invoke a concept that is vastly different from what the Framers barely began to construct two centuries ago.

For a sense of the evolving nature of the Constitution we need look no further than the first three words of the document's preamble: "We the People." When the founding Fathers used this phrase in 1787, they did not have in mind the majority of America's citizens. "We the People" included, in the words of the Framers, "the whole Number of free Persons." On a matter so basic as the right to vote, for example, Negro slaves were excluded, although they were counted for representational purposes—at three-fifths each. Women did not gain the right to vote for over a hundred and thirty years.

These omissions were intentional. The record of the Framers' debates on the slave question is especially clear: the Southern States acceded to the demands of the New England States for giving Congress broad power to regulate commerce, in exchange for the right to continue the slave trade. The economic interests of the regions coalesced: New Englanders engaged in the "carrying trade" would profit from transporting slaves from Africa as well as goods produced in America by slave labor. The perpetuation of slavery ensured the primary source of wealth in the Southern States.

Despite this clear understanding of the role slavery would play in the new republic, use of the words "slaves" and "slavery" was carefully avoided in the original document. Political representation in the lower House of Congress was to be based on the population of "free Persons" in each State, plus three-fifths of all "other Persons." Moral principles against slavery, for those who had them, were compromised, with no explanation of the conflicting principles for which the American Revolutionary War had ostensibly been fought: the self-evident truths "that all men are created equal, that they are endowed by their Creator with certain unalienable Rights, that among these are Life, Liberty and the pursuit of Happiness."

It was not the first such compromise. Even these ringing phrases from the Declaration of Independence are filled with irony, for an early draft of what became that Declaration assailed the King of England for suppressing legislative attempts to end the slave trade and for encouraging slave rebellions. The final draft adopted in 1776 did not contain this criticism. And so again at the Constitutional Convention eloquent objections to the institution of slavery went unheeded, and its opponents eventually consented to a document which laid a foundation for the tragic events that were to follow. . . .

No doubt it will be said, when the unpleasant truth of the history of slavery in America is mentioned during this bicentennial year, that the Constitution was a product of its times, and embodied a compromise which, under other circumstances, would not have been made. But the effects of the Framers' compromise have remained for generations. They arose from the contradiction between guaranteeing liberty and justice to all, and denying both to Negroes. . . .

While the Union survived the Civil War, the Constitution did not. In its place arose a new, more promising basis for justice and equality, the 14th Amendment, ensuring protection of the life, liberty, and property of *all* persons against deprivations without due process, and guaranteeing equal protection of the laws. And yet almost another century would pass before any significant recognition was obtained of the rights of black Americans to share equally even in such basic opportunities as education, housing, and employment, and to have their votes counted, and counted equally. In the meantime, blacks joined America's military to fight its wars and invested untold hours working in its factories and on its farms, contributing to the development of this country's magnificent wealth and waiting to share in its prosperity.

What is striking is the role legal principles have played throughout America's history in determining the condition of Negroes. They were enslaved by law, emancipated by law, disenfranchised and segregated by law; and finally, they have begun to win equality by law. Along the way, new constitutional principles have emerged to meet the challenges of a changing society. The progress has been dramatic, and it will continue.

The men who gathered in Philadelphia in 1787 could not have envisioned these changes. They could not have imagined, nor would they have accepted, that the document they were drafting would one day be construed by a Supreme Court to which had been appointed a woman and the descendent of an African slave. "We the People" no longer enslave, but the credit does not belong to the Framers. It belongs to those who refused to acquiesce in outdated notions of "liberty," "justice," and "equality," and who strived to better them.

And so we must be careful, when focusing on the events which took place in Philadelphia two centuries ago, that we not overlook the momentous events which followed, and thereby lose our proper sense of perspective. Otherwise, the odds are that for many Americans the bicentennial celebration will be little more than a blind pilgrimage to the shrine of the original document now stored in a vault in the National Archives. If we seek, instead, a sensitive understanding of the Constitution's inherent defects, and its promising evolution through 200 years of history, the celebration of the "Miracle at Philadelphia" will, in my view, be a far more meaningful and humbling experience. We will see that the true miracle was not the birth of the Constitution, but its life, a life nurtured through two turbulent centuries of our own making, and a life embodying much good fortune that was not.

Thus, in this bicentennial year, we may not all participate in the festivities with flag-waving fervor. Some may more quietly commemorate the suffering, struggle, and sacrifice that has triumphed over much of what was wrong with the original document, and observe the anniversary with hopes not realized and promises not fulfilled. I plan to celebrate the bicentennial of the Constitution as a living document, including the Bill of Rights and the other amendments protecting individual freedoms and human rights.

Questions for Review and Reflection

1. Why does Marshall believe it is "unfortunate" that the planned celebration for the birth of the U.S. Constitution is concentrating exclusively on positive elements?
2. What is this compromise in Philadelphia to which Marshall speaks?
3. Why does Marshall refuse to accept the invitation to celebrate the Constitution?
4. What were some of the faults in the Founders' document that required adjustment over the years?
5. Who did the Founding Fathers include in "We the People"?
6. What was exchanged for the right to continue with the slave trade?
7. What two words were carefully avoided in the Constitution? What words were used in their place?
8. What were the lasting effects of the Framers' compromise?
9. How does Marshall plan to celebrate the bicentennial of the Constitution? How is the Constitution a living document?

Reading 4

Henry Cisneros, 1988

"American Dynamism and the New World Culture"

Henry Cisneros, newly appointed Director of Housing and Urban Development in the Clinton administration, is a leading spokesperson on Latino concerns. At the time of this article, he was the mayor of San Antonio, Texas, and a leading Latino political officeholder in the southwest.

Cisneros predicted that prosperity and success would come to America by the year 2000 because of its pluralistic system that encourages many groups of people to come to the country with their energy and vitality. Eager to contribute and to become a part of American society, these individuals who create America's "ethnic heterogeneity" are a source of strength and richness for American society, said Cisneros. He stressed that it is necessary to have "leadership that believes in inclusiveness and consensus."

America is not declining. It is changing.

In the year 2000, just 12 years from now, 46% of the population of California will be Hispanic, Asian and black. In San Francisco County that figure will be 65%, mostly Asian. In Los Angeles, "minorities," mostly Hispanic, will account for 60% of the population. Even in traditional white, conservative bastions like Orange County, 40% of the population will be Hispanic and Asian. In San Diego, 40% of the population will be non-white, mostly Hispanic.

The most stunning statistic of all: 92% of Californians will live in counties where the "minority" population is more than 30%—a dimension that truly changes the complexion of a community, politically and culturally.

Similar demographic changes are taking place in most central cities and metropolitan areas across this nation: Baltimore, Philadelphia, Chicago, Miami, Atlanta, San Antonio, Denver, Dallas, Houston, New York. These changes will, in time, alter not only the state of California as a whole, but also the other major anchor states of American political and economic life: New York, Illinois, Florida and Texas.

These demographic changes, largely the result of immigration, don't worry me. They may be the very source of the renewal of this country.

I would worry more about the future of America if the large immigrant and young minority populations were not here, and all we had was a classic, northern-hemispheric, advanced industrial nation with an aging white population and a birth dearth.

I would worry more about a nation with too few workers saddled with immense health-care and income-security costs for the aged. I would worry more about a country that had little future orientation because the heaviest voting bloc in the country—elderly whites—felt they already had their best day.

These things would worry me a great deal more than to see young Asians populating the West Coast and commanding the valedictory positions in high schools and colleges. Or young Hispanics with a strong faith in family values and the basic American ethic of hard work, and saving for the future.

Many people fail to see that the immigrants who come to America today, whether Asian or Hispanic, are predisposed to the American way of life. Immigrants come to America from other nations because they are dissatisfied with where they have lived. Those coming from Mexico, for example, have no inclination to go back because they have seen the fallacies and failure of other systems—economically, politically and in terms of personal freedom and upward mobility. Therefore, the commitment they are making to the United States is total.

That dedication brings with it the same kind of raw energy and talent that has characterized previous waves of immigration to America. These immigrants place a great premium on values that relate to the future. They have faith in the future—the most precious resource any nation can have.

A New Southwest Culture

Over time, the immigrants that settle here are fostering an important evolution in American culture. Traditional ethnic values are being matched to the new economy and American rationalism.

What we find in the Hispanic community is the melding of a certain "heart" to American rationalism. By "heart" I mean an affection for the extended family, compassionate values and a sense of sharing that is very deeply rooted in the Catholic tradition, a tradition that is almost synonymous with the Hispanic culture.

Those Catholic values are a useful leavening against the rootless, strictly rationalistic dimensions of American life. On the other hand, American life and education provides an Hispanic, for example, with a strong sense of discipline, management of time, respect for deadlines, mastery over routine and a results-orientation.

Contrary to the belief that this collision of values and principles is going to create cultural tension and confusion, in reality it produces a person who is a very complete human being. It produces a human being whose ability to cope with the essence of life—human trauma, pain, sharing and compassion—is matched with the imperative to succeed.

In some sense, what we are seeing in the Southwest is the development of a new culture.

I suspect the same kind of fusion is taking place within the Asian community; where Confucian values of the extended family and group loyalty are a leavening influence on the rootless rationalism which comes from the Protestant foundation of American society.

The identification of the model of a new culture in which people have sorted these things out is very useful for American society. Out of this cultural tension, I believe, comes a richness, even a higher order of human development.

America in 2000

By the year 2000, the dominant characteristic of this nation will be its ethnic heterogeneity. Hispanics will serve in the Senate. Blacks will serve as governors. An Asian will serve as president of Stanford University. Prestigious institutions like the Bohemian Grove will be composed of Hispanics, Asians and blacks. First Interstate Bank will be run by a woman.

I think Mario Cuomo would have been elected president this year, had he run. He's likely to be replaced by a Greek-American, Michael Dukakis. That is a precursor of times to come, when people more clearly defined as "minorities," as opposed to ethnics," will be in the same position. The present is a transition to that future time.

By the year 2000, I see an American economy that manages, during the 1990s, to restore some of its basic industries. While the future economy will ride on the advantages of technology and research, it will be a diversified economy that stresses everything from tourism to urban redevelopment, from construction to retailing and financial services.

By the year 2000, America's share of Gross World Product will decline to a lower percentage, but we will still be the single most important force in the global economy. We will have an intertwined and productive relationship with Japan, and a Europe that will, by then, have been integrated for nearly a decade. The Soviet Union and Eastern Europe will also be sizable trading partners of the US due to Gorbachev's reforms, which will be in their 15th year by the turn of the century. Korea, Taiwan, Thailand, Singapore, Hong Kong and China, Indonesia and Malaysia will be active trading partners with America. Brazil will arrive as a world-class economic challenger to the advanced nations.

In short, America won't be a nation in decline, but a trading state interlinked in a consensus-oriented world economy. I say consensus because we will all learn the Japanese way in time. It is the only effective mechanism for organizing affairs in the globally intertwined economic and financial setting of a world with plural centers of power.

Worrying Obstacles

America's demographic trends do worry me a great deal, however, if we fail to educate America's rising population groups and if we fail to produce a growth economy.

A couple of years ago, then Japanese Prime Minister Nakasone said that America would never be able to compete with the Japanese head-on in the next century because of its large population of blacks and Hispanics. He was properly criticized for that remark.

But had Nakasone altered the statement slightly he would have been correct. Had he said America will not be able to compete because it is failing to educate its large population of blacks and Hispanics, and as a result, America will have a large part of its population that is illiterate and under-productive—a permanent underclass—Nakasone would have been correct. Had he said that no nation can carry 10 or 15 or 20 million people in an underclass and still remain competitive, he would have been correct.

This question transcends civil rights, Christian compassion and national ideals. The growth of a permanent underclass has reached the dimensions of an American survival issue. How does America compete in the world? How does America penetrate technological barriers? How does America keep civil order? How does America develop its middle class? How does America maintain its centrist political values? How do we do any of these things if we fail to bring our large and growing minority populations into the economic mainstream?

This nation must realize there is a real potential explosion between growing minority populations and the traditional aging white population that has an increasing tendency to say, "We're going to vote against bond issues, and property taxes and capital expenditures because our children have already finished school. We have no interest in the future." That's a real political risk on the horizon.

My concerns with economic growth have to do with the changing pattern of the distribution of income in this country. In 1985, the top 20% of Americans earned 43% of the national income, the largest percentage earned by that group since World War II. The bottom 20% earned only 4.7% of the national income, the smallest percentage in 25 years.

That suggests to me a new polarization along income lines that is a result, primarily, of a transformation in the American economy. We've lost millions of jobs paying $12 and $13 an hour and replaced them with millions paying $5 and $6 an hour. We've shipped millions of jobs offshore and continue to lose our basic industries.

And economic growth rates have fallen by half, exacerbating the industrial dislocation. In 1947, 33% of Americans lived under the poverty line. By 1960 that number was down to 22% and by 1973 it reached its lowest point at 11%. Throughout this whole period, from 1947–1973, the American economy grew at an average rate of nearly 4% per year.

In the late 70s and early 80s, our growth rate has been 2% and below. As a result, poverty has begun to grow again. It's now back up around 15%.

This trend must not be allowed to develop further. A prosperous economy, whether national, regional or urban, is an essential precondition for creating a sense of upward mobility. It is the precondition for any social justice program. A job is clearly more effective than any poverty program.

To the extent that investment in education and economic growth is hampered by massive deficits, by a whopping trade deficit and by the loss of basic industry, much of what we must do to harness the new economy to meet both our demographic challenges and global competition is severely restricted. A recommitment to growth and education is vital to this nation's future.

The New Politics

Finally, there is a great danger that, absent the commitment to education, the demographic realities will collide with the economic trend of class polarization. That would result in a society in which politics as we have traditionally known it in this country will cease to function.

Instead of politicians addressing the middle class and the middle view, instead of the Democratic and Republican parties both vying for and capturing the center, leaving the extremes with nowhere to go, we will find political figures pitching to the outsides of the spectrum.

Traditional politics that are slightly right or left of center will crumble if large numbers of people are in a permanent underclass; or, conversely, if large numbers of people feel insecure about their income because they're older and the economy doesn't work for them anymore.

When combined with voter apathy, the breakdown of traditional authority structures due to unprecedented heterogeneity and the excessive tendency of this society to litigate every conflict, moves us away from the political center toward paralysis and gridlock.

In my view, American society is becoming so culturally diverse that the center can no longer be held together by the older structures of elites with their school ties and cocktail parties. New and innovative structures of governance and goal-setting need to evolve.

There are precedents. I'm reminded of the brown bag lunches held between the black community and the business community in Atlanta during the 1960s. The phrase "a city too busy to hate" came from that experience.

In Minneapolis, the business community committed itself to annual contributions for social programs—the so-called "5% Club"—which William Ouchi cited in *The M Form Society* as the best example of consensus decision making in any American city.

These kinds of new structures of goal-setting and consensus building are models for future forms of governance in America.

The US still has immense resources. It has a unique capability to draw on the energies of its people through the free-market system. The US still calls forth the loyalties and patriotic spirit of its people. With a commitment to harness the new economy for our rising population groups, and leadership that believes in inclusiveness and consensus, this nation will prosper materially and enrich itself culturally.

Questions for Review and Reflection

1. What was the author's purpose in listing the various statistics about the projected growth of the "minorities" in California and the rest of the nation? How might these figures frighten the conservative right?
2. The author maintains that immigrants coming to America, whether Asian or Hispanic, are predisposed to the American way of life. What, precisely, does he mean by this? Do you agree?
3. In what ways does this "collision of values and principles," created by the influx of immigrants into American society, produce a "complete human being"? According to the author, what will be the dominant characteristic of the American nation by the year 2000? Do you agree?
4. According to the author, what is the cause and result of polarization as it occurs along economic lines in America?
5. What dangers does the author see in the nation's reduced commitment to education? How is this experienced along demographic lines? How does this lead to class polarization?

Reading 5

Herbert Hill, 1988

"Race, Affirmative Action, and the Constitution"

Despite government's reinvigorated effort to guarantee equal protection and freedom from discrimination, imbalances continued in education, employment, and job training for women and minorities. Past practices had left them lagging behind other groups, unable to compete on an equal playing field. Government responded by ordering that affirmative action steps be taken to make up for the past.

Affirmative action programs were widely supported by black organizations to promote economic and educational opportunities for African Americans. Recruiting efforts, special training programs, and numerically based goals that took race and ethnicity into account were seen as one way to open doors so long closed.

Professor of African American Studies at the University of Wisconsin and author of many writings on race, Dr. Herbert Hill presented his views on affirmative action in a lecture at the City College of New York. He concluded that such programs "can be a major instrument for social change."

1988 begins the third century of the United States Constitution and having survived the ritual celebration of the 1987 bicentennial, it is appropriate that we take a fresh critical look at that document and its legacy. As we examine the historical circumstances in which the Constitution emerged, we must acknowledge the continuing centrality of race in the evolution of the Constitution and of this nation.

Under the original Constitution, a system of slavery based on race existed for many generations, a system that legally defined black people as property and declared them to be less than human. Under its authority an extensive web of racist statutes and judicial decisions emerged over a long period. The Naturalization Law of 1790 explicitly limited citizenship to "white persons," the Fugitive Slave Acts of 1793 and 1850 made a travesty of law and dehumanized the nation, and the Dred Scott Decision of 1857, where Chief Justice Taney declared that blacks were not people but "articles of merchandise," are but a few of the legal monuments grounded on the assumption that this was meant to be a white man's country and that all others had no rights in the law.

With the ratification of the 13th, 14th, and 15th Amendments in 1865, 1868 and 1870 respectively and the adoption of the Civil Rights Acts of 1866, 1870 and 1875, a profoundly different set of values was asserted. This new body of law affirmed that justice and equal treatment were not for white persons exclusively, and that black people, now citizens of the nation, also were entitled to "the equal protection of the laws."

The Civil Rights Amendments and the three related Acts proclaim a very different concept of the social order than that implicit in the "three-fifths" clause contained in Section 2 of Article 1 of the Constitution. A concept that required the reconstruction of American society so that it could be free of slavery, free of a racism that was to have such terrible long-term consequences for the entire society.

The struggle to realize the great potential of the Reconstruction amendments to the Constitution, the struggle to create a just, decent and compassionate society free of racist oppression, is a continuing struggle that has taken many different forms in each era since the Reconstruction Period and one that continues today. In our own time the old conflict between those interests intent on perpetuating racist patterns rooted in the past and the forces that struggle for a society free of racism and its legacy continues in the raging battle for and against affirmative action.

During the late 1950's and early 1960's, as a result of direct confrontation with the system of state imposed segregation, together with the emergence of a new body of constitutional law on race, a hope was born that the legacy of centuries of slavery and racism would finally come to an end. But the hope was not yet to be realized. The high moral indignation of the 1960's was evidently but a passing spasm which was quickly forgotten.

A major manifestation of the sharp turning away from the goals of justice and equality is to be found in the shrill and paranoid attacks against affirmative action. The effort to eliminate the present effects of past discrimination, to correct the wrongs of many generations was barely underway when it came under powerful attack. And now, even the very modest gains made by racial minorities through affirmative action are being erased, as powerful institutions try to turn the clock of history back to the dark and dismal days of a separate and unequal status for black Americans.

Judging by the vast outcry, it might be assumed that the remedy of affirmative action to eliminate racist and sexist patterns has become as widespread and destructive as discrimination itself. And once again, the defenders of the racial *status quo* have succeeded in confusing the remedy with the original evil. The term "reverse discrimination," for example, has become another code word for resisting the elimination of prevailing patterns of discrimination.

The historic dissent of Justice John Marshall Harlan in the 1883 decision of the Supreme Court in the Civil Rights Cases defines the constitutional principle requiring the obligation of the government to remove all the "badges and incidents" of slavery. Although initially rejected, the rationale of Harlan's position was of course vindicated in later Supreme Court decisions, as in *Brown v. Board of Education* in 1954 and *Jones v. Mayer* in 1968, among others.

The adoption by Congress of the Civil Rights Act of 1964 further confirmed this constitutional perception of the equal protection clause of the 14th Amendment and reinforced the legal principle that for every right there is a remedy. I believe that what Justice Harlan called the "badges and incidents" of slavery include every manifestation of racial discrimination, not against black people alone, but also against other people of color who were engulfed by the heritage of racism that developed out of slavery.

In this respect, I believe that an interpretation of the law consistent with the meaning of the 13th and 14th Amendments to the Constitution holds that affirmative action programs carry forth the contemporary legal obligation to eradicate the consequences of slavery and racism. In order to do that, it is necessary to confront the present effects of past discrimination and the most effective remedy to achieve that goal is affirmative action. Mr. Justice Blackmun in his opinion in *Bakke* wrote, " . . . in order to get beyond racism, we must first take account of race. There is no other way."

By now it should be very clear, that the opposition to affirmative action is based on perceived group interest rather than on abstract philosophical differences about "quotas," "reverse discrimination," "preferential treatment" and the other catch-phrases commonly raised in public debate. After all the pious rhetoric equating affirmative action with "reverse discrimination" is stripped away, it is evident that the opposition to affirmative action is in fact the effort to perpetuate the privileged position of white males in American society.

In his dissent in *Bakke,* Justice Thurgood Marshall wrote, "The experience of Negroes in America has been different in kind, not just in degree, from that of other ethnic groups. It is not merely the history of slavery alone but also that a whole people were marked as inferior by the law. And that mark has endured. The dream of America as the great melting pot has not been realized for the Negro; because of his skin color he never even made it into the pot." . . .

Before the emergence of affirmative action remedies, the legal prohibitions against job discrimination were for the most part declarations of abstract morality that rarely resulted in any change. Pronouncements of public policy such as state and municipal fair employment practice laws were mainly symbolic, and the patterns of job discrimination remained intact. Because affirmative action programs go beyond individual relief to attack long-established patterns of discrimination and, if vigorously enforced by government agencies over a sustained period can become a major instrument for social change, they have come under powerful and repeated attack.

As long as Title VII litigation was concerned largely with procedural and conceptual issues, only limited attention was given to the consequences of remedies. However, once affirmative action was widely applied and the focus of litigation shifted to the adoption of affirmative action plans, entrenched interests were threatened. And as the gains of the 1960's are eroded, the nation becomes even more mean-spirited and self-deceiving.

Racism in the history of the United States has not been an aberration. It has been systematized and structured into the functioning of the society's most important institutions. In the present as in the past, it is widely accepted as a basis for promoting the interests of whites. For many generations the assumptions of white supremacy were codified in the law, imposed by custom and often enforced by violence. While the forms have changed, the legacy of white supremacy is expressed in the continuing patterns of racial discrimination, and for the vast majority of black and other non-white people, race and racism remain the decisive factors in their lives.

The current conflict over affirmative action is not simply an argument about abstract rights or ethnic bigotry. In the final analysis it is an argument between those who insist upon the substance of a long-postponed break with the traditions of American racism, and those groups that insist upon maintaining the valuable privileges and benefits they now enjoy as a consequence of that dismal history.

Questions for Review and Reflection

1. According to the author, is racism in America an aberration, or is it part of the permanent fabric of American culture?
2. What is the author's attitude toward the concept of government-sponsored affirmative action? Do you agree with his position? Why? What have the defenders of the status quo managed to do with their charges of "reverse discrimination" in America?
3. What does the term "badge of slavery" mean? Which Supreme Court decision recognized the truth and reality of this concept?
4. According to Hill, what is the basis for the opposition to affirmative action? How might this opposition be overcome?
5. What distinctions does Justice Thurgood Marshall see between black Americans and other minorities in the United States? Do you agree with his assessment? Why?

Reading 6

Joaquin Avila, 1988

Latino Political Empowerment

A graduate of Harvard Law School, Joaquin Avila has served as counsel for the Mexican-American Legal Defense and Education Fund. He used litigation to challenge "discriminatory election systems," and his lawsuits brought an end to some redistricting plans and at-large elections that diluted minority voices in California and Texas. Now in private law practice in California, Avila continues to challenge districts where minority votes are not afforded sufficient weight, so that true equality in the voting booth can be achieved. He says in this essay published in 1988, "Presently, the Latino community is engaged in a struggle for political equality . . . evidenced by aggressive legislation to enforce the Voting Rights Act, and by legislative and community political advocacy to secure the implementation of non-discriminatory electoral systems."

Latinos in California are not politically integrated. Although permitted to vote, their voting power in many communities is ineffective.

This ineffective voting power is due to discriminatory election structures. These election structures deny Latinos their right to effective participation in the political process.

This denial of effective political participation serves only to contribute to the growing alienation experienced by the Latino community. California cannot afford to have this alienation, especially from a growing Latino community. This alienation is not conducive toward the creation of a cohesive society.

The ability of California to achieve a more cohesive society is inextricably tied to the well-being of the Latino community. A characteristic of such a healthy community is the presence of political activity. Political participation contributes to the cohesiveness of the body politic.

Active political participation can only be achieved by the removal of discriminatory election systems.

Presently the Latino community is engaged in a struggle for political equality. This struggle is evidenced by aggressive litigation to enforce the Voting Rights Act, and by legislative and community political advocacy to secure the implementation of non-discriminatory election systems.

The timing of this political struggle is critical. The changing of boundaries for congressional, state legislative, and local governmental districts through the redistricting process will occur in 1991. The Latino community must be prepared to participate in these redistrictings. These redistrictings are important since this redistribution of political power occurs only once every ten years.

These efforts to eliminate discriminatory election systems should not be viewed simply as another minority issue. All racial and ethnic groups have a vested interest in having an active political community. Such a community will create leadership and community institutions at the local level.

The issue of voting rights for the Latino community is not simply another equity issue to resolve. Rather, the key to the advancement of the Latino community will be dependent upon the community's degree of integration into the political process. Thus, for Latinos, successful resolution of the voting rights issue will determine the political survival of our community.

The purpose of this essay is to emphasize the importance of Latino voting rights. This emphasis hopefully will play a role in convincing key decision makers of the importance of eliminating discriminatory election systems.

The time for action is now. These key decision makers cannot continue to ignore our problems. We simply do not have the luxury of waiting any longer. . . .

Political Empowerment

The quality of representation is an issue which will eventually have to be addressed by Latino communities. A non-discriminatory election system will provide the minority community with an opportunity for holding elected officials accountable. This accountability in turn will result in more responsive officials.

More responsive elected officials will aggressively seek to improve the community's quality of life standards. Basic employment and educational needs will be addressed. These officials and community leaders can create opportunities for small businesses to provide more employment opportunities and to support educational programs. The first priority of any educational program should be to address the high dropout rates within urban and barrio schools.

For the moment, the issue of the quality of representation for many communities must be subordinated to the basic issue of securing access to the political process. Such access will only be accomplished if discriminatory election systems are eliminated.

Conclusion

The issue of political integration is not just a minority issue. A state such as California can not continue to have a growing population which is under-educated, unemployed, and not involved in the political process. Maintenance of the status quo is a recipe for disaster. To change this status quo, the Latino community and its leadership must seize the initiative of aggressively pursuing litigative, legislative, and other advocacy strategies to remove discriminatory election systems. This aggressive promotion must be premised upon the notion that every vote counts. . . .

The Latino community cannot afford to wait for responsive governmental actions to accomplish the task. The initiative and preserverance must come from within. And action from the Latino community must begin now.

The first step is the investment: registering to vote and participating in elections. The second step is to support and become involved in the advocacy strategies to enforce the Voting Rights Act. These two steps are critical for the political survival of the Latino community and for the future of California.

The agenda has been established; and the call to action has been announced. It's our future; let us take charge.

Questions for Review and Reflection

1. Why do you suppose Avila believes that Latino voting power in many communities is ineffective? What are his suggestions to make it more effective?
2. What is the effect of the denial of effective political participation of the Latino community? What will be the result in the Latino community if this is reversed?
3. How is the issue of Latino voting different from other issues of equity that need to be solved?
4. According to the author, how might "accountability" be instilled in the political process if a system of non-discriminatory elections is established in America? Why is the issue of political integration not just another minority issue?

Reading 7

Susan Faludi, 1991

Backlash: The Undeclared War against American Women

Harvard graduate and Pulitzer Prize-winning journalist Susan Faludi wrote an award-winning book in which she exposed what she saw as a diminution of the women's rights movement since the 1980s. Faludi disputed "conventional wisdom," which said that women were achieving full equality. Instead, she charged that a "powerful counter-assault" had been waged to halt the progress that women had made. Faludi declared that equal opportunities for women had regressed due to this backlash. "Just when women's quest for equal rights seemed closest to achiev ing its objectives, the backlash struck it down." She produced an itemized agenda of what must be achieved in employment, education, and reproductive rights in order to remedy discrimination and win back all that had been lost.

The backlash decade produced one long, painful, and unremitting campaign to thwart women's progress. And yet, for all the forces the backlash mustered—the blistering denunciations from the New Right, the legal setbacks of the Reagan years, the powerful resistance of corporate America, the self-perpetuating myth machines of the media and Hollywood, the "neotraditional" marketing drive of Madison Avenue—women never really surrendered. The federal government may have crippled equal employment enforcement and the courts may have undermined twenty-five years of antidiscrimination law— yet women continued to enter the work force in growing numbers each year. Newsstands and airwaves may have been awash with frightening misinformation on spinster booms, birth dearths, and deadly day care—yet women continued to postpone their wedding dates, limit their family size, and combine work with having children. Television sets and movie screens may have been filled with nesting goodwives, but female viewers still gave their highest ratings to shows with strong-willed and independent heroines. Backlash dressmakers couldn't even get women to follow the most trivial of fashion prescriptions; while retailers crammed their racks with garter belts and teddies, women just kept reaching for the all-cotton Jockeys. . . .

American women have always fought the periodic efforts to force them back behind the curtain. The important question to ask about the current backlash, then, is not *whether* women are resisting, but how effectively. Millions of individual women, each in her own way, spent the last decade kicking against the backlash barricades. But much of that effort proved fruitless. While women didn't succumb to the backlash agenda, they didn't gain sufficient momentum to crash its steel-reinforced gates, either. Instead, when women tried to drive privately against the antifeminist forces of the '80s, they most often found their wheels spinning, frustration and disappointment building as they sank deeper in the same old ruts.

There are so many ways to rebel that pose no real or useful challenge to the system—like the proverbial exploited worker who screws the bolts in backward or the dutiful daughter chronically late to Sunday dinner. Some women tried to slip by the backlash checkpoint by mouthing the backlash passwords or trying to tailor the "pro-family" agenda to their own ends or by insisting that *they* were certainly not feminists. Still others resorted to the old "feminine" strategy—just be good and patient; the world will eventually take pity on women who wait.

While the '80s was an era that trumpeted the "one person can make a difference" credo, this strategy proved a blind alley on the road to equal rights. To remove the backlash wall rather than to thrash continually against it, women needed to be armed with more than their privately held grievances and goals. Indeed, to instruct each woman to struggle alone was to set each woman up, yet again, for defeat.

In the past, women have proven that they can resist in a meaningful way, when they have had a clear agenda that is unsanitized and unapologetic, a mobilized mass that is forceful and public, and a conviction that is uncompromising and relentless. On the rare occasions when these three elements have coalesced in the last two centuries, women have won their battles. The suffrage campaign faltered when its leaders resorted to accommodation and deception—daintily claiming they just viewed the vote as a form of "enlarged housekeeping." Ultimately, it was the combination of a forthright agenda, mass action, and sheer physical resistance that won the day. Suffragists organized thousands of women, filed 480 appeals to the state legislatures, launched fifty-six referendum efforts and staged forty-seven campaigns at state constitutional conventions. Even so, it wasn't until the National Woman's Party members began picketing the Capitol, chaining themselves to the White House gates and enduring imprisonment and forced feedings, that half the population finally got the vote.

Likewise, the women's liberation movement had many false starts. As political scientist Ethel Klein has observed, despite individual women's repeated efforts only 10 of the 884 women's rights bills introduced in Congress in the '60s ever passed. It took a sheer display of numbers and determination for the women's movement to force its way into public consciousness. The

1970 Women's Strike for Equality, then the largest demonstration for women's rights in history, turned the tide—inspiring a vast growth in feminist organization memberships and a flood of legal victories. Before the strike, the politicians ignored feminists. Afterward, seventy-one women's rights bills were signed into law in a matter of a few years—nearly 40 percent of all the legislation on women's rights passed in the century. . . .

Under the '80s backlash, in the very few instances where women have tried such a vocal and unapologetic strategy, they *have* managed to transform the public climate, set the agenda on their own terms, and change the minds of many individual men. The spectacular turnaround in abortion politics, pulled off by a rejuvenated pro-choice movement in 1989, is a textbook case in point. It happened when women who believed in the right to control their own bodies finally made a mighty showing of those bodies in 1989—a half billion marched on the Capitol on April 9, Washington, D.C.'s largest demonstration ever—and confronted the anti-abortion protesters at the clinic doors. Among female students, too, pro-choice protests drew more undergraduates than came to the antiwar marches in the '60s. Their vast numbers steamrolled over an antiabortion crusade that seemed, only weeks earlier, on the verge of wiping out women s reproductive rights. The mass mobilization of a pro-choice coalition defused all but a few of the hundreds of antiabortion bills introduced in the state legislatures in 1989, swept pro-choice candidates into gubernatorial and congressional office and even scared Republican National Committee chairman Lee Atwater enough to relabel the GOP "an umbrella party" on the abortion question. In Idaho in 1990, one of the nation's most restrictive abortion bills was vetoed by Cecil Andrus, the state's "pro-life" governor—after pro-choice women declared a boycott of Idaho potatoes. Some feminist leaders argued against such forceful tactics. "Let the governor make his decision based on the seriousness of this issue and the Constitution, not potatoes," National Abortion Rights Action League's executive director Kate Michelman advised. But it was the boycott that clinched it. "Anytime someone threatens one of our major cash crops," Governor Andrus explained, "it becomes significant."

For most of the decade, however, the increasingly reinforced fortress of an antifeminist culture daunted women more than it galvanized them. The backlash watchtowers flashed their warning signals without cease, and like high-security floodlights, they served to blind women to their own prodigious strengths. Women of the '80s were the majority in the general population, the college campuses, the voting booths, the bookstores, at the newsstands, and before the television sets. They represented nearly half the workers in offices and spent nearly 80 percent of the consumer dollars in stores. They enjoyed an unprecedented and expanding gender advantage in both national and state elections—by the end of the '80s, a Democratic female candidate could command an instant 12- to 20-point lead from female voters simply by declaring herself pro-choice. Yet so often in this era, women seemed unaware of the weight and dynamism of their own formidable presence. . . .

That women have in their possession a vast and untapped vitality also explains one of the more baffling phenomena of the backlash—the seeming "overreaction" with which some men have greeted even the tiniest steps toward women's advancement. Maybe these men weren't overreacting after all. In the '80s, male politicians saw the widening gender gap figures. Male policymakers saw the polls indicating huge and rising majorities of women demanding economic equality, reproductive freedom, a real participation in the political process, as well as a real governmental investment in social services and a real commitment to peace. (A record gender gap of 25 percent divided the sexes on the 1991 Persian Gulf war; on the eve of battle, a majority of women opposed military intervention, while a majority of men supported it.) Male corporate heads saw the massive female consensus for child care and family leave policies and the vast female resentment over indecent pay and minimal promotions. Male evangelical leaders saw the huge numbers of "traditional" wives who were ignoring their teachings or heading for the office. All of these men understood the profound force that an American women's movement could exert if it got half a chance. It was women, tragically, who were still in the dark.

"The reason men 'overreact' is *they* get it," Eleanor Smeal, founder of the Fund for the Feminist Majority, says. "If women all got together on the same day, on the same hour, we would go over the top." That day could have been any one of the 3,650 days in the last backlash decade. But women never did capitalize on the historic advantage they enjoyed; and as the attack on equal rights gathered momentum, women's energies were diverted and ultimately exhausted in fending off antifeminism's punishing blows. What is perhaps most depressing to contemplate is what might have been. The '80s could have become American women's great leap forward.

At the start of the '90s, some forecasters—most of them advertisers and political publicists—began declaring that the next ten years was going to be "the Decade of Women." What they meant by this prognosis was not entirely clear. Were they divining a real phenomenon or just coining another "trend"? Were they suggesting that women would wield more authority in the '90s, or were they simply envisioning another nostalgia-drenched epoch in which women would adopt a softer, more "feminine" pose?

In any event, when the media set out to report this story, they had the usual trouble rounding up evidence. "I get press calls every election season," Ruth Mandel, director of the Center for the American Woman and Politics, wearily told a reporter. "But the answer is no, this isn't the year (for women)—it wasn't the year in 1986 or 1988, and it won't be in '90 or '92."

One might hope, or dream, that Mandel's gloomy prediction is proved wrong. But more productively, women can act. Because there really is no good reason why the '90s can't be their decade. Because the demographics and the opinion polls are on women's side. Because women's hour on the stage is long, long overdue. Because, whatever new obstacles are mounted against the future march toward equality, whatever new myths invented, penalties levied, opportunities rescinded, or degradations imposed, no one can ever take from the American woman the justness of her cause.

Questions for Review and Reflection

1. How does Faludi describe the backlash?
2. Why does she feel women would turn against the women's movement?
3. Why does she feel that men "overreact" to women's advancement?
4. Why does Faludi say the 90's is the decade of the woman?

Reading 8

Shelby Steele, 1991

The Content of Our Character

Some black leaders opposed what was called "preferential treatment," calling it social engineering that demoralized rather than uplifted blacks. These critics contended that entitlements were based on victim status rather than on true merit. Shelby Steele, an outspoken critic, termed such programs "manufacturing parity."

Steele, a professor of English at California State University at San Jose, has written several essays on the subject of race for *Harper's* magazine, one of which was included in *The Best American Essays of 1989*. He followed these writings with the book from which this reading was taken, a critical examination of the whole policy of affirmative action. He writes, "Under affirmative action the quality that earns us preferential treatment is an implied inferiority." Steele argues that government should use its vast power to offer preferential treatment based on disadvantage regardless of race, while imposing severe sanctions for discrimination. This dilemma over the proper exercise of government authority to guarantee opportunity remains a nagging question in making public policy.

So, in theory, affirmative action certainly has all the moral symmetry that fairness requires—the injustice of historical and even contemporary white advantage is offset with black advantage; preference replaces prejudice, inclusion answers exclusion. It is reformist and corrective, even repentant and redemptive. And I would never sneer at these good intentions. . . .

Yet good intentions, because of the opportunity for innocence they offer us, are very seductive and can blind us to the effects they generate when implemented. In our society, affirmative action is, among other things, a testament to white goodwill and to black power, and in the midst of these heavy investments, its effects can be hard to see. But after twenty years of implementation, I think affirmative action has shown itself to be more bad than good and that blacks—whom I will focus on in this essay—now stand to lose more from it than they gain.

In talking with affirmative action administrators and with blacks and whites in general, it is clear that supporters of affirmative action focus on its good intentions while detractors emphasize its negative effects. Proponents talk about "diversity" and "pluralism"; opponents speak of "reverse discrimination," the unfairness of quotas and set-asides. It was virtually impossible to find people outside either camp. The closest I came was a white male manager at a large computer company who said, "I think it amounts to reverse discrimination, but I'll put up with a little of that for a little more diversity." I'll live with a little of the effect to gain a little of the intention, he seemed to be saying. But this only makes him a halfhearted supporter of affirmative action. I think many people who don't really like affirmative action support it to one degree or another anyway. . . .

I think that one of the most troubling effects of racial preferences for blacks is a kind of demoralization, or put another way, an enlargement of self-doubt. Under affirmative action the quality that earns us preferential treatment is an implied inferiority. However this inferiority is explained—and it is easily enough explained by the myriad deprivations that grew out of our oppression—it is still inferiority. . . .

The effects of this may be a subject for another essay. The point here is that the implication of inferiority that racial preferences engender in both the white and black mind expands rather than contracts this doubt. . . .

Preferential treatment, no matter how it is justified in the light of day, subjects blacks to a midnight of self-doubt, and so often transforms their advantage into a revolving door.

Another liability of affirmative action comes from the fact that it indirectly encourages blacks to exploit their own past victimization as a source of power and privilege. Victimization, like implied inferiority, is what justifies preference, so that to receive the benefits of preferential treatment one must, to some extent, become invested in the view of one's self as a victim. In this way, affirmative action nurtures a victim-focused identity in blacks. The obvious irony here is that we become inadvertently invested in the very condition we are trying to overcome. Racial preferences send us the message that there is more power in our past suffering than our present achievements— none of which could bring us a *preference* over others.

When power itself grows out of suffering, then blacks are encouraged to expand the boundaries of what qualifies as racial oppression, a situation that can lead us to paint our victimization in vivid colors, even as we receive the benefits of preference. The same corporations and institutions that give us preference are also seen as our oppressors. At Stanford University minority students—some of whom enjoy as much as $15,000 a year in financial aid—recently took over the president's office demanding, among other things, more financial aid. The power to be found in victimization, like any power, is intoxicating and can lend itself to the creation of a new class of super-victims who can feel the pea of victimization under twenty mattresses. Preferential treatment rewards us for being underdogs rather than for moving beyond that status—a displacement of incentives that, along with its deepening of our doubt, is more a yoke than a spur.

But, I think, one of the worst prices that blacks pay for preference has to do with an illusion. I saw this illusion at work recently in the mother of a middle-class black student who was going off to his first semester of college. "They owe us this, so don't think for a minute that you don't belong there." This is the logic by which many blacks, and some whites, justify affirmative action—it is something "owed," a form of reparation. But this logic overlooks a much harder and less digestible reality, that it is impossible to repay blacks living today for the historic suffering of the race. If all blacks were given a million dollars tomorrow morning it would not amount to a dime on the dollar of three centuries of oppression, nor would it obviate the residues of that oppression that we still carry today. The concept of historic reparation grows out of man's need to impose a degree of justice on the world that simply does not exist. Suffering can be endured and overcome, it cannot be repaid. Blacks cannot be repaid for the injustice done to the race, but we can be corrupted by society's guilty gestures of repayment.

Affirmative action is such a gesture. It tells us that racial preferences can do for us what we cannot do for ourselves. The corruption here is in the hidden incentive *not* to do what we believe preferences will do. This is an incentive to be reliant on others just as we are struggling for self-reliance. And it keeps alive the illusion that we can find some deliverance in repayment. The hardest thing for any sufferer to accept is that his suffering excuses him from very little and never has enough currency to restore him. To think otherwise is to prolong the suffering. . . .

I believe affirmative action is problematic in our society because it tries to function like a social program. Rather than ask it to ensure equal opportunity we have demanded that it create parity between the races. But preferential treatment does not teach skills, or educate, or instill motivation. It only passes out entitlement by color, a situation that in my profession has created an unrealistically high demand for black professors. The social engineer's assumption is that this high demand will inspire more blacks to earn Ph.D.'s and join the profession. In fact, the number of blacks earning Ph.D.'s has declined in recent years. A Ph.D. must be developed from preschool on. He requires family and community support. He must acquire an entire system of values that enables him to work hard while delaying gratification. There are social programs, I believe, that can (and should) help blacks *develop* in all these areas, but entitlement by color is not a social program; it is a dubious reward for being black. . . .

But if not preferences, then what? I think we need social policies that are committed to two goals: the educational and economic development of disadvantaged people, regardless of race, and the eradication from our society—through close monitoring and severe sanctions—of racial, ethnic, or gender discrimination. Preferences will not deliver us to either of these goals, since they tend to benefit those who are not disadvantaged—middle-class white women and middle-class blacks—and attack one form of discrimination with another. Preferences are inexpensive and carry the glamour of good intentions—change the numbers and the good deed is done. To be against them is to be unkind. But I think the unkindest cut is to bestow on children like my own an undeserved advantage while neglecting the development of those disadvantaged children on the East Side of my city who will likely never be in a position to benefit from a preference. Give my children fairness; give disadvantaged children a better shot at development—better elementary and secondary schools, job training, safer neighborhoods, better financial assistance for college, and so on.

Questions for Review and Reflection

1. To what famous speech does the title of Steele's book allude? Why do you suppose he chose this particular sentiment to entitle his work?
2. According to the author, what does the existence of affirmative action policy reveal about the nature of American society? Do you agree?
3. What is the author's position on affirmative action? What are some of its positive elements, according to Steele?
4. The author refers to the concept of victimization in this selection and suggests that it is intoxicating. What is victimization, and how is it intoxicating?
5. If the policy of affirmative action is unwise for the nation, what two social policies does the author recommend instead?

Reading 9

Linda Chavez, 1991

Out of the Barrio

Linda Chavez served as a public official in a variety of federal posts during the 1980s and was one of the first women appointed to the Civil Rights Commission. She has edited *American Educator* magazine and has written many articles as well as the book from which this reading was taken.

In this study of Hispanics in American society, Chavez objects to abandoning the "melting pot" approach to assimilation and defends its successful incorporation of an ethnically diverse population during the nineteenth and twentieth centuries.

The role of government, according to Chavez, is to promote the common culture and language. The protection and advancement of native cultures should be accomplished by the communities themselves. Chavez points to Chinese, Jewish, and other groups who "have long established after-school and weekend programs to teach [their own] language and culture to children from these groups."

She credits both education and politics as great "equalizers" and encourages assimilation in politics by reaching out to broadly based constituencies and community issues. She is describing a pluralist system with a sense of community for all Americans.

Assimilation has become a dirty word in American politics. It invokes images of people, cultures, and traditions forged into a colorless alloy in an indifferent melting pot. But, in fact, assimilation, as it has taken place in the United States, is a far more gentle process, by which people from outside the community gradually became part of the community itself. Descendants of the German, Irish, Italian, Polish, Greek, and other immigrants who came to the United States bear little resemblance to the descendants of the countrymen their forebears left behind. America changed its immigrant groups—and was changed by them. Some groups were accepted more reluctantly than others—the Chinese, for example—and some with great struggle. Blacks, whose ancestors were forced to come here, have only lately won their legal right to full participation in this society; and even then civil rights gains have not been sufficiently translated into economic gains. Until quite recently, however, there was no question but that each group desired admittance to the mainstream. No more. Now ethnic leaders demand that their groups remain separate, that their native culture and language be preserved intact, and that whatever accommodation takes place be on the part of the receiving society. . . .

The government should not be obliged to preserve any group's distinctive language or culture. Public schools should make sure that all children can speak, read, and write English well. When teaching children from non-English-speaking backgrounds, they should use methods that will achieve English proficiency quickly and should not allow political pressure to interfere with meeting the academic needs of students. No children in an American school are helped by being held back in their native language when they could be learning the language that will enable them to get a decent job or pursue higher education. More than twenty years of experience with native-language instruction fails to show that children in these programs learn English more quickly or perform better academically than children in programs that emphasize English acquisition.

If Hispanic parents want their children to be able to speak Spanish and know about their distinctive culture, they must take the responsibility to teach their children these things. Government simply cannot—and should not—be charged with this responsibility. Government bureaucracies given the authority to create bicultural teaching materials homogenize the myths, customs, and history of the Hispanic peoples of this hemisphere, who, after all, are not a single group but many groups. It is only in the United States that "Hispanics" exist; a Cakchiquel Indian in Guatemala would find it remarkable that anyone could consider his culture to be the same as a Spanish Argentinean's. The best way for Hispanics to learn about their native culture is in their own communities. Chinese, Jewish, Greek, and other ethnic communities have long established after-school and weekend programs to teach language and culture to children from these groups. . . .

The real barriers to Hispanic political power are apathy and alienage. Too few native-born Hispanics register and vote; too few Hispanic immigrants become citizens. The way to increase real political power is not to gerrymander districts to create safe seats for Hispanic elected officials or treat illegal aliens and other immigrants as if their status were unimportant to their political representation; yet those are precisely the tactics Hispanic organizations have urged lately. Ethnic politics is an old and honored tradition in the United States. . . .

Politics has traditionally been a great equalizer. One person's vote was as good as another's, regardless of whether the one was rich and the other poor. But politics requires that people participate. The great civil rights struggles of the 1960s were fought in large part to guarantee the right to vote. Hispanic leaders demand representation but do not insist that individual

Hispanics participate in the process. The emphasis is always on rights, never on obligations. Hispanic voter organizations devote most of their efforts toward making the process easier—election law reform, postcard registration, election materials in Spanish—to little avail; voter turnout is still lower among Hispanics than among blacks and white. Spanish posters urge Hispanics to vote because it will mean more and better jobs and social programs, but I've never seen one that mentions good citizenship. Hispanics (and others) need to be reminded that if they want the freedom and opportunity democracy offers, the least they can do is take the time to register and vote. These are the lessons with which earlier immigrants were imbued, and they bear reviving. . . .

The government can do only so much in promoting higher education for Hispanics or any group. It is substantially easier today for a Hispanic student to go to college than it was even twenty or thirty years ago, yet the proportion of Mexican Americans who are graduating from college today is unchanged from what it was forty years ago. When the former secretary of education Lauro Cavazos, the first Hispanic ever to serve in the Cabinet, criticized Hispanic parents for the low educational attainment of their children, he was roundly attacked for blaming the victim. But Cavazos's point was that Hispanic parents must encourage their children's educational aspirations and that, too often, they don't. Those groups that have made the most spectacular socioeconomic gains—Jews and Chinese, for example—have done so because their families placed great emphasis on education.

Hispanics cannot have it both ways. If they want to earn as much as non-Hispanic whites, they have to invest the same number of years in schooling as these do. The earnings gap will not close until the education gap does. Native-born Hispanics are already enjoying earnings comparable to those of non-Hispanic whites, once educational differences are factored in. If they want to earn more, they must become better educated. But education requires sacrifices, especially for persons from lower-income families. Poverty, which was both more pervasive and severe earlier in this century, did not prevent Jews or Chinese from helping their children get a better education. These families were willing to forgo immediate pleasures, even necessities, in order to send their children to school. Hispanics must be willing to do the same—or else be satisfied with lower socioeconomic status. The status of second- and third-generation Hispanics will probably continue to rise even without big gains in college graduation; but the rise will be slow. Only a substantial commitment to the education of their children on the part of this generation of Hispanic parents will increase the speed with which Hispanics improve their social and economic status. . . .

Affirmative action politics treats race and ethnicity as if they were synonymous with disadvantage. The son of a Mexican American doctor or lawyer is treated as if he suffered the same disadvantage as the child of a Mexican farm worker; and both are given preference over poor, non-Hispanic whites in admission to most colleges or affirmative action employment programs. Most people think this is unfair, especially white ethnics whose own parents and grandparents also faced discrimination in this society but never became eligible for the entitlements of the civil rights era. It is inherently patronizing to assume that all Hispanics are deprived and grossly unjust to give those who aren't preference on the basis of disadvantages they don't experience. Whether stated or not, the essence of affirmative action is the belief that Hispanics—or any of the other eligible groups—are not capable of measuring up to the standards applied to whites. This is a pernicious idea.

Ultimately, entitlements based on their status as "victims" rob Hispanics of real power. The history of American ethnic groups is one of overcoming disadvantage, of competing with those who were already here and proving themselves as competent as any who came before. Their fight was always to be treated the same as other Americans, never to be treated as special, certainly not to turn the temporary disadvantages they suffered into the basis for permanent entitlement. Anyone who thinks this fight was easier in the early part of this century when it was waged by other ethnic groups does not know history. Hispanics have not always had an easy time of it in the United States. Even though discrimination against Mexican Americans and Puerto Ricans was not as severe as it was against blacks, acceptance has come only with struggle, and some prejudices still exist. Discrimination against Hispanics, or any other group, should be fought, and there are laws and a massive administrative apparatus to do so. But the way to eliminate such discrimination is not to classify all Hispanics as victims and treat them as if they could not succeed by their own efforts. Hispanics can and will prosper in the United States by following the example of the millions before them.

Q uestions for Review and Reflection

According to Chavez,
1. Why is assimilation a dirty word?
2. What is the role of government vis-à-vis culture and language?
3. How can culture be preserved?
4. What are the real barriers to Hispanic political power?
5. What is the great equalizer? Explain why this is so.

Reading **10**

Patricia Ireland, 1992

"The State of NOW"

Patricia Ireland's early experiences as a student and flight attendant led to her membership in the National Organization for Women, of which she is now president. The bias and discrimination that she confronted brought about her active support of women's rights.

This retrospective of the National Organization for Women and the issues it has chosen to tackle over the past 20 years underscores the new direction in which the group is moving. NOW has become more inclusive and pluralistic, taking stands on racism, welfare reform, homelessness, and rights for gays and the disabled. Membership and management reflect efforts to increase diversity within the group and to forge alliances with other civil rights groups. This approach calls for a new unity among all people who face discrimination and need advocacy.

When I became active, only 39 percent of women in the U.S. supported the idea of a women's rights movement. Today, 78 percent of women say they are supporters of the women's movement, including 20 percent who say they are strong supporters. The gains of the past two decades have confirmed the strength of the entire women's movement.

The first words of NOW's statement of purpose are "To take action," a mandate NOW members have always taken seriously. While we lobbied for child care, activists also marched in Mother's Day parades chained to baby carriages. We picketed the Pittsburgh *Press* to end sex-segregated help-wanted ads, and occupied offices of the Equal Employment Opportunity Commission to pressure the agency to enforce Title VII on behalf of women. When I was arrested in 1987 for nonviolently protesting at the Vatican Embassy (against Reagan's recognition of Rome and papal intervention in U.S. policy), some people questioned the target as well as the tactic. In 1967, when NOW activists voted to support the Equal Rights Amendment, members who felt that women needed protective labor laws left the organization. We lost members again the following year when NOW took a stand in favor of legalizing birth control and abortion. NOW was Red-baited for supporting child care. Richard Nixon vetoed the child care bill in 1971, with a scathing message—written by Pat Buchanan—calling child care the "Sovietization of American children." . . .

As the entire women's movement gains strength and momentum, attacks on all of us increase. Predictably, one of the divide-and-conquer tactics used is lesbian-baiting. But in 1992, the tactic is less effective than it was 20 years ago. The fight for lesbian rights and against heterosexism was, in an earlier period, a source of great controversy in NOW (and in the movement as a whole). All this time later, memories of the attempted purge of the "Lavender Menace" by some NOW leaders and chapters remain painful. But the overwhelming majority of the organization fought back in 1971 with a strong resolution clearly identifying lesbian rights as a feminist issue and a NOW issue. We can take pride that NOW's work since then has been an important part of shaping the movement and changing public opinion on lesbian rights. . . .

NOW has also been enhanced by our commitment to fighting racism and by the affirmative action we have taken internally. The Reverend Pauli Murray, an African American and a NOW cofounder, was one of the authors of our statement of purpose. Other women who led NOW in the early years included Addie Wyatt, Shirley Chisholm, Fannie Lou Hamer, and Coretta Scott King. Aileen Hernandez was elected the first African American president of NOW, in 1971. Still, women of color in NOW's early leadership must have felt isolated. But in 1980, NOW activists voted to require affirmative action on our national board, and since 1987 programs to increase diversity at the chapter and state levels have been mandated.

Ginny Montes, who took office as national secretary last December, brings to our new team of four officers an important perspective as a woman of color and an immigrant from Honduras. She serves an organization with at least 30 percent racial and ethnic diversity represented on the national board and far greater participation by women of color at all levels than NOW had two decades ago. We continue to pursue greater diversity within NOW, including stronger alliances with civil rights groups and organizations of women of color. We have also begun more work on disability rights issues. And as "welfare reform" proposals sweep the country, NOW is determined to fight against those who blame poor women for the nation's economic mess; we have made a major commitment to work with welfare rights, antihunger, and homelessness coalitions.

Change, even strongly desired change, is never easy. Communication between diverse communities and activists can be difficult and confusing. But such a process is crucial if we are to succeed in building the backlash to the backlash. We must empower more women to move into policy-making positions, not just in government but in all institutions—including NOW. . . .

The entire women's movement deserves credit for helping to transform righteous indignation into the concerted political action that expresses itself in Braun and Yeakel. But we all know that our work is not finished. Like the rest of the feminist movement (and despite misperceptions of the extent of our resources), NOW's reach always exceeds our grasp. There are never enough hours in the day, monies in the till, staff in the Action Center, or activists in the field. But we at NOW believe that, working together, women have the strength and determination to change the balance of power in state legislatures, Congress, and even the White House. In this season of discontent, it will be women who can transform the national rage and demoralization into hope. We have been building toward this moment for 20 years.

Questions for Review and Reflection

1. Compare the women's movement today to what it was when Ireland joined NOW.
2. What kinds of action has NOW taken in its history?
3. What issue is provoking controversy in NOW today?
4. What civil rights issues is NOW confronting?
5. Account for the changes in leadership that have taken place recently.

Reading 11

John Mohawk, 1992

"Looking for Columbus: Thoughts on the Past, Present, and Future of Humanity"

John Mohawk is a member of the Seneca tribe of Native Americans, an associate professor of American studies at State University of New York, and editor of *Daybreak* newsletter, a national publication of Indian news.

Mohawk criticized the "melting pot" theory as a failed ideology for a pluralist society. He recommends an end to the "clashing and intermixing" and urges a respect for the "multiplicity of cultures" that make up America. His concept of pluralism embraces people from all over the world. He views America as only part of a much larger society where "difference is just a simple fact of life." The global world is made up of so many different cultures and languages; it is past time to understand and accept this reality, according to Mohawk.

I s it possible at last to look at the modern period, not as a process of crisis and decline, but as a wonderful opportunity to amalgamate and pull things together?"

No area of the globe has a bloodier history than Europe. And the reason for this is the outrageous intolerance of people claiming for centuries and centuries to be the chosen ones of God, to be a special people, a "superior race of men." . . .

It is essential that we understand that the intolerance arising out of Eurocentrism is what has caused the crisis of our times. Eurocentrism not only creates anthropocentrism—which comes directly from the tradition calling upon "man" to go out and assert "dominion" over nature—but ordains that people are not open to any other thinking. I was at a discussion at the Harvard Divinity School not long ago when a speaker got up and said, "Humans are obviously superior to all other life forms on Earth." I wanted to ask him to define "superior." Without trees to create oxygen, humans can't breathe, so they are a *dead* life form. If we don't understand ourselves in relation to the very big picture of the planet, as a biological living thing, then we don't understand the world we are living in. We can make abysmally ignorant statements such as "mankind is superior to all other life forms on Earth," but, *however* you define "superior," it is immaterial to nature. Nature doesn't care what your ideologies are.

Toward a Viable Future

For 500 years we have seen both a clashing and an intermixing of cultures. Over all but the last decade or so, America has espoused the ideology of "the melting pot," and yet that approach has failed to enrich this culture. So, we're beginning to arrive at the realization that we might have to adopt a more pluralistic approach; instead of requiring everybody to be the same, maybe we should learn to live with one another, and allow for a genuine multiplicity of cultures. We are living in a world in which difference is just a simple fact of life, but our collective thinking has yet to truly come to grips with this reality. This *has* to change.

A workable world mentality means that we are going to have to make peace with those who are different from us. We must also come together in the realization that social initiatives, social justice, and ecology have to go hand in hand. As long as people don't have enough to eat, as long as people are driven off their lands, as long as investment banks in the industrialized world finance dams that displace people in the Third and Fourth Worlds, there will be people scrambling down hillsides cutting down the forests in order to find a place to live and a way to make a living.

I offer you the suggestion that we need to reevaluate our thinking. We need to look at the old philosophies and ask ourselves whether that is where we want to put our energies. Or should we look at other peoples' ways of thinking about the world and its societies, and decide anew how human priorities and human societies ought to be constructed? We need to give ourselves permission to trust our own thinking and not allow bureaucrats and crazed guys at the pulpit to do our thinking for us. And we need to take *this* kind of ideology and make it work for us on *the land.*

We are going to have to ask ourselves what our resources are. Our first resource is human compassion, gained through the clear use of our minds, which will allow us to make the best use of the human family. And another of our best resources emerges when we think clearly about the peoples who have alternative answers to the questions that are not being answered by the society we live in. For the first time in human history it is possible to talk to the jungle-dwelling Indians of South America in a European language at a North American conference and find out what they think about the world they live in and the world we live in. It is possible for the first time to take all the knowledge of the whole family of humanity and start plotting a course toward a viable future. It is possible at last to look at the modern period, not as a process of crisis and decline, but as a wonderful opportunity to amalgamate and pull things together, and to make the world our library. It at last is possible, in other words, not only to finally find the real meaning of Columbus, but to bury it.

Questions for Review and Reflection

1. How does Mohawk define Eurocentrism?
2. What kinds of differences does he say exist in the world that are simple facts of life?
3. What resources does Mohawk feel can be utilized to achieve a more pluralistic society?

Reading 12

Vine Deloria Jr., 1992

"Afterword"

A member of the Standing Rock Sioux, Vine Deloria Jr., is a scholar of Indian affairs. He has written many books, including *Custer Died for Your Sins; An Indian Manifesto; We Talk, You Listen;* and *Behind the Trail of Broken Treaties*. He holds degrees in law and theology, and is considered a leading spokesman for American Indians.

Deloria calls for a redefinition of American democracy. This will require a revision of history that provides a true accounting of the "smallest and least significant people" in order that they be part of "the complete human heritage." Deloria maintains that we live in a global society, that "the world is now irretrievably one." A full understanding of the contributions and "virtues" represented by these previously ignored people is vital to future human development, according to Deloria, and is a step necessary for future progress.

Increasingly, American Indians are understanding the European invasion as a failure. That is to say, in spite of severe oppression, almost complete displacement, and substantial loss of religion and culture, Indians have not been completely defeated. Indeed, the hallmark of today's Indian psyche is the realizaiton that the worst has now passed and that it is the white man with his careless attitude toward life and the environment who is actually in danger of extinction. The old Indian prophecies say that the white man's stay on these western continents will be the shortest of any who have come here. From an Indian point of view, the general theme by which to understand the history of the hemisphere would be the degree to which the whites have responded to the rhythms of the land—the degree to which they have become indigenous. From that perspective, the judgment of Europeans is severe.

American history is usually cast in the light of progress—how a wilderness was tamed and brought to production by a hardy people who created a society in which the benefits of the earth were distributed to the largest percentage of people. From a short-term perspective, there is much to be said for this interpretation. Luxuries virtually inundate the United States, and even the poorest person in this society is in a much more comfortable position than the majority of people in most other human societies. This evaluation cannot be true for all nations of the Americas, of course, but for the peoples influenced by the English tradition it is most certainly a fact. The people of the United States prefer to credit their success to an intense commitment to progress, although at odd moments the Deity does get a bit of a compliment, and progress is almost always defined as an increase in material wealth. But in recent years, as the United States has begun to resemble a Third World nation saddled with insurmountable debts, the argument about the superiority of the United States is wearing a little thin. We are now living on future wealth, not on what we are able to produce ourselves. Today we have mortgaged the future.

It is fitting that we understand the conditions which once existed in this hemisphere, because this generation is facing a particularly difficult time grasping the meaning of the American experience. History, it appears to some people, is drawing to a close—at least the view of history that has nourished, inspired, and oriented us for most of our lives. The titanic struggle known as the Cold War is over and it is no longer clear in which direction world history is moving, if indeed there is movement at all.

In a rare and almost eerie prophetic analysis of the potential contained in the world situation in 1830, Alexis de Tocqueville observed:

> The American fights against natural obstacles; the Russian is at grips with men. The former combats the wilderness and barbarism; the latter, civilization with all its arms. America's conquests are made with the plowshare, Russia's with the sword.
>
> To attain their aims, the former relies on personal interest and gives free scope to the unguided strength and common sense of individuals.
>
> The latter in a sense concentrates the whole power of society in one man.
>
> One has freedom as the principal means of action; the other has servitude.
>
> Their point of departure is different and their paths diverse; nevertheless, each seems called by some secret design of Providence one day to hold in its hands the destinies of half the world.

To what degree has this prediction been fulfilled? Russia no longer fights men and apparently has abandoned one-man rule, but has the United States transcended its struggle with nature so that it is, in a sense, the leader of the beginning of a new global history shared by everyone?

If we have understood the rage for democracy that has recently swept the earth, toppling long-established dictatorships and gnawing at the foundations of the monolith of Chinese communism, we must come to see that even American democracy, the oldest and most prosperous on earth, faces a gigantic task of redefinition. It may well be that the United States has worn out the democratic forms which were once so comfortable and reassuring. The United States must either make a gargantuan leap forward to a new global society of peace and justice or become a relic of vested privilege that will be swept aside with the old political structures of the Old World.

Russian communism and the American experiment with democracy represented two paths which the European emergence from feudalism could have taken. That these possibilities were realized on lands away from Europe is significant because the Old World could not have survived the stresses which the escape from feudalism required. Indeed, Nazism can be regarded as the true response of Europe to its declining role in the world: the *Lebensraum* of the National Socialists was simply Russian and American imperialsim written in the small space of Central Europe. If the struggle for living space has ended, and it was always a quest for a secure national identity, then our present and future task is to create, once and for all, an adequate history of the human race, a history in which even the smallest and least significant people are understood in the light of their own experiences. For Americans that means coming to grips with the real meaning of the past five centuries and understanding what actually happened between the original inhabitants of this hemisphere and those who tried to erase and replace them. . . .

We now stand at a similar threshold in human history. We do not know how the pieces will fit together yet, but we do know that the world is now irretrievably one. And the Americas stand as the crucial elements in the new order. The future writing of American hsitory must seek to integrate the American experience into the much larger context of human strivings. It cannot be regarded as the final product of an evolutionary march toward greatness or as a unique experiment in how people should organize themselves as a society. America and Canada, Australia and New Zealand, remain the primary lands where the native and immigrant histories have not yet been reconciled. These lands yet contain mysteries about the human past which we cannot fathom. We must solve them so that they can become part of the complete human heritage.

Scott Momaday suggests at the beginning of this book that Columbus made a voyage in time as well as space, that he moved the world from the Middle Ages to the Renaissance. Since that time, we have moved beyond the Renaissance, through the Reformation and the Industrial Revolution, suffered a series of world wars, and now envision a period of relative global peace. The native peoples of the American continents suffered total inundation, lost a substantial portion of their population, and in coming into the modern world surrendered much of the natural life which had given them comfort and dignity. But they have managed to survive. Now, at a time when the virtues they represented, and continue to represent, are badly needed by the biosphere struggling to remain alive, they must be given the participatory role which they might have had in the world if the past five centuries had been different. The attitudes and beliefs that have kept the natives of the Western Hemisphere hidden and neglected must be changed so that world history becomes the story of mankind on this planet and not the selected history of a few people and their apology for what has happened to our species.

There are old Indian prophecies that forecast the coming of the white man, and some of them predict the disappearance of tribes because of the actions of these invaders. Other prophecies declare that the white man will be the shortest-lived of all those who have sought to live on these lands. We have yet to write the final chapter of the human story and we must now attempt to live out the final chapter of the American story. How closely it will resemble the contents of this book in another five centuries is for this and future generations to determine.

Questions for Review and Reflection

1. What do Indian prophecies predict for the future of the white man?
2. Analyze de Tocqueville's predictions for the world and compare them to what has happened.
3. Why is it necessary to redefine democracy, according to Deloria?
4. What world view does Deloria take?

One Nation, Many Peoples: The Essence of a Democratic Society

The United States of America is one nation made up of many different people. It began with a population of four million in 13 states. Today there are over 250 million people in 50 states, with diverse backgrounds, languages, cultures, religions, and attitudes. Combining diversity and democracy requires both tolerance for the differences that exist among people and a shared set of values that unify and create a spirit of community.

The basic components of the U.S. Constitution are compromises reached by diverse groups and interests. The authors of the document recognized that it would have to adapt to changing circumstances. The Constitution was written in language broad enough to allow for reinterpretation and prescient enough to include an amending process.

One set of changing circumstances has led to a new government-to-government relationship between the United States and Native American tribes. In 1992, Congress declared that the nation's obligations included "the protection of the sovereignty of each tribal government." To that end, Congress authorized a commitment and financial support to an internal tribal justice system.

Spurred by another set of changing circumstances, the United States redefined its relationships with African Americans through Congress's initiation of the Thirteenth, Fourteenth, and Fifteenth Amendments. The Fourteenth Amendment has since been reinterpreted to encompass other minorities and women under its equal protection umbrella. This expansion of rights has led to such legislation as the Women in Apprenticeship and Nontraditional Occupations Act, which aims to increase equal opportunities for women.

Maintaining a sense of community has always been difficult among people who do not share a common culture or history. The United States Civil Rights Commission confronted one such instance when they found newly arriving Asian Americans to be "victims of stereotype," facing "significant cultural and linguistic barriers," and an "inability to use the political process effectively."

Is assimilation the answer? The "melting pot" theory was used to incorporate large numbers of immigrants who entered the country in the nineteenth and twentieth centuries, and they gradually became part of their new community.

Public education has been a particularly effective means of achieving commonality. Teaching core values and principles of democracy has reinforced and perpetuated the system. Education has also contributed to a tolerance for difference through an understanding of and appreciation for the existence of other cultures. Recognizing that "a primary means by which a child learns is through the use of such child's native language and cultural heritage," Congress passed the Bilingual Education Act to help preserve immigrants' native cultures while they were being assimilated into American culture. Following the federal example, the State of New York incorporated a multicultural curriculum into its educational program that reflects the multiethnic, multiracial society that it serves.

Another way in which a pluralistic society manages diversity and democracy is by acknowledging the existence of distinct groups and their right to exist. Like-minded individuals form associations, which then compete for power. A variety of such interest groups, representing many minorities and women, complained to Congress that they were underrepresented in management and decision-making positions in business. Such organized complaints contributed to the passage of the Civil Rights Act of 1991, which was designed to prevent employment practices with a "disparate impact" on minorities and to provide more access to job opportunities.

To exercise the right to vote is "the essence of a democratic society," the Supreme Court said in its 1964 *Reynolds v. Sims* case (see Chapter 7, Reading 1). In voting, "the individual is important, not his race, his creed, or his color," wrote Justice William O. Douglas when he dissented from the majority opinion in *Wright v. Rockefeller,* a case also deliberated in 1964. The *Wright* plaintiffs argued that New York State's reapportionment plan, which created one white and three nonwhite congressional districts, was based solely on race. Justice Hugo Black's majority decision upheld the redistricting on the grounds that its racial motivation had not been proven. In 1993, however, the Court rejected a reapportionment plan that it found was based solely on race, because it resulted in "irrational" political districts. In this *Shaw v. Reno* decision, the Court posited that such a plan "threatens to carry us further from the goal of a political system in which race no longer matters," and "reinforces the perception that members of the same racial group . . . think alike. . . . We have rejected such perceptions elsewhere as impermissible racial stereotypes."

"Liberty is an unfinished business," wrote the American Civil Liberties Union some years ago. Similarly unfinished are the full extension of equality and other principles that make up a democratic form of government. As this century ends, the United States continues to struggle with its diversity and democracy. How much of a role should government play in guaranteeing equal opportunities? Should affirmative action bring about equality of results? Are gays entitled to equal opportunities in the military? What are basic rights, and how far should government go to provide for them? Is health care one of those basic rights? Can diverse groups agree on some core values, or do cultural differences make that impossible? These and many other questions will continue to be raised in a democracy of one nation and many peoples.

Reading 1

United States Congress, 1988

The Bilingual Education Act

"Recognizing . . . that the federal government has a special and continuing obligation to assist in providing equal educational opportunities to limited English proficient children," the United States Congress passed the Bilingual Education Act.

Bilingual education is seen as one means of preserving immigrants' native cultures while assimilating them into their new culture. Students are permitted to learn in their own language while they are making the transition to English. This acknowledgement of the effectiveness of other languages as teaching tools is now prevalent in states with large populations of minorities. Nevertheless, the policy remains controversial. Opponents say that it slows down the learning process and hinders the mainstreaming of students. Proponents defend the program as a means of keeping students up to date in their other subjects, preserving the cultural integrity of their language, and introducing their fellow students to other languages.

§ 3282. Policy; appropriations

(a) Policy

Recognizing—

(1) that there are large and growing numbers of children of limited English proficiency;

(2) that many of such children have a cultural heritage which differs from that of English proficient persons;

(3) that the Federal Government has a special and continuing obligation to assist in providing equal educational opportunity to limited English proficient children;

(4) that, regardless of the method of instruction, programs which serve limited English proficient students have the equally important goals of developing academic achievement and English proficiency;

(5) that the Federal Government has a special and continuing obligation to assist language minority students to acquire the English language proficiency that will enable them to become full and productive members of society;

(6) that the instructional use and development of a child's non-English native language promotes student self-esteem, subject matter achievement, and English-language acquisition;

(7) that a primary means by which a child learns is through the use of such child's native language and cultural heritage;

(8) that, therefore, large numbers of children of limited English proficiency have educational needs which can be met by the use of bilingual educational methods and techniques;

(9) that in some school districts establishment of bilingual education programs may be administratively impractical due to the presence of small numbers of students of a particular native language or because personnel who are qualified to provide bilingual instructional services are unavailable;

(10) that States and local school districts should be encouraged to determine appropriate curricula for limited English proficient students within their jurisdictions and to develop and implement appropriate instructional programs;

(11) that children of limited English proficiency have a high dropout rate and low median years of education;

(12) that the segregation of many groups of limited English proficient students remains a serious problem;

(13) that reliance on student evaluation procedures which are inappropriate for limited English proficient students have resulted in the disproportionate representation of limited English proficient students in special education, gifted and talented, and other special programs;

(14) that there is a serious shortage of teachers and educational personnel who are professionally trained and qualified to serve children of limited English proficiency;

(15) that many schools fail to meet the full instructional needs of limited English proficient students who also may be handicapped or gifted and talented;

(16) that both limited English proficient children and children whose primary language is English can benefit from bilingual education programs, and that such programs help develop our national linguistic resources and promote our international competitiveness;

(17) that research, evaluation, and data collection capabilities in the field of bilingual education need to be strengthened so as to better identify and promote those programs and instructional practices which result in effective education;

(18) that parent and community participation in bilingual education programs contributes to program effectiveness; and

(19) that because of limited English proficiency, many adults are not able to participate fully in national life, and that limited English proficient parents are often not able to participate effectively in their children's education,

the Congress declares it to be the policy of the United States, in order to establish equal educational opportunity for all children and to promote educational excellence (A) to encourage the establishment and operation, where appropriate, of educational programs using bilingual educational practices, techniques, and methods, (B) to encourage the establishment of special alternative instructional programs for students of limited English proficiency in school districts where the establishment of bilingual educational programs is not practicable or for other appropriate reasons, and (C) for those purposes, to provide financial assistance to local educational agencies, and, for certain related purposes, to State educational agencies, institutions of higher education, and community organizations. The programs assisted under this subchapter include programs in elementary and secondary schools as well as related preschool and adult programs which are designed to meet the educational needs of individuals of limited English proficiency, with particular attention to children having the greatest need for such programs. Such programs shall be designed to enable students to achieve full competence in English and to meet school grade-promotion and graduation requirements. Such programs may additionally provide for the development of student competence in a second language.

(b) Authorization

(1) For the purpose of carrying out the provisions of this subchapter, there are authorized to be appropriated, subject to paragraph (6), $200,000,000 for the

fiscal year 1989 and such sums as may be necessary for the fiscal year 1990 and for each succeeding fiscal year ending prior to October 1, 1993.

(2) There are further authorized to be appropriated to carry out the provisions of section 3302 of this title, subject to paragraph (6), such sums as may be necessary for the fiscal year 1989 and each of the 4 succeeding fiscal years.

(3) From the sums appropriated under paragraph (1) for part A of this subchapter for any fiscal year, the Secretary may reserve not to exceed 25 percent for special alternative instructional programs and related activities authorized under section 3291(a)(3) of this title and may include programs under paragraphs (2), (4), (5), and (6) of section 3291(a) of this title.

(4) From the sums appropriated under paragraph (1) for any fiscal year, the Secretary shall reserve at least 60 percent for the programs carried out under part A of this subchapter; and of this amount, at least 75 percent shall be reserved for the programs of transitional bilingual education carried out under section 3291(a)(1) of this title, and may include programs under paragraphs (2), (4), (5), and (6) of section 3291(a) of this title.

(5) From the sums appropriated under paragraph (1) for any fiscal year, the Secretary shall reserve at least 25 percent for training activities carried out under part C of this subchapter.

(6) Notwithstanding paragraphs (1) and (2), no amount in excess of $200,000,000 may be appropriated for the fiscal year 1989 to carry out the provisions of this subchapter (including section 3302 of this title).

(7) The reservation required by paragraph (3) shall not result in changing the terms, conditions, or negotiated levels of any grant awarded in fiscal year 1987 to which section 3291(d)(1)(A), 3291(d)(1)(C), or 3291(d)(2) of this title applies.

(Pub.L. 89–10, Title VII, § 7002, as added Pub.L. 100–297, Title I, § 1001, Apr. 28, 1988, 102 Stat. 274.)

|Q| uestions for Review and Reflection

1. What are the positive aspects of the ideal of bilingual education? What are the negative aspects? Do you believe that bilingual education benefits or detracts from American society? Why?
2. The Bilingual Education Act begins with a series of statements that establish certain assumptions. Which assumptions do you agree with? Which don't you agree with?
3. In what ways does this legislation empower local school districts? In what ways does it diminish the power and autonomy of local school districts? Why?

4. Might there be any hidden agenda behind the move for bilingual education? If so, what might it be?

Reading 2

United States Congress, 1991

The Civil Rights Act

Traditionally, some employers have practiced discrimination in their hiring policies, claiming it is necessary to their business to do so. Others have tolerated workplace harassment of individuals based on their race, ethnicity, or gender. Under the 1991 Civil Rights Act, employers must prove a business necessity when an employment practice results in a "disparate impact" on protected groups (categories based on race, sex, religion or national origin). The employer is required to seek other means of achieving the business purpose before such an employment policy will be tolerated. The act also offers limited compensation for intentional discrimination or harassment. Punitive damages can be awarded when it is proven that the defendant acted with reckless disregard for the rights of the individual.

Congress stated that this legislation was necessary to provide additional protection against unlawful discrimination and to strengthen and improve civil rights laws.

Civil Rights Act of 1991

For Legislative History of Act, see Report for P.L. 102–166 in U.S.C.C. & A.N. Legislative History Section.

An Act to amend the Civil Rights Act of 1964 to strengthen and improve Federal civil rights laws, to provide for damages in cases of intentional employment discrimination, to clarify provisions regarding disparate impact actions, and for other purposes.

Be it enacted by the Senate and House of Representatives of the United States of America in Congress assembled,

Section 1. Short Title.

This Act may be cited as the "Civil Rights Act of 1991".

Sec. 2. Findings.

The Congress finds that—

(1) additional remedies under Federal law are needed to deter unlawful harassment and intentional discrimination in the workplace;

(2) the decision of the Supreme Court in Wards Cove Packing Co. v. Atonio, 490 U.S. 642 (1989) has weakened the scope and effectiveness of Federal civil rights protections; and

(3) legislation is necessary to provide additional protections against unlawful discrimination in employment.

Sec 3. Purposes.

The purposes of this Act are—

(1) to provide appropriate remedies for intentional discrimination and unlawful harassment in the workplace;

(2) to codify the concepts of "business necessity" and "job related" enunciated by the Supreme Court in Griggs v. Duke Power Co., 401 U.S. 424 (1971), and in the other Supreme Court decisions prior to Wards Cove Packing Co. v. Atonio, 490 U.S. 642 (1989);

(3) to confirm statutory authority and provide statutory guidelines for the adjudication of disparate impact suits under title VII of the Civil Rights Act of 1964 (42 U.S.C. 2000e et seq.); and

(4) to respond to recent decisions of the Supreme Court by expanding the scope of relevant civil rights statutes in order to provide adequate protection to victims of discrimination. . . .

Sec. 105. Burden of Proof in Disparate Impact Cases.

(a) Section 703 of the Civil Rights Act of 1964 (42 U.S.C. 2000e–2) is amended by adding at the end of the following new subsection:

"(k)(1)(A) An unlawful employment practice based on disparate impact is established under this title only if—

"(i) a complaining party demonstrates that a respondent uses a particular employment practice that causes a disparate impact on the basis of race, color, religion, sex, or national origin and the respondent fails to demonstrate that the challenged practice is job related for the position in question and consistent with business necessity; or

"(ii) the complaining party makes the demonstration described in subparagraph (C) with respect to an alternative employment practice and the respondent refuses to adopt such alternative employment practice.

"(B)(i) With respect to demonstrating that a particular employment practice causes a disparate impact as described in subparagraph (A)(i), the complaining party shall demonstrate that each particular challenged employment practice causes a disparate impact, except that if the complaining party can demonstrate to the court that the elements of a respondent's decisionmaking process are not capable of separation for analysis, the decisionmaking process may be analyzed as one employment practice.

"(ii) If the respondent demonstrates that a specific employment practice does not cause the disparate impact, the respondent shall not be required to demonstrate that such practice is required by business necessity.

"(C) The demonstration referred to by subparagraph (A)(ii) shall be in accordance with the law as it existed on June 4, 1989, with respect to the concept of 'alternative employment practice'. . . .

"(2) A demonstration that an employment practice is required by business necessity may not be used as a defense against a claim of intentional discrimination under this title.

"(3) Notwithstanding any other provision of this title, a rule barring the employment of an individual who currently and knowingly uses or possesses a controlled substance, as defined in schedules I and II of section 102(6) of the Controlled Substances Act (21 U.S.C. 802(6)), other than the use of possession of a drug taken under the supervision of a licensed health care professional, or any other use or possession authorized by the Controlled Substances Act or any other provision of Federal law, shall be considered an unlawful employment practice under this title only if such rule is adopted or applied with an intent to discriminate because of race, color, religion, sex, or national origin."

(b) No statements other than the interpretive memorandum appearing at Vol. 137 Congressional Record S 15276 (daily ed. Oct. 25, 1991) shall be considered legislative history of, or relied upon in any way as legislative history in construing or applying, any provision of this Act that relates to Wards Cove—Business necessity/cumulation/alternative business practice. . . .

Title II—Glass Ceiling

Sec. 201. Short Title.

This title may be cited as the "Glass Ceiling Act of 1991".

Sec. 202. Findings and Purpose.

(A) Findings.—Congress finds that—

(1) despite a dramatically growing presence in the workplace, women and minorities remain underrepresented in management and decisionmaking positions in business;

(2) artificial barriers exist to the advancement of women and minorities in the workplace;

(3) United States corporations are increasingly relying on women and minorities to meet employment requirements and are increasingly aware of the advantages derived from a diverse work force;

(4) the "Glass Ceiling Initiative" undertaken by the Department of Labor, including the release of the report entitled "Report on the Glass Ceiling Initiative", has been instrumental in raising public awareness of—

> (A) the underrepresentation of women and minorities at the management and decisionmaking levels in the United States work force;
> (B) the underrepresentation of women and minorities in line functions in the United States work force;
> (C) the lack of access for qualified women and minorities to credential-building developmental opportunities; and
> (D) the desirability of eliminating artificial barriers to the advancement of women and minorities to such levels;

(5) the establishment of a commission to examine issues raised by the Glass Ceiling Initiative would help—

> (A) focus greater attention on the importance of eliminating artificial barriers to the advancement of women and minorities to management and decisionmaking positions in business; and
> (B) promote work force diversity.

Questions for Review and Reflection

1. Why did Congress find additional remedies necessary to protect civil rights?
2. What are the major purposes of the 1991 act?
3. Who has the burden of proof as of 1991?
4. Define disparate impact, according to this statute and the courts.
5. Define the glass ceiling and describe who is affected by it.

Reading 3

New York State Social Studies and Review Committee, 1991

"One Nation, Many Peoples: A Declaration of Cultural Independence"

Education is one of the primary institutions which advances the ideals and values of a democracy. States all across the country, responding to the distinct groups of peoples with prominent cultures, have begun to advance a pluralistic approach to education. Textbooks and general curricula are infusing multi-cultural learning into mainstream academic disciplines. Separate ethnic- and gender-based programs and studies are being developed in high schools and colleges all over America.

A leader in this movement has been the New York State Social Studies Department, which issued a lengthy report on behalf of pluralism and inclusion, recommending a full multicultural curriculum for history and the social sciences. They wrote, "We see the social studies as the primary avenue through which the school addresses our cultural diversity and interdependence."

Preamble

The United States is a microcosm of humanity today. No other country in the world is peopled by a greater variety of races, nationalities, and ethnic groups. But although the United States has been a great asylum for diverse peoples, it has not always been a great refuge for diverse cultures. The country has opened its doors to a multitude of nationalities, but often their cultures have not been encouraged to survive or, at best, have been kept marginal to the mainstream.

Since the 1960s, however, a profound reorientation of the self-image of Americans has been under way. Before this time the dominant model of the typical American had been conditioned primarily by the need to shape a unified nation out of a variety of contrasting and often conflicting European immigrant communities. But following the struggles for civil rights, the unprecedented increase in non-European immigration over the last two decades and the increasing recognition of our nation's indigenous heritage, there has been a fundamental change in the image of what a resident of the United States is.

With this change, which necessarily highlights the racial and ethnic pluralism of the nation, previous ideals of assimilation to an Anglo-American model have been put in question and are now slowly and sometimes painfully being set aside. Many people in the United States are no longer comfortable with the requirement, common in the past, that they shed their specific cultural differences in order to be considered American. Instead, while busily adapting to and shaping mainstream cultural ideals commonly identified as American, in recent decades many in the United States—from European and non-European backgrounds—have been encouraging a more tolerant, inclusive, and realistic vision of American identity than any that has existed in the past.

This identity, committed to the democratic principles of the nation and the nation-building in which all Americans are engaged, is progressively evolving from the past model toward a new model marked by respect for pluralism and awareness of the virtues of diversity. This situation is a current reality, and a multicultural education, anchored to the shared principles of a liberal democracy, is today less an educational innovation than a national priority.

It is fitting for New York State, host to the Statue of Liberty, to inaugurate a curriculum that reflects the rich cultural diversity of the nation. The beacon of hope welcomes not just the "wretched and poor" individuals of the world, but also the dynamic and rich cultures all people bring with them.

Two centuries after this country's founders issued a Declaration of Independence, focused on the political independence from which societies distant from the United States have continued to draw inspiration, the time has come to *recognize cultural interdependence*. We propose that the principle of respect for diverse cultures is critical to our nation, and we affirm that a right to cultural diversity exists. We believe that the schoolroom is one of the places where this cultural *interdependence* must be reflected.

It is in this spirit that we have crafted this report, "One Nation, Many Peoples." We see the social studies as the primary avenue through which the school addresses our cultural diversity and interdependence. But the study of cultural diversity and interdependence is only one goal. It is through such studies that we seek to strengthen our national commitment and world citizenship, with the development of intellectual competence in our students as the foundation. We see the social studies as directed at the development of intellectual competence in learners, with the capacity to view the world and understand it from multiple perspectives as one of the main components of such competence. Multicultural knowledge in this conception of the social studies becomes a vehicle and not a goal. Multicultural content and experience become instruments by which we enable students to develop their intelligence and to function as human and humane persons.

I. Introduction

Affirmation of Purpose

This Committee affirms that multicultural education should be a source of strength and pride. Multicultural education is often viewed as divisive and even as destructive of the values and beliefs which hold us together as Americans. Certainly, contemporary trends toward separation and dissolution in such disparate countries as the Soviet Union, South America, Canada, Yugoslavia, Spain, and the United Kingdom remind us that different ethnic and racial groups have often had extraordinary difficulty remaining together in nation-states. But national unity does not require that we eliminate the very diversity that is the source of our uniqueness and, indeed, of our adaptability and viability among the nations of the world. *If the United States is to continue to prosper in the 21st century, then all of its citizens, whatever their race or ethnicity, must believe that they and their ancestors have shared in the building of the country and have a stake in its success.* Thus, multicultural education, far from being a source of dissolution, is necessary for the cultural health, social stability, and economic future of New York State and the nation.

Questions for Review and Reflection

1. In what ways is the United States a microcosm of humanity, according to the committee? Do you agree, or do you think that the American experience somehow separates us from the rest of the world?
2. How is this report a repudiation of the concept of assimilation for minority cultures? How is this an argument for a new model of multicultural pluralism? How is this a declaration of cultural interdependence?
3. How might a multicultural education policy lead to strength and pride? Which societal groups might feel threatened by this policy of multicultural education? Is there common ground?
4. Why is the social studies class important in the development of intellectual competence and learning in American society?
5. How does the committee employ recent events in the former Soviet Union, South Africa, Canada, Yugoslavia, Spain, and the United Kingdom to argue that separatism is destructive, while a multicultural approach benefits society more? How do events following the publication of this document further strengthen the committee's argument?

Reading 4

United States Commission on Civil Rights, February 1992

"Civil Rights Issues Facing Asian Americans in the 1990s"

The 1957 Civil Rights Act established a commission appointed by the president to investigate and make recommendations on the status of civil rights in America. Its initial focus was an investigation of the civil rights of African Americans, but its agenda expanded to include other minorities, as well as women and the disabled.

The civil rights of Asian Americans became an issue as floods of refugees came to the United States from Southeast Asia following the Vietnam War. Immigration from that part of the world surpassed Latino immigration during the 1980s.

Many Asian Americans were highly educated and professionally skilled. They often succeeded in business and other occupations, and their children became high achievers in school. At times, this caused resentment among other minority populations. Interracial animosity became very open in some neighborhoods of cities like New York and Los Angeles.

The U.S. Civil Rights Commission held a series of conferences to examine the problems facing these arriving immigrants from Vietnam, Thailand, Cambodia, Laos, and elsewhere in Asia. The report concluded that an image of the "model minority" had been cast upon the Asian American, an image that was damaging, because government agencies overlooked them when drawing up antidiscrimination policies.

The report found that, much like some of the other minority groups, Asian Americans faced language and cultural barriers as well as a lack of political representation. Recommendations were made that could provide some relief and could, in the Commission's view, "be applicable to other minority groups as well."

This report presents the results of an investigation into the civil rights issues facing Asian Americans that was undertaken as a followup to the Commission's 1989 Asian Roundtable Conferences. Contrary to the popular perception that Asian Americans have overcome discriminatory barriers, Asian Americans still face widespread prejudice, discrimination, and denials of equal opportunity. In addition, many Asian Americans, particularly those who are immigrants, are deprived of equal access to public services, including police protection, education, health care, and the judicial system.

Several factors contribute to the civil rights problems facing today's Asian Americans. First, Asian Americans are the victims of stereotypes that are widely held among the general public. These stereotypes deprive Asian Americans of their individuality and humanity in the public's perception and often foster prejudice against Asian Americans. The "model minority" stereotype, the often-repeated contention that Asian Americans have overcome all barriers facing them and that they are a singularly successful minority group, is perhaps the most damaging of these stereotypes. This stereotype leads Federal, State, and local agencies to overlook the problems facing Asian Americans, and it often causes resentment of Asian Americans within the general public.

Second, many Asian Americans, particularly immigrants, face significant cultural and linguistic barriers that prevent them from receiving equal access to public services and from participating fully in the American political process. Many Asian American immigrants arrive in the United States with minimal facility in the English language and with little familiarity with American culture and the workings of American society. There has been a widespread failure of government at all levels and of the Nation's public schools to provide for the needs of immigrant Asian Americans. Such basic needs as interpretive services to help limited-English-proficient Asian Americans in their dealings with government agencies, culturally appropriate medical care, bilingual/English as a Second Language education, and information about available public services are largely unmet.

A third, but equally important, problem confronting Asian Americans today is a lack of political representation and an inability to use the political process effectively. Asian Americans face many barriers to participation in the political process, in addition to the simple fact that many Asian Americans are not yet citizens and hence ineligible to vote. Although some Asian Americans are politically active, the large majority have very little access to political power. This lack of political empowerment leads the political leadership of the United States to overlook and sometimes ignore the needs and concerns of Asian Americans. It also leads to a failure of the political leadership to make addressing Asian American issues a national priority.

This chapter lays out specific conclusions and recommendations. Many of the civil rights issues facing Asian Americans also confront other minority groups. For example, issues related to the rights of language minorities are equally important for other language-minority groups. Thus, many of our conclusions with respect to violations of Asian Americans' civil rights and our recommendations for enhancing the protection of their civil rights are applicable to other minority groups as well. . . .

Recommendation 12:

Every school system with immigrant students should have in place a comprehensive program to ease the transition of newly arrived immigrant students and their families into the American school system and into American society at large. Such a program should include intensive English as a Second Language classes offered to adults, as well as classes for children in school. . . .

Recommendation 13:

Colleges and universities should examine thoroughly their admissions policies for adverse effects or unintentional bias against Asian Americans and put in place safeguards to prevent them. Such safeguards should include:

- providing training to admissions staff;
  routinely reviewing new policies for adverse impact;
  including Asian Americans in the admissions process; and
- making data on the racial and ethnic breakdown of applicants and admitted students available to the public when requested. . . .

Recommendation 19:

Federal and State enforcement agencies should take aggressive steps to enforce antidiscrimination provisions with respect to the glass ceiling, including initiating compliance reviews of firms' employment practices that follow the lead of the Office of Federal Contract Compliance Programs' pilot studies of Fortune 500 companies. . . .

Recommendation 29:

Congress should reauthorize section 203(c) of the Voting Rights Act of 1982 with the following change:

- The section should be modified to apply to language-minority groups with more than a specified minimum number rather than a percentage of citizens of voting age.

Recommendation 30:

The Bureau of the Census should release detailed data on Asian Americans promptly, as promised.

Recommendation 31:

The major political parties and civic organizations (e.g., the League of Women Voters) should launch a major effort to promote voter registration and political participation among Asian Americans.

Questions for Review and Reflection

1. Identify the kinds of discrimination faced by Asian Americans, according to the commission. Are the issues any different than for other minorities, in your opinion?
2. Which government institutions does the commission feel can most effectively address the problems faced by Asian Americans?
3. Some of the commission's recommendations can apply to other minority groups. Can you identify which of those recommendations may be helpful and which may not?

Reading 5

United States Congress, October 1992

The Women in Apprenticeship and Nontraditional Occupations Act

Following the demise of the Equal Rights Amendment, the women's movement focused on economic issues. Activists lobbied for government assistance in creating more equal opportunities in employment, more child care, and more protection from fathers who fail to follow through on child support responsibilities.

The federal government was able to assist both women and the economy by affording the means to develop much-needed skilled labor in some of the trades while at the same time creating new and nontraditional employment opportunities for women.

Congress defined nontraditional occupations as those jobs in which women made up less than 25% of the work force. They appropriated money for outreach programs and technical assistance to employers and unions "to encourage employment of women in apprenticeable . . . and nontraditional occupations."

Efforts in child care and enforcement of child support orders continue. Congresswoman Lynn Woolsey, D-(Petaluma) CA, recently proposed legislation to the House of Representatives, under which the Internal Revenue Service would collect delinquent child support payments and disburse the money to the child's custodial parent.

Women in Apprenticeship and Nontraditional Occupations Act

An Act to assist business in providing women with opportunities in apprenticeship and nontraditional occupations.

Be it enacted by the Senate and House of Representatives of the United States of American in Congress assembled,

Section 1. Short Title.

This Act shall be cited as the "Women in apprenticeship and Nontraditional Occupations Act".

Sec. 2. Findings; Statement of Purpose.

(a) FINDINGS.—The Congress finds that—

> (1) American businesses now and for the remainder of the 20th century will face a dramatically different labor market than the one to which they have become accustomed;
>
> (2) two in every three new entrants to the work force will be women, and to meet labor needs such women must work in all occupational areas including in apprenticeable occupations and nontraditional occupations;
>
> (3) women face significant barriers to their full and effective participation in apprenticeable occupations and nontraditional occupations;
>
> (4) the business community must be prepared to address the barriers that women have to such jobs in order to successfully integrate them into the work force; and
>
> (5) few resources are available to employers and unions who need assistance in recruiting, training, and retaining women in apprenticeable occupations and other nontraditional occupations.

(b) PURPOSE.—It is the purpose of this Act to provide technical assistance to employers and labor unions to encourage employment of women in apprenticeable occupations and nontraditional occupations. Such assistance will enable business to meet the challenge of Workforce 2000 by preparing employers to successfully recruit, train, and retain women in apprenticeable occupations and non-traditional occupations and will expand the employment and self-sufficiency options of women. This purpose will be achieved by—

> (1) promoting the program to employers and labor unions to inform them of the availability of technical assistance which will assist them in preparing the workplace to employ women in apprenticeable occupations and nontraditional occupations;
>
> (2) providing grants to community-based organizations to deliver technical assistance to employers and labor unions to prepare them to recruit, train, and employ women in apprenticeable occupations and nontraditional occupations;
>
> (3) authorizing the Department of Labor to serve as a liaison between employers, labor, and the community-based organizations providing technical assistance, through its national office and its regional administrators; and
>
> (4) conducting a comprehensive study to examine the barriers to the participation of women in apprenticeable occupations and nontraditional occupations and to develop recommendations for the workplace to eliminate such barriers.

Sec. 3. Outreach to Employers and Labor Unions

(a) IN GENERAL.—With funds available to the Secretary of Labor to carry out the operations of the Department of Labor in fiscal year 1994 and subsequent fiscal years, the Secretary shall carry out an outreach program to inform employers of technical assistance available under section 4(a) to assist employers to prepare the workplace to employ women in apprenticeable occupations and other nontraditional occupations.

> (1) Under such program the Secretary shall provide outreach to employers through, but not limited to, the private industry councils in each service delivery area.
> (2) The Secretary shall provide outreach to labor unions through, but not limited to, the building trade councils, joint apprenticeable occupations councils, and individual labor unions.

(b) PRIORITY.—The Secretary shall give priority to providing outreach to employers located in areas that have nontraditional employment and training programs specifically targeted to women.

Sec. 4. Technical Assistance.

(a) IN GENERAL.—With funds appropriated to carry out this section, the Secretary shall make grants to community-based organizations to provide technical assistance to employers and labor unions selected under subsection (b). Such technical assistance may include—

> (1) developing outreach and orientation sessions to recruit women into the employers' apprenticeable occupations and nontraditional occupations;
> (2) developing preapprenticeable occupations or nontraditional skills training to prepare women for apprenticeable occupations or nontraditional occupations;
> (3) providing ongoing orientations for employers, unions, and workers on creating a successful environment for women in apprenticeable occupations or nontraditional occupations;
> (4) setting up support groups and facilitating networks for women in nontraditional occupations on or off the job site to improve their retention;
> (5) setting up a local computerized data base referral system to maintain a current list of tradeswomen who are available for work;
> (6) serving as a liaison between tradeswomen and employers and tradeswomen and labor unions to address workplace issues related to gender; and
> (7) conducting exit interviews with tradeswomen to evaluate their on-the-job experience and to assess the effectiveness of the program.

(b) SELECTION OF EMPLOYER AND LABOR UNIONS.—The Secretary shall select a total of 50 employers or labor unions to receive technical assistance provided with grants made under subsection (a).

Questions for Review and Reflection

1. In what ways can government assist employers and unions under this law?
2. What role can the Department of Labor play?
3. Outline some programs in this law that provide technical assistance.
4. Why does the law say women should be singled out for help?

Reading 6

United States Supreme Court, 1993

Shaw v. Reno, 509 US—, 125 L. Ed. 2d 511, 113

Gerrymandering, a term that dates back to 1812, describes the practice of drawing voting district boundaries for political advantage. Named for Massachusetts governor Elbridge Gerry, who created a district shaped like a salamander, the skewing practice has been employed by some states to draw district boundaries that dilute minority voting power. With this racial gerrymandering, a group was fragmented into several districts so that its power was not congregated in any one.

The 1965 Voting Rights Act (see Chapter 7, Reading 7) prohibited racial gerrymandering, but the 1982 Voting Rights Amendment changed this policy, requiring states to draw lines where possible that took race into account in order to foster minority voting strength.

In 1991 North Carolina produced a redistricting plan that was challenged by voters because it appeared to have been drawn solely on the basis of race, without taking any other factors such as community or contiguousness into account.

The Supreme Court ruled 5-4 that such a plan violated the Constitution because it "reinforces the perception that members of the same racial group—regardless of their age, education, economic status, or the community in which they live—think alike." The Court feared that such a form of gerrymandering, even for remedial purposes, may "balkanize us into competing factions." Furthermore, they stated that it threatened to "carry us further from the goal of a political system in which race no longer matters . . . a goal . . . to which the Nation continues to aspire."

Justice O'Connor delivered the opinion of the Court.

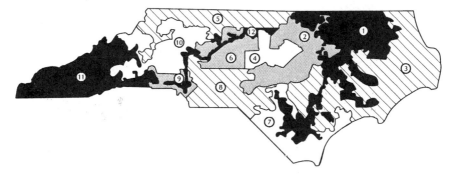

[1a] This case involves two of the most complex and sensitive issues this Court has faced in recent years: the meaning of the constitutional "right" to vote, and the propriety of race-based state legislation designed to benefit members of historically disadvantaged racial minority groups. As a result of the 1990 census, North Carolina became entitled to a twelfth seat in the United States House of Representatives. The General Assembly enacted a reapportionment plan that included one majority-black congressional district. After the Attorney General of the United States objected to the plan pursuant to § 5 of the Voting Rights Act of 1965, 79 Stat 439, as amended, 42 USC § 1973c [42 USCS § 1973c], the General Assembly passed new legislation creating a second majority-black district. Appellants allege that the revised plan, which contains district boundary lines of dramatically irregular shape, constitutes an unconstitutional racial gerrymander. The question before us is whether appellants have stated a cognizable claim. . . .

Appellants contended that the General Assembly's revised reapportionment plan violated several provisions of the United States Constitution, including the Fourteenth Amendment. They alleged that the General Assembly deliberately "create[d] two Congressional Districts in which a majority of black voters was concentrated arbitrarily—without regard to any other considerations, such as compactness, contiguousness, geographical boundaries, or political subdivisions" with the purpose "to create Congressional Districts along racial lines" and to assure the election of two black representatives to Congress. App to Juris Statement 102a. Appellants sought declaratory and injunctive relief against the state appellees. They sought similar relief against the federal appellees, arguing, alternatively, that the federal appellees had miscontrued the Voting Rights Act or that the Act itself was unconstitutional. . . .

[2] It is against this background that we confront the questions presented here. In our view, the District Court properly dismissed appellants' claims against the federal appellees. Our focus is on appellants' claim that the State engaged in unconstitutional racial gerrymandering. That argument strikes a powerful historical chord: It is unsettling how closely the North Carolina plan resembles the most egregious racial gerrymanders of the past. . . .

An understanding of the nature of appellants' claim is critical to our resolution of the case. In their complaint, appellants did not claim that the General Assembly's reapportionment plan unconstitutionally "diluted" white voting strength. They did not even claim to be white. Rather, appellants' complaint alleged that the deliberate segregation of voters into separate districts on the basis of race violated their constitutional right to participate in a "color-blind" electoral process. . . .

What appellants object to is redistricting legislation that is so extremely irregular on its face that it rationally can be viewed only as an effort to segregate the races for purposes of voting, without regard for traditional districting principles and without sufficiently compelling justification. . . .

A reapportionment plan that includes in one district individuals who belong to the same race, but who are otherwise widely separated by geographical and political boundaries, and who may have little in common with one another but the color of their skin, bears an uncomfortable resemblance to political apartheid. It reinforces the perception that members of the same racial group—regardless of their age, education, economic status, or the community in which they live—think alike, share the same political interests, and will prefer the same candidates at the polls. We have rejected such perceptions elsewhere as impermissible racial stereotypes. . . .

When a district obviously is created solely to effectuate the perceived common interests of one racial group, elected officials are more likely to believe that their primary obligation is to represent only the members of that group, rather than their constituency as a whole. This is altogether antithetical to our system of representative democracy. As Justice Douglas explained in his dissent in Wright v. Rockefeller nearly 30 years ago:

"Here the individual is important, not his race, his creed, or his color. The principle of equality is at war with the notion that District A must be represented by a Negro, as it is with the notion that District B must be represented by a Caucasian, District C by a Jew, District D by a Catholic, and so on." . . .

For these reasons, we conclude that a plaintiff challenging a reapportionment statute under the Equal Protection Clause may state a claim by alleging that the legislation, though race-neutral on its face, rationally cannot be understood as anything other than an effort to separate voters into different districts on the basis of race, and that the separation lacks sufficient justification. . . .

[1e, 9c] Racial classifications of any sort pose the risk of lasting harm to our society. They reinforce the belief, held by too many for too much of our history, that individuals should be judged by the color of their skin. Racial classifications with respect to voting carry particular dangers. Racial gerrymandering, even for remedial purposes, may balkanize us into competing racial factions; it threatens to carry us further from the goal of a political system in which race no longer matters—a goal that the Fourteenth and Fifteenth Amendments embody, and to which the Nation continues to aspire. It is for these reasons that race-based districting by our state legislatures demands close judicial scrutiny.

In this case, the Attorney General suggested that North Carolina could have created a reasonably compact second majority-minority district in the south-central to southeastern part of the State. We express no view as to whether appellants successfully could have challenged such a district under the Fourteenth Amendment. We also do not decide whether appellants' complaint stated a claim under constitutional provisions other than the Fourteenth Amendment. Today we hold only that appellants have stated a claim under the Equal Protection Clause by alleging that the North Carolina General Assembly adopted a reapportionment scheme so irrational on its face that it can be understood only as an effort to segregate voters into separate voting districts because of their race, and that the separation lacks sufficient justification. If the allegation of racial gerrymandering remains uncontradicted, the District Court further must determine whether the North Carolina plan is narrowly tailored to further a compelling governmental interest. Accordingly, we reverse the judgment of the District Court and remand the case for further proceedings consistent with this opinion.

It is so ordered.

 uestions for Review and Reflection

1. According to this decision:
   a) What is the basis for the appellants' complaint?
   b) What constitutional rights were at issue?
   c) What constitutes political apartheid?
   d) How would the creation of these districts affect the roles of elected officials?
   e) Why are racial classifications harmful?

2. Examine the North Carolina Congressional Plan. Do you agree that the districts are unjustifiably irregular?

Reading 7

United States Congress, December 1993

The Indian Tribal Justice Act

Among the many diverse peoples of the United States, Native American tribes occupy a unique position in the American democracy, constituting quasi-sovereign dependent nations within, and surrounded by, the larger country.

With the end of armed conflict between Indians and other Americans, the tribes and the federal government began their prolonged struggle to establish an appropriate relationship. The search continues for a balance that allows Native Americans to retain both their cultural identity and independence and the legal and economic protections of the United States government. Over and over again, the parties have struggled to determine where the responsibility for medical, legal, and educational services to the tribes should lie. That responsibility has shifted among Congress, state and local governments, and the tribes themselves in a changing series of federal laws—the 1924 act declaring Indians to be U.S. citizens, the Indian Reorganization Act of 1934, the Termination Acts of 1953-54, the Indian Civil Rights Act of 1968, and the Self-Determination and Assistance Act of 1975.

The Indian Tribal Justice Act of 1993 joins this list of legislative attempts to afford Native Americans such services as legal counsel for the indigent, law libraries, probation systems, and other technical assistance, without curtailing the tribes' sovereignty and self-governance.

Indian Tribal Justice Act

An Act to assist the development of tribal judicial systems, and for other purposes.

Be it enacted by the Senate and House of Representatives of the United States of America in Congress assembled,

Section 1. Short Title.

This Act may be cited as the "Indian Tribal Justice Act."

Sec. 2. Findings.

The Congress finds and declares that—

(1) there is a government-to-government relationship between the United States and each Indian tribe;

(2) the United States has a trust responsibility to each tribal government that includes the protection of the sovereignty of each tribal government;

(3) Congress, through statutes, treaties, and the exercise of administrative authorities, has recognized the self-determination, self-reliance, and inherent sovereignty of Indian tribes;

(4) Indian tribes possess the inherent authority to establish their own form of government, including tribal justice systems;

(5) tribal justice systems are an essential part of tribal governments and serve as important forums for ensuring public health and safety and the political integrity of tribal governments;

(6) Congress and the Federal courts have repeatedly recognized tribal justice systems as the appropriate forums for the adjudication of disputes affecting personal and property rights;

(7) traditional tribal justice practices are essential to the maintenance of the culture and identity of Indian tribes and to the goals of this Act;

(8) tribal justice systems are inadequately funded, and the lack of adequate funding impairs their operation; and

(9) tribal government involvement in and commitment to improving tribal justice systems is essential to the accomplishment of the goals of this Act.

Sec. 3. Definitions.

For purposes of this Act:

(1) The term "Bureau" means the Bureau of Indian Affairs of the Department of the Interior.

(2) The term "Courts of Indian Offenses" means the courts established pursuant to part 11 of title 25, Code of Federal Regulations.

(3) The term "Indian tribe" means any Indian tribe, band, nation, pueblo, or other organized group or community, including any Alaska Native entity, which administers justice under its inherent authority or the authority of the United States and which is recognized as eligible for the special programs and services provided by the United States to Indian tribes because of their status as Indians.

(4) The term "judicial personnel" means any judge, magistrate, court counselor, court clerk, court administrator, bailiff, probation officer, officer of the court, dispute resolution facilitator, or other official, employee, or volunteer within the tribal justice system.

(5) The term "Office" means the Office of Tribal Justice Support within the Bureau of Indian Affairs.

(6) The term "Secretary" means the Secretary of the Interior.

(7) The term "tribal organization" means any organization defined in section 4(1) of the Indian Self-Determination and Education Assistance Act.

(8) The term "tribal justice system" means the entire judicial branch, and employees thereof, of an Indian tribe, including (but not limited to) traditional methods and forums for dispute resolution, lower courts, appellate courts (including intertribal appellate courts), alternative dispute resolution systems, and circuit rider systems, established by inherent tribal authority whether or not they constitute a court of record.

Title I—Tribal Justice Systems

Sec. 101. Office of Tribal Justice Support.

(a) ESTABLISHMENT.—There is hereby established within the Bureau the Office of Tribal Justice Support. The purpose of the Office shall be to further the development, operation, and enhancement of tribal justice systems and Courts of Indian Offenses.

(b) TRANSFER OF EXISTING FUNCTIONS AND PERSONNEL.—All functions performed before the date of the enactment of this Act by the Branch of Judicial Services of the Bureau and all personnel assigned to such Branch as of the date of the enactment of this Act are hereby transferred to the Office of Tribal Justice Support. Any reference in any law, regulation, executive order, reorganization plan, or delegation of authority to the Branch of Judicial Services is deemed to be a reference to the Office of Tribal Justice Support.

(c) FUNCTIONS.—In addition to the functions transferred to the Office pursuant to subsection (b), the Office shall perform the following functions:

(1) Provide funds to Indian tribes and tribal organizations for the development, enhancement, and continuing operation of tribal justice systems.

(2) Provide technical assistance and training, including programs of continuing education and training for personnel of Courts of Indian Offenses.

(3) Study and conduct research concerning the operation of tribal justice systems.

(4) Promote cooperation and coordination among tribal justice systems and the Federal and State judiciary systems.

(5) Oversee the continuing operations of the Courts of Indian Offenses.

Questions for Review and Reflection

1. According to this law:
   a) What is the importance of tribal justice systems?
   b) What is the responsibility of the United States government toward tribes and their justice systems?
   c) What steps will the United States take in order to provide for the Indian justice system?
2. Do you see any fundamental change in United States-Indian relations as a result of this act?

Sources

Chapter 1

Reading 1: Thomas Jefferson, The Declaration of Independence. In F. N. Thorpe, ed., *The Federal and State Constitutions* (Washington, DC: U.S. Government Printing Office).

Reading 2: John Adams, Thoughts on Government. In Charles Francis Adams, ed., *The Works of John Adams,* vol. 14 (Boston: Little, Brown, 1851), pp. 193–200.

Reading 3: Benjamin Franklin, Letter to Europeans Seeking a New Life in America. In U. Waldo Cutler, ed., *Selections from the Writings of Benjamin Franklin* (New York: Thomas Y. Crowell, 1905), pp. 150–62.

Reading 4: Thomas Jefferson, Letter to James Madison. In Adrienne Koch and William Pedden, eds., *The Life and Selected Writings of Thomas Jefferson* (New York: Modern Library, 1944), pp. 436–41.

Reading 5: Constitutional Convention, The Constitution of the United States. In F. N. Thorpe, ed., *The Federal and State Constitutions* (Washington, DC: U.S. Government Printing Office).

Reading 6: United States Congress, The Bill of Rights. In F. N. Thorpe, ed., *The Federal and State Constitutions* (Washington, DC: U.S. Government Printing Office).

Chapter 2

Reading 1: Abigail Adams, Letter to John Adams. In L. H. Butterfield, ed., *The Adams Family Correspondence* (Cambridge, MA: Belknap Press of Harvard University Press). Copyright © 1963, 1973 by the Massachusetts Historical Society. Reprinted by permission.

Reading 2: Manumitted Slaves of North Carolina, Petition to Redress Set of Grievances. *Debates and Proceedings in the Congress of the U.S.,* 4th Cong., 2nd sess. (Gales and Seaton, 1855), pp. 2015–18.

Reading 3: The Cherokee Nation, Appeal to the People of the United States. In Myron Marty and Theodore Finkelston, eds., *Retracing Our Steps* (San Francisco: Canfield Press, 1972), pp. 217–23.

Reading 4: Sarah Grimké, Letters on Equality of the Sexes. In Elizabeth Ann Bartless, ed., *Letters on the Equality of the Sexes* (New Haven: Yale University Press, 1988), pp. 31–41.

Reading 5: Seneca Falls Convention, Declaration of Sentiments. In Elizabeth Cady Stanton, Susan B. Anthony, and Matilda Joslyn Gage, eds., *History of Woman Suffrage,* vol. 1 (1881; reprint, New York: Arno Press, 1969), pp. 70-72.

Reading 6: William Wells Brown, Letter to Enoch Price. In Herbert Aptheker, ed., *A Documentary History of the Negro People in the United States* (New York: Citadel Press, 1951), pp. 293–97. Copyright © 1951 by Herbert Aptheker. Published by arrangement with Carol Publishing Group. A Citadel Press book.

Reading 7: Norman Assing, Letter to Governor Bigler. In David Brion Davis, ed., *Antebellum American Culture* (Washington, DC: D. C. Heath, 1979), pp. 263–65.

Chapter 3

Reading 1: John Quincy Adams, Diaries. *Diaries of John Quincy Adams* (New York: Longmans, Green, 1928), pp. 230–32, 246–47.

Reading 2: Abraham Lincoln, Fragments on Slavery. In Mario Cuomo and Harold Holzer, eds., *Lincoln on Democracy* (New York: HarperCollins, 1990), pp. 62–63.

Reading 3: United States Congress, Thirteenth Amendment. In F. N. Thorpe, ed., *The Federal and State Constitutions* (Washington, DC: U.S. Government Printing Office).

Reading 4: United States Congress, Fourteenth Amendment. In Benjamin Poore, ed., *The Federal and State Constitutions* (Washington, DC: U.S. Government Printing Office).

Reading 5: United States Congress, Fifteenth Amendment. Ibid.

Chapter 4

Reading 1: Red Cloud, Speech at Cooper Institute. In Myron Marty and Theodore Finkelston, eds., *Retracing Our Steps* (San Francisco: Canfield Press, 1972), pp. 43–44.

Reading 2: Victoria Woodhull, Testimony before Congress. In Madeleine B. Stern, ed., *The Victoria Woodhull Reader* (Weston, MA: M & S Press, 1973), pp. 31–33. Courtesy of M & S Press, Inc., Providence, RI. Reprinted by permission.

Reading 3: Congressman R. H. Cain, Speech to the House of Representatives. In Leslie H. Fishel Jr. and Benjamin Quarles, eds., *The Black American* (Glenview, IL: Scott Foresman, 1970), pp. 183–89.

Reading 4: Chief Joseph, "An Indian's View of Indian Affairs." In Paul Boller, ed., *A More Perfect Union,* vol. 2 (Boston: Houghton Mifflin, 1992), pp. 67–71.

Reading 5: Frederick Douglass, Address to Black Convention. In Richard Current et al., eds., *Words That Made American History* (Boston: Little, Brown, 1972), pp. 69–71.

Reading 6: Mary Putnam Jacobi, Address to New York State Constitutional Convention. Mary Putnam Jacobi, *Common Sense as Applied to Woman Suffrage* (New York: G. P. Putnam, 1894), appendix, pp. 199–236.

Reading 7: Elizabeth Cady Stanton, "The Solitude of Self." In Susan B. Anthony and Ida H. Harper, eds., *History of Woman Suffrage,* vol. 3 (1892; reprint, New York: Arno Press, 1969).

Reading 8: Booker T. Washington, Speech at the Atlanta Exposition. In *Up from Slavery* (Dodd Mead, 1965), pp. 138–51.

Reading 9: Susan B. Anthony, "The Status of Women." In *Annals of America,* vol. 12 (Chicago: Encyclopaedia Britannica, 1968), pp. 144–48. © 1968, 1976 by Encyclopaedia Britannica, Inc.

Reading 10: W. E. B. Du Bois, *The Souls of Black Folks* (1903; reprint, New York: Vintage Books, 1990), pp. 36–48.

Reading 11: Margaret Sanger, *Women and the New Race.* In Diane Ravitch, ed., *The American Reader* (New York: Harper Perennial, 1990), pp. 250–52.

Reading 12: Luther Standing Bear, *Land of the Spotted Eagle.* In *What the Indian Means to America* (Lincoln: University of Nebraska Press, 1933), pp. 247–59.

Reading 13: Ralph Bunche, *The Political Status of the Negro after FDR,* Dewey Grantham, ed. (Chicago: University of Chicago Press, 1973), pp. 103–18.

Chapter 5

Reading 1: Woodrow Wilson, *The New Freedom* (New York: Doubleday, Page, 1913).

Reading 2: United States Congress, Nineteenth Amendment. In Benjamin Poore, ed., *The Federal and State Constitutions* (Washington, DC: U.S. Government Printing Office).

Reading 3: Franklin D. Roosevelt, Economic Bill of Rights. In Bertell Ollmann and Jonathan Birnbaum, eds., *The U.S. Constitution* (New York: New York University Press, 1990), pp. 298–99.

Reading 4: Harry Truman, Executive Order 9981. *Federal Register* (Washington, DC: U.S. Government Printing Office), p. 4313.

Reading 5: United States Supreme Court, *Brown v. Board of Education,* 347 U.S. 483 (1954).

Reading 6: Dwight D. Eisenhower, Address to the Nation. In *Public Papers of the Presidents of the United States, January 1–December 31, 1957* (Washington, DC: U.S. Government Printing Office).

Chapter 6

Reading 1: Martin Luther King Jr., Letter from a Birmingham Jail. In Martin Luther King Jr., *Why We Can't Wait* (New York: Harper & Row, 1964), pp. 77–100.

Reading 2: Betty Friedan, *The Feminine Mystique* (New York: Dell Books, 1963), pp. 362–64. Reprinted with the permission of W. W. Norton & Company, Inc. Copyright © 1963, 1973, 1974, 1983 by Betty Friedan.

Reading 3: Martin Luther King Jr., "I Have a Dream" Speech. In James M. Washington, ed., *A Testament of Hope: The Essential Writings of Martin L. King* (New York: HarperCollins, 1986), pp. 217–20.

Reading 4: Malcolm X, Speech to New York Meeting. In George Breitman and Betty Shabazz, eds., *Malcolm X Speaks* (New York: Pathfinder Press, 1989), pp. 45–59. © 1965, 1989 by Betty Shabazz and Pathfinder Press. Reprinted by permission.

Reading 5: The National Organization for Women, Organizing Statement. In Betty Friedan, *It Changed My Life* (New York: Random House, 1976), pp. 87–92. Reprinted by permission of Curtis Brown, Ltd., copyright © 1963, 1964, 1966, 1970, 1971, 1972, 1973, 1974, 1975, 1976, 1985, 1991 by Betty Friedan.

Reading 6: American Indian Task Force, Statement to the U.S. House of Representatives. *Congressional Record* for 91st Cong., 1st sess., November 13, 1969.

Reading 7: Reies Tijerina, Letter from a Santa Fe Jail. In Wayne Moquin and Charles van Doren, *A Documen-*

tary History of the Mexican-Americans (New York: Praeger, 1971), pp. 374-77.

Reading 8: Delano Grape Workers, Proclamation. In Wayne Moquin and Charles van Doren, *A Documentary History of the Mexican-Americans* (New York: Praeger, 1971), pp. 363-65.

Reading 9: National Council on Indian Opportunity, Statement of Indian Members. In Alvin Josephy, ed., *Red Power* (American Heritage Press, 1971), pp. 192-208. Copyright © 1971 by Alvin Josephy. Reprinted by permission of the author.

Reading 10: Armando Rodriguez, Testimony to Congress. *Congressional Record* for 91st Cong., 2nd sess., pp. 5154-56.

Reading 11: Mary Frances Berry, *Black Resistance/White Law* (Appleton-Century Crofts, 1971), pp. 235-39. Reprinted by permission of Viking Penguin, Inc.

Reading 12: Cesar Chavez, An Interview. In Jacques Levy, *Cesar Chavez: Autobiography of La Causa* (New York: W. W. Norton, Inc., 1975), pp. 536-39.

Chapter 7

Reading 1: United States Supreme Court, *Reynolds v. Sims,* 377 U.S. 533 (1964).

Reading 2: United States Congress, The Civil Rights Act of 1964. *U.S. Code Annotated,* P.L. 88-352, 78 Stat. 241, Title 42.

Reading 3: Hubert Humphrey, Civil Rights Commission Report. In *Congress and the Nation* (Washington, DC: Congressional Quarterly Press, 1965), p. 1642.

Reading 4: Lyndon B. Johnson, Howard University Speech. In *Public Papers of Lyndon B. Johnson,* vol. 2 (Washington, DC: U.S. Government Printing Office, 1966).

Reading 5: United States Congress, The Voting Rights Act. *U.S. Code Annotated,* P.L. 89-110, 79 Stat. 437, Title 42.

Reading 6: Lyndon B. Johnson, Executive Order 11246. *Federal Register,* no. 12319 (Washington, DC: U.S. Government Printing Office, 1965).

Reading 7: Richard M. Nixon, Message to Congress. In *Public Papers of the Presidents of the United States, January 1-December 31, 1970* (Washington, DC: U.S. Government Printing Office, 1971).

Reading 8: United States Supreme Court, *Reed v. Reed,* 404 U.S. 71 (1971).

Reading 9: United States Supreme Court, *Roe v. Wade,* 410 U.S. 113 (1973).

Reading 10: United States Congress, The Indian Self-Determination and Assistance Act. In *U.S. Statutes at Large,* vol. 88, part 2 (Washington, DC: U.S. Government Printing Office, 1976), pp. 2203-17.

Reading 11: State of California, The California Agricultural Labor Relations Act. In *West Annotated Code,* Labor Sections (St. Paul: West Publishing, 1989), pp. 298-305.

Chapter 8

Reading 1: Phyllis Schlafly, *The Power of the Positive Woman* (New York: Arlington House, 1977). Copyright © 1977 by Phyllis Schlafly. Reprinted by permission of Crown Publishers, Inc.

Reading 2: Gloria Steinem, *Outrageous Acts and Everyday Rebellions* (New York: Holt, Rinehart & Winston, 1983), pp. 341-62. Copyright © 1983 by Gloria Steinem. Copyright © 1984 by East Toledo Productions, Inc. Reprinted by permission of Henry Holt and Company, Inc.

Reading 3: Thurgood Marshall, Speech on the Bicentennial of the Constitution. In Bruce Stinebrickner, ed., *Annual Editions: American Government, 1994/95* (Guilford, CT: The Dushkin Publishing Group), pp. 53-54.

Reading 4: Henry Cisneros, "American Dynamism and the New World Culture," *New Perspective Quarterly* (Summer 1988), 36-38.

Reading 5: Herbert Hill, "Race, Affirmative Action, and the Constitution." In George McKenna and Stanley Feingold, eds., *Taking Sides: Clashing Views on Controversial Political Issues* (Guilford, CT: The Dushkin Publishing Group, 1993), pp. 194-99. Herbert Hill is professor of Afro-American studies and industrial relations at the University of Wisconsin-Madison. Formerly national labor director of the NAACP, he is the author of *Black Labor and the American Legal System* and other books.

Reading 6: Joaquin Avila, "Latino Political Empowerment." Pamphlet published privately by Joaquin Avila, 1988, Linda Stone, ed., pp. 20-25.

Reading 7: Susan Faludi, *Backlash: The Undeclared War against American Women* (New York: Crown, 1991), pp. 454-61. Copyright © 1991 by Susan Faludi. Reprinted by permission of Crown Publishers, a division of Random House, Inc.

Reading 8: Shelby Steele, *The Content of Our Character: A New Vision of Race in America* (New York: St. Martin's Press, 1990), chap. 7.

Reading 9: Linda Chavez, *Out of the Barrio: Toward a New Politics of Hispanic Assimilation* (New York: Basic Books, 1991), pp. 162-71. Copyright © 1991 by BasicBooks. Reprinted by permission of BasicBooks, a division of HarperCollins Publishers, Inc.

Reading 10: Patricia Ireland, "The State of NOW." *Ms. Magazine,* July/August 1992, pp. 24-27. Reprinted by permission of Ms. Magazine, © 1992.

Reading 11: John Mohawk, "Looking for Columbus: Thoughts on the Past, Present, and Future of Humanity." In M. Annette Jaimes, ed., *The State of Native-Americans, Genocide, Colonization and Resistance* (Boston: South End Press, 1992), pp. 439-44.

Reading 12: Vine Deloria Jr., "Afterword." In Alvin Josephy, ed., *America in 1492* (New York: Alfred A. Knopf, 1992), pp. 429-43. Copyright © 1992 by Alfred A. Knopf, a division of Random House, Inc. Reprinted by permission of the publisher.

Chapter 9

Reading 1: United States Congress, The Bilingual Education Act. P.L. 88-10, 102 Stat. 274, Title 20.

Reading 2: United States Congress, The Civil Rights Act of 1991. *U.S. Congressional and Administrative Codes,* P.L. 102-166 (St. Paul: West Publishing, 1991).

Reading 3: New York State Social Studies and Review Committee, "One Nation, Many Peoples: A Declaration of Cultural Independence." In *Historic Documents* (Washington, DC: Congressional Quarterly Press, 1992), pp. 333-48.

Reading 4: United States Commission on Civil Rights, "Civil Rights Issues Facing Asian Americans in the 1990s." Pursuant to P.L. 98-183 (Washington, DC: U.S. Government Printing Office, 1992).

Reading 5: United States Congress, The Women in Apprenticeship and Nontraditional Occupations Act. *U.S. Code Annotated,* P.L. 102-530, October 27, 1992.

Reading 6: United States Supreme Court, *Shaw v. Reno* 509 U.S.___, 125 L. Ed. 2d 511, 513 S.Ct. ___ (1993).

Reading 7: United States Congress, The Indian Tribal Justice Act. *U.S. Code Annotated,* P.L. 103-176, December 3, 1993.